Research Navigator.com Guide: Psychology

Brian M. Kelley

Bridgewater College

Linda R. Barr

University of the Virgin Islands

PEARSON

Boston | New York | San Francisco
Mexico City | Montreal | Toronto | London | Madrid | Munich | Paris
Hong Kong | Singapore | Tokyo | Cape Town | Sydney

For related titles and support materials, visit our online catalog at
www.ablongman.com

Copyright © 2007 Pearson Education, Inc.

Between the time Web site information is gathered and then
published, it is not unusual for some sites to have closed. Also,
the transcription of URLs can result in unintended typographical
errors. The publisher would appreciate notification where
these errors occur so that they may be corrected in subsequent
editions.

ISBN   0-205-51708-0

Printed in the United States of America

10 9 8 7 6 5 4 3 2 1   11 10 09 08 07 06

Contents

Introduction

Your professor assigns a ten-page research paper that's due in two weeks—and you need to make sure you have up-to-date, credible information. Where do you begin? Today, the easiest answer is the Internet—because it can be so convenient and there is so much information out there. But therein lies part of the problem. How do you know if the information is reliable and from a trustworthy source?

ResearchNavigator.com Guide is designed to help you select and evaluate research from the Web to help you find the best and most credible information you can. Throughout this guide, you'll find:

- **A practical and to-the-point discussion of search engines.**
  Find out which search engines are likely to get you the information you want and how to phrase your searches for the most effective results.
- **Detailed information on evaluating online sources.** Locate credible information on the Web and get tips for thinking critically about Web sites.
- **Citation guidelines for Web resources.** Learn the proper citation guidelines for Web sites, email messages, listservs, and more.
- **ResearchNavigator.com Guide.** All you need to know to get started with ResearchNavigator.com, a research database that gives you immediate access to hundreds of scholarly journals and other popular publications, such as *Scientific American, U.S. News & World Report,* and many others.

So before running straight to your browser, take the time to read through this copy of *ResearchNavigator.com Guide* and use it as a reference for all of your Web research needs.

P A R T 1

Research
Navigator.com

What Is ResearchNavigator.com?

ResearchNavigator.com is the easiest way for you to start a research assignment or research paper. Complete with extensive help on the research process and four exclusive databases of credible and reliable source material (including EBSCO's ContentSelect™ Academic Journal and Abstract Database, *New York Times* Search by Subject Archive, Link Library, and the *Financial Times* Article Archive), ResearchNavigator.com helps you quickly and efficiently make the most of your research time.

ResearchNavigator.com includes four databases of dependable source material to get your research process started:

1. EBSCO's ContentSelect™ Academic Journal and Abstract Database, organized by subject, contains 50–100 of the leading academic journals per discipline. Instructors and students can search the online journals by keyword, topic, or multiple topics. Articles include abstract and citation information and can be cut, pasted, emailed, or saved for later use.

2. The *New York Times* Search by Subject Archive is organized by academic subject and searchable by keyword, or multiple keywords. Instructors and students can view full-text articles from the world's leading journalists from *The New York Times*. The *New York Times* Search by Subject Archive is available exclusively to instructors and students through ResearchNavigator.com.

3. Link Library, organized by subject, offers editorially selected "Best of the Web" sites. Link libraries are continually scanned and kept up to date, providing the most relevant and accurate links for research assignments.
4. The *Financial Times* Article Archive and Company Financials provides a searchable one-year archive and five-year financials for the 500 largest U.S. companies (by gross revenue).

In addition, ResearchNavigator.com includes extensive online content detailing the steps in the research process including:

- Understanding the Research Process
- Finding Sources for your Assignment
- Using your Library for Research, with library guides to 31 core disciplines. Each library guide includes an overview of major databases and online journals, key associations and newsgroups, and suggestions for further research.
- Writing Your Research Assignment
- Finishing with Endnotes and a Bibliography

Registering with ResearchNavigator.com

`http://www.researchnavigator.com`

ResearchNavigator.com is simple to use and easy to navigate. The goal of ResearchNavigator.com is to help you complete research assignments or research papers quickly and efficiently. The site is organized around the following five tabs:

- The Research Process
- Finding Sources
- Using Your Library
- Start Writing
- Endnotes & Bibliography

In order to begin using ResearchNavigator.com, you must first register using the personal access code that appears in the front cover of this book.

To Register:

4. Go to **http://www.researchnavigator.com**
5. Click "Register" under "New Users" on the left side of the screen.
6. Enter the access code exactly as it appears on the inside front cover of this book. (Note: Access codes can only be used once to com-

plete one registration. If you purchased a used guide, the access code may not work. Please go to **www.researchnavigator.com** for information on how to obtain a new access code.)

7. Follow the instructions on screen to complete your registration—you may click the Help button at any time if you are unsure how to respond.

8. Once you have successfully completed registration, write down the Login Name and Password you just created and keep it in a safe place. You will need to enter it each time you want to revisit ResearchNavigator.com.

9. Once you register, you have access to all the resources in ResearchNavigator.com for twelve months.

Getting Started

From the ResearchNavigator.com homepage, you have easy access to all of the site's main features, including a quick route to four exclusive databases of source content that will be discussed in greater detail on the following pages. If you are new to the research process, you may want to start by clicking the *Research Process* tab, located in the upper right hand section of the page. Here you will find extensive help on all aspects of the research process, including:

- Overview of the Research Process
- Understanding a Research Assignment
- Finding a Topic
- Creating Effective Notes
- Research Paper Paradigms
- Understanding and Finding "Source" Material
- Understanding and Avoiding Plagiarism
- Summary of the Research Process

For those of you who are already familiar with the research process, you already know that the first step in completing a research assignment or research paper is to select a topic. (In some cases, your instructor may assign you a topic.) According to James D. Lester in *Writing Research Papers,* choosing a topic for the research paper can be easy (any topic will serve) yet very complicated (an informed choice is critical). He suggests selecting a person, a person's work, or a specific issue to study—President George W. Bush, John Steinbeck's *Of Mice and Men,* or learned dexterity with Nintendo games. Try to select a topic that will meet three demands.

1. It must examine a significant issue.

2. It must address a knowledgeable reader and carry that reader to another level of knowledge.

3. It must have a serious purpose, one that demands analysis of the issues, argues from a position, and explains complex details.

You can find more tips from Lester in the *Research Process* section of ResearchNavigator.com.

ResearchNavigator.com simplifies your research efforts by giving you a convenient launching pad for gathering data on your topic. The site has aggregated four distinct types of source material commonly used in research assignments: academic journals (Content-Select™); newspaper articles (*New York Times*), World Wide Web sites (Link Library), and international news and business data (*Financial Times*).

EBSCO's ContentSelect Academic Journal and Abstract Database

EBSCO's ContentSelect Academic Journal and Abstract Database contains scholarly, peer-reviewed journals (like the *Journal of Clinical Psychology* or the *Journal of Anthropology*). A scholarly journal is an edited collection of articles written by various authors and is published several times per year. All the issues published in one calendar year comprise a volume of that journal. For example, the *American Sociological Review* published volume 65 in the year 2000. This official journal of the American Sociological Association is published six times a year, so issues 1–6 in volume 65 are the individual issues for that year. Each issue contains between 4 and 8 articles written by a variety of authors. Additionally, journal issues may contain letters from the editor, book reviews, and comments from authors. Each issue of a journal does not necessarily revolve around a common theme. In fact, most issues contain articles on many different topics.

Scholarly journals, are similar to magazines in that they are published several times per year and contain a variety of articles in each issue, however, they are NOT magazines. What sets them apart from popular magazines like *Newsweek* or *Science News* is that the content of each issue is peer-reviewed. This means that each journal has, in addition to an editor and editorial staff, a pool of reviewers. Rather than a staff of writers who write something on assignment, journals accept submissions from academic researchers all over the world. The editor relies on these peer reviewers both to evaluate the articles, which are submitted, and to decide if they should be accepted for publication. These published articles provide you with a specialized knowledge and information about your research topic. Academic journal articles adhere to strict scientific guidelines for methodology and theoretical grounding. The information obtained in these individual articles is more scientific than information you would find in a popular magazine, newspaper article, or on a Web page.

Using ContentSelect

Searching for articles in ContentSelect is easy! Here are some instructions and search tips to help you find articles for your research paper.

Select a Database

ContentSelect's homepage features a list of databases. To search within a single database, click the name of the database. To search in more than one database, hold down the alt or command key while clicking on the name of the database.

Basic Search.   After selecting one or more databases, you must enter a keyword or keywords, then click on "go." This will take you to the basic search window. If you've selected a precise and distinctive keyword, your search may be done. But if you have too many results—which is often the case—you need to narrow your search.

Standard Search (Boolean).
- **AND** combines search terms so that each result contains all of the terms. For example, search **education AND technology** to find only articles that contain both terms.
- **OR** combines search terms so that each result contains at least one of the terms. For example, search **education OR technology** to find results that contain either term.
- **NOT** excludes terms so that each result does not contain the term that follows the "not" operator. For example, search **education NOT technology** to find results that contain the term education but not the term technology.

Search by Article Number.   Each and every article in the EBSCO ContentSelect Academic Journal and Abstract Database is assigned its own unique article number. In some cases, you may know the exact article number for the journal article you'd like to retrieve. Perhaps you noted it during a prior research session on ResearchNavigator.com. Such article numbers might also be found on a companion web site for your text, or in the text itself.

   To retrieve a specific article, simply type that article number in the "Search by Article Number" field and click the **GO** button.

Advanced Search. On the tabbed tool bar, click **Advanced Search.** The advanced search window appears. Enter your search terms in the **Find** field. Your search terms can be keywords or selections from search history. Boolean operators (AND, OR, NOT) can also be included in your search.

You can also use **field codes** with your search terms. Fields refer to searchable aspects of an article or Web page; in the case of ContentSelect, they include author, title, subject, abstract, and journal name. Click **Field Codes** to display a list of field codes available with the databases you are using. Type the field code before your search terms to limit those words to the field you entered. For example, **AU Naughton** will find records that contain Naughton in the author field.

To **print, e-mail, or save** several search results, click on the folder next to the result; then print, e-mail, or save from the folder at the top of the results field. (You can still print, e-mail, or save individual results from the open article or citation.)

You can remove specific results, or clear the entire folder and collect new results, during your session. If you end your session, or it times out due to inactivity, the folder is automatically cleared.

Full-Text Results. Some ContentSelect results will be available in full text—that is, if you click on the full text logo at the bottom of an entry, you will be able to call up the entire journal or magazine article. If you want to limit your search to results available in full text, click on the "search options" tab, and then on "full text." Then renew your search.

Abstract and Citation Results. Many ContentSelect results are in the form of citations containing abstracts. A **citation** is a bibliographic reference to an article or document, with basic information such as ISSN (International Standard Serial Number, the standard method for identifying publications) and publisher that will help you locate it. An **abstract** is a brief description of an article, usually written by the author. An abstract will help you decide whether you want to locate the work—either in an electronic database or a print version—through your college library.

A handy tip: once you have found an article that meets your research needs, you can search fields easily from the article citation to turn up similar articles. For example, suppose a particular 2005 story from the *Christian Science Monitor* suits your paper perfectly. Go to the citation and click on the subject field to find similar articles. Or, if you want to see what else the author has written, click on the author field to produce a list of articles he or she has written.

In many cases you can search the full text of articles using electronic databases and then read the entire article online. Typically, in order to use these databases you need to have a library card number or special password provided by the library. But sometimes when you use an electronic database you will find that the text of an article won't be accessible online, so you'll have to go to the library's shelves to find the magazine or newspaper in which the article originally appeared.

The *New York Times* Search by Subject Archive

Newspapers, also known as periodicals because they are issued in periodic installments (e.g., daily, weekly, or monthly), provide contemporary information. Information in periodicals—journals, magazines, and newspapers—may be useful, or even critical, when you are ready to focus in on specific aspects of your topic, or to find more up-to-date information.

There are some significant differences between newspaper articles and journal articles, and you should consider the level of scholarship that is most appropriate for your research. Popular or controversial topics may not be well covered in journals, even though coverage in newspapers and "general interest" magazines like *Newsweek* and *Science* for that same topic may be extensive.

ResearchNavigator.com gives you access to a one-year, "search by subject" archive of articles from one of the world's leading newspapers—*The New York Times*. To learn more about *The New York Times,* visit them on the Web at **http://www.nytimes.com**.

Using the search-by-subject archive is easy. Simply select a subject and type a word, or multiple words separated by commas, into the search box and click "go." The *New York Times* search by subject archive sorts article results by relevance, with the most relevant appearing first. To view the most recently published articles first, use the "Sort by" pull-down menu located just above the search results. You can further refine your search as needed. Articles can be printed or saved for later use in your research assignment. Be sure to review the citation rules for how to cite a newspaper article in endnotes or a bibliography.

"Best of the Web" Link Library

The third database included on ResearchNavigator.com, Link Library, is a collection of Web links, organized by academic subject and key terms. To use this database, simply select an academic subject from the dropdown list, and then find the key term for the topic you are searching. Click on the key term and see a list of five to seven editorially reviewed Web sites that offer educationally relevant and reliable content. For example, if your research topic is "Allergies," you may want to select the academic subject Biology and then click on "Allergies" for links to web sites that explore this topic. Simply click on the alphabet bar to view other key terms in Biology, and their corresponding links. The web links in Link Library are monitored and updated each week, reducing your incidence of finding "dead" links.

International *Financial Times* Article Archive

ResearchNavigator.com's fourth database of content is the *Financial Times* Article Archive and Company Financials Database. Through an exclusive agreement with the *Financial Times,* a leading daily newspaper covering national and international news and business, you can search this publication's one-year archive for news stories affecting countries, companies, and people throughout the world. Simply enter your keyword(s) in the text box and click the **GO** button.

Using Your Library

After you have selected your topic and gathered source material from the three databases of content on ResearchNavigator.com, you may need to complete your research by going to your school library. ResearchNavigator.com does not try to replace the library, but rather helps you understand how to use library resources effectively and efficiently.

You may put off going to the library to complete research assignments or research papers because the library can seem overwhelming. ResearchNavigator.com provides a bridge to the library by taking you through a simple step-by-step overview of how to make the most of your library time. Written by a library scientist, the *Using Your Library* tab explains:

- Major types of libraries
- What the library has to offer
- How to choose the right library tools for a project
- The research process
- How to make the most of research time in the library

In addition, when you are ready to use the library to complete a research assignment or research paper, ResearchNavigator.com includes 31 discipline-specific "library guides" for you to use as a roadmap. Each guide includes an overview of the discipline's major subject databases, online journals, and key associations and newsgroups.

For more information and detailed walk-throughs, please visit
www.researchnavigator.com/about

Start Writing

Once you've become well acquainted with the steps in the research process and gathered source materials from ResearchNavigator.com and your school library, it's time to begin writing your assignment. Content found in this tab will help you do just that, beginning with a discussion on how to draft a research paper in an academic style. Other areas addressed include:

- Blending reference material into your writing
- Writing the introduction, body, and conclusion
- Revising, proofreading, and formatting the rough draft
- Online *Grammar Guide* that spells out some of the rules and conventions of standard written English. Included are guidelines and examples for good sentence structure; tips for proper use of articles, plurals and possessives, pronouns, adjectives and adverbs; details on subject-verb agreement and verb tense consistency; and help with the various forms of punctuation.

This is also the tab where you will find sample research papers for your reference. Use them as a guide to writing your own assignment.

Endnotes & Bibliography

The final step in a research assignment is to create endnotes and a bibliography. In an era dubbed "The Information Age," knowledge and words are taking on more significance than ever. Laws requiring writers to document or give credit to the sources of information, while evolving, must be followed.

Various organizations have developed style manuals detailing how to document sources in their particular disciplines. For writing in the humanities and social sciences, the Modern Language Association (MLA) and American Psychological Association (APA) guidelines are the most commonly used, but others, such as those in *The Chicago Manual of Style* (CMS), are also required. The purpose of this Research Navigator™ tab is to help you properly cite your research sources. It contains detailed information on MLA, APA, CMS, and CBE styles. You'll also find guidance on how to cite the material you've gathered right from ResearchNavigator.com!

This Research Navigator tab also provides students with the option to use **AutoCite.** Students just select their documentation style (MLA or APA), and then fill in the fields with information about their source. **AutoCite** will do the rest! It will automatically create the entry in the proper format. Once completed, **AutoCite** will also generate a "Works Cited" or "References" list that students can print or save (cut and paste).

P A R T **2**

Conducting
Online
Research

Finding Sources:
Search Engines and Subject Directories

Your professor has just given you an assignment to give a five minute speech on the topic "gun control." After a (hopefully brief) panic attack, you begin to think of what type of information you need before you can write the speech. To provide an interesting introduction, you decide to involve your class by taking a straw poll of their views for and against gun control, and to follow this up by giving some statistics on how many Americans favor (and oppose) gun control legislation and then by outlining the arguments on both sides of the issue. If you already know the correct URL for an authoritative Web site like Gallup Opinion Polls (www.gallup.com) or other sites you are in great shape! However, what do you do when you don't have a clue as to which Web site would have information on your topic? In these cases, many, many people routinely (and mistakenly) go to Yahoo! and type in a single term (e.g., guns). This approach is sure to bring first a smile to your face when the results offer you 200,874 hits on your topic, but just as quickly make you grind your teeth in frustration when you start scrolling down the hit list and find sites that range from gun dealerships, to reviews of the video "Young Guns," to aging fan sites for "Guns and Roses."

Finding information on a specific topic on the Web is a challenge. The more intricate your research need, the more difficult it is to find the one or two Web sites among the billions that feature the information you want. This section is designed to help you to avoid frustration and to focus in on the right site for your research by using search engines, subject directories, and meta-sites.

Search Engines

Search engines (sometimes called search services) are becoming more numerous on the Web. Originally, they were designed to help users search the Web by topic. More recently, search engines have added features which enhance their usefulness, such as searching a particular part of the Web (e.g., only sites of educational institutions—dot.edu), retrieving just one site which the search engine touts as most relevant (like Ask.com {www.ask.com}), or retrieving up to 10 sites which the search engine rank as most relevant (like Google {www.google.com}).

Search Engine Defined

According to Cohen (1999):

> "A search engine service provides a searchable database of Internet files collected by a computer program called a wanderer, crawler, robot, worm, or spider. Indexing is created from the collected files, and the results are presented in a schematic order. There are no selection criteria for the collection of files.
>
> A search service therefore consists of three components: (1) a spider, a program that traverses the Web from link to link, identifying and reading pages; (2) an index, a database containing a copy of each Web page gathered by the spider; and (3) a search engine mechanism, software that enables users to query the index and then returns results in a schematic order (p. 31)."

One problem students often have in their use of search engines is that they are deceptively easy to use. Like our example "guns," no matter what is typed into the handy box at the top, links to numerous Web sites appear instantaneously, lulling students into a false sense of security. Since so much was retrieved, surely SOME of it must be useful. WRONG! Many Web sites retrieved will be very light on substantive content, which is not what you need for most academic endeavors. Finding just the right Web site has been likened to finding diamonds in the desert.

As you can see by the definition above, one reason for this is that most search engines use indexes developed by machines. Therefore they are indexing terms not concepts. The search engine cannot tell the difference between the keyword "crack" to mean a split in the sidewalk and "crack" referring to crack cocaine. To use search engines properly takes some skill, and this chapter will provide tips to help you use search engines more effectively. First, however, let's look at the different types of search engines with examples:

TYPES OF SEARCH ENGINES

TYPE	DESCRIPTION	EXAMPLES
1st Generation	• Non-evaluative, do not evaluate results in terms of content or authority. • Return results ranked by relevancy alone (number of times the term(s) entered appear, usually on the first paragraph or page of the site)	AltaVista (www.altavista.com) Excite (www.excite.com) HotBot (www.HotBot.com) Ixquick Metasearch (ixquick.com) Lycos (www.lycos.com)
2nd Generation	• More creative in displaying results. • Results are ordered by characteristics such as: concept, document type, Web site, popularity, etc. rather than relevancy.	Ask (www.ask.com) Direct Hit (www.directhit.com) Google! (www.google.com) HotLinks (www.hotlinks.com) Simplifind (www.simpli.com) SurfWax (www.surfwax.com) Also see Meta-Search engines below. EVALUATIVE SEARCH ENGINES About.Com (www.about.com) WebCrawler (www.webcrawler.com)
Commercial Portals	• Provide additional features such as: customized news, stock quotations, weather reports, shopping, etc. • They want to be used as a "one stop" Web guide. • They profit from prominent advertisements and fees charged to featured sites.	GONetwork (www.go.com) Google Web Directory (directory.google.com) LookSmart (www.looksmart.com) My Starting Point (www.stpt.com) Open Directory Project (dmoz.org) NetNow (www.inetnow.com) Yahoo! (www.yahoo.com)
Meta-Search Engines	Run searches on multiple search engines.	There are different types of meta-search engines. See the next 2 boxes.

(continued)

TYPES OF SEARCH ENGINES, *continued*

TYPE	DESCRIPTION	EXAMPLES
Meta-Search Engines *Integrated Result*	• Display results for search engines in one list. • Duplicates are removed. • Only portions of results from each engine are returned.	Beaucoup.com (www.beaucoup.com) Highway 61 (www.highway61.com) Cyber411 (www.cyber411. com) Mamma (www.mamma.com) MetaCrawler (www. metacrawler.com) Visisimo (www.vivisimo.com) Northern Light (www.nlsearch.com) SurfWax (www.surfwax.com)
Meta-Search Engines *Non-Integrated Results*	• Comprehensive search. • Displays results from each search engine in separate results sets. • Duplicates remain. • You must sift through all the sites.	Dogpile (www.dogpile.com) GoHip (www.gohip.com) Searchalot (www.searchalot.com) ProFusion (www. profusion.com)

QUICK TIPS FOR MORE EFFECTIVE USE OF SEARCH ENGINES

1. Use a search engine:
   - When you have a narrow idea to search.
   - When you want to search the full text of countless Web pages
   - When you want to retrieve a large number of sites
   - When the features of the search engine (like searching particular parts of the Web) help with your search

2. Always use Boolean Operators to combine terms. Searching on a single term is a sure way to retrieve a very large number of Web pages, few, if any, of which are on target.
   - Always check search engine's HELP feature to see what symbols are used for the operators as these vary (e.g., some engines use the & or + symbol for AND).
   - Boolean Operators include:
     AND to narrow search and to make sure that **both** terms are included
       e.g., children AND violence
     OR to broaden search and to make sure that **either** term is included
       e.g., child OR children OR juveniles
     NOT to **exclude** one term
       e.g., eclipse NOT lunar

3. Use appropriate symbols to indicate important terms and to indicate phrases (Best Bet for Constructing a Search According to Cohen (1999): Use a plus sign (+) in front of terms you want to retrieve: +solar +eclipse. Place a phrase in double quotation marks: "solar eclipse" Put together: "+solar eclipse" "+South America").

4. Use word stemming (a.k.a. truncation) to find all variations of a word (check search engine HELP for symbols).
   - If you want to retrieve child, child's, or children use child* (some engines use other symbols such as !, #, or $)
   - Some engines automatically search singular and plural terms, check HELP to see if yours does.

5. Since search engines only search a portion of the Web, use several search engines or a meta-search engine to extend your reach.

6. Remember search engines are generally mindless drones that do not evaluate. Do not rely on them to find the best Web sites on your topic, use *subject directories* or meta-sites to enhance value (see below).

Finding Those Diamonds in the Desert: Using Subject Directories and Meta-sites

Although some search engines, like WebCrawler (www.webcrawler.com) do evaluate the Web sites they index, most search engines do not make any judgment on the worth of the content. They just return a long—sometimes very long—list of sites that contained your keyword. However, *subject directories* exist that are developed by human indexers, usually librarians or subject experts, and are defined by Cohen (1999) as follows:

> "A subject directory is a service that offers a collection of links to Internet resources submitted by site creators or evaluators and organized into subject categories. Directory services use selection criteria for choosing links to include, though the selectivity varies among services (p. 27)."

World Wide Web Subject directories are useful when you want to see sites on your topic that have been reviewed, evaluated, and selected for their authority, accuracy, and value. They can be real time savers for students, since subject directories weed out the commercial, lightweight, or biased Web sites.

Metasites are similar to subject directories, but are more specific in nature, usually dealing with one scholarly field or discipline. Some examples of subject directories and meta-sites are found in the table on the next page.

SMART SEARCHING—SUBJECT DIRECTORIES AND META-SITES

TYPES—SUBJECT DIRECTORIES	EXAMPLES
General, covers many topics	Access to Internet and Subject Resources (www2.lib.udel.edu/subj/) Best Information on the Net (BIOTN) (http://library.sau.edu/bestinfo/) INFOMINE: Scholarly Internet Resource Collections (http://infomine.ucr.edu/) Librarian's Index to the Internet (www.lii.org/) Martindale's "The Reference Desk" (www.martindalecenter.com) PINAKES: A Subject Launchpad (www.hw.ac.uk/libWWW/irn/pinakes/pinakes.html) Refdesk.com (www.refdesk.com) Search Engines and Subject Directories (College of New Jersey) (www.tcnj.edu/~library/research/internet_search.html) Scout Report Archives (www.scout.cs.wisc.edu/archives) WWW Virtual Library (http://vlib.org)
Subject Oriented	
• Communication Studies	The Media and Communication Studies Site (www.aber.ac.uk/media) University of Iowa Department of Communication Studies (www.uiowa.edu/~commstud/resources)
• Cultural Studies	Sara Zupko's Cultural Studies Center (www.popcultures.com)
• Education	Educational Virtual Library (www.csu.edu.au/education/library.html) ERIC [Education ResourcesInformation Center] (www.eduref.org) Kathy Schrock's Guide for Educators (http://kathyschrock.net/abceval/index.htm)
• Journalism	Journalism Resources (https://bailiwick.lib.uiowa.edu/journalism/) Journalism and Media Criticism page (www.chss.montclair.edu/english/furr/media.html)
• Literature	Norton Web Source to American Literature (www.wwnorton.com/naal) Project Gutenberg [Over 3,000 full text titles] (www.gutenberg.org)

SMART SEARCHING, *continued*

TYPES—SUBJECT DIRECTORIES	EXAMPLES
• Medicine & Health	PubMed [National Library of Medicine's index to Medical journals, 1966 to present] (www.ncbi.nlm.nih.gov/PubMed/) RxList: The Internet Drug Index (http://rxlist.com) Go Ask Alice (www.goaskalice.columbia.edu) [Health and sexuality]
• Technology	CNET.com (www.cnet.com)

Choose subject directories to ensure that you are searching the highest quality Web pages. As an added bonus, subject directories periodically check Web links to make sure that there are fewer dead ends and out-dated links.

Another closely related group of sites are the *Virtual Library sites,* also referred to as Digital Library sites (see the table below). Hopefully, your campus library has an outstanding Web site for both on-campus and off-campus access to resources. If not, there are

VIRTUAL LIBRARY SITES

PUBLIC LIBRARIES	
• Internet Public Library	www.ipl.org
• Library of Congress	http://lcweb.loc.gov/homepage/lchp.html
• New York Public Library	www.nypl.org
University/College Libraries	
• Case Western	www.cwru.edu/uclibraries.html
• Dartmouth	www.dartmouth.edu/~library
• Duke	www.lib.duke.edu/
• Franklin & Marshall	www.library.fandm.edu
• Harvard	www.harvard.edu/museums/
• Penn State	www.libraries.psu.edu
• Stanford	www.slac.stanford.edu/FIND/spires.html
• ULCA	www.library.ucla.edu
Other	
• Perseus Project [subject specific—classics, supported by grants from corporations and educational institutions]	www.perseus.tufts.edu

several virtual library sites that you can use, although you should realize that some of the resources would be subscription based, and not accessible unless you are a student of that particular university or college. These are useful because, like the subject directories and meta-sites, experts have organized Web sites by topic and selected only those of highest quality.

You now know how to search for information and use search engines more effectively. In the next section, you will learn more tips for evaluating the information that you found.

BIBLIOGRAPHY FOR FURTHER READING

Books

Basch, Reva. (1996). *Secrets of the Super Net Searchers.*

Berkman, Robert I. (2000). *Find It Fast: How to Uncover Expert Information on Any Subject Online or in Print.* NY: HarperResource.

Glossbrenner, Alfred & Glossbrenner, Emily. (1999). *Search Engines for the World Wide Web,* 2nd Ed. Berkeley, CA: Peachpit Press.

Hock, Randolph, & Berinstein, Paula. (1999). *The Extreme Searcher's Guide to Web Search Engines: A Handbook for the Serious Searcher.* Information Today, Inc.

Miller, Michael. (2000). *Complete Idiot's Guide to Yahoo!* Indianapolis, IN: Que.

Miller, Michael. (2000). *Complete Idiot's Guide to Online Search Secrets.* Indianapolis, IN: Que.

Paul, Nora, Williams, Margot, & Hane, Paula. (1999). *Great Scouts!: Cyber-Guides for Subject Searching on the Web.* Information Today, Inc.

Radford, Marie, Barnes, Susan, & Barr, Linda. (2001). *Web Research: Selecting, Evaluating, and Citing* Boston. Allyn and Bacon.

Journal Articles

Cohen, Laura B. (1999, August). The Web as a research tool: Teaching strategies for instructors. *CHOICE Supplement 3,* 20–44.

Cohen, Laura B. (August 2000). Searching the Web: The Human Element Emerges. *CHOICE Supplement 37,* 17–31.

Introna, Lucas D., & Nissenbaum, Helen. (2000). Shaping the web: Why the politics of search engines matters. The Information Society, Vol. 16, No. 3, pp. 169–185.

Evaluating Sources on the Web

Congratulations! You've found a great Web site. Now what? The Web site you found seems like the perfect Web site for your research.

But, are you sure? Why is it perfect? What criteria are you using to determine whether this Web site suits your purpose?

Think about it. Where else on earth can anyone "publish" information regardless of the *accuracy, currency,* or *reliability* of the information? The Internet has opened up a world of opportunity for posting and distributing information and ideas to virtually everyone, even those who might post misinformation for fun, or those with ulterior motives for promoting their point of view. Armed with the information provided in this guide, you can dig through the vast amount of useless information and misinformation on the World Wide Web to uncover the valuable information. Because practically anyone can post and distribute their ideas on the Web, you need to develop a new set of *critical thinking skills* that focus on the evaluation of the quality of information, rather than be influenced and manipulated by slick graphics and flashy moving java script.

Before the existence of online sources, the validity and accuracy of a source was more easily determined. For example, in order for a book to get to the publishing stage, it must go through many critiques, validation of facts, reviews, editorial changes and the like. Ownership of the information in the book is clear because the author's name is attached to it. The publisher's reputation is on the line too. If the book turns out to have incorrect information, reputations and money can be lost. In addition, books available in a university library are further reviewed by professional librarians and selected for library purchase because of their accuracy and value to students. Journal articles downloaded or printed from online subscription services, such as Infotrac, ProQuest, EbscoHost, or other fulltext databases, are put through the same scrutiny as the paper versions of the journals.

On the World Wide Web, however, Internet service providers (ISPs) simply give Web site authors a place to store information. The Web site author can post information that may not be validated or tested for accuracy. One mistake students typically make is to assume that all information on the Web is of equal value. Also, in the rush to get assignments in on time, students may not take the extra time to make sure that the information they are citing is accurate. It is easy just to cut and paste without really thinking about the content in a critical way. However, to make sure you are gathering accurate information and to get the best grade on your assignments, it is vital that you develop your critical ability to sift through the dirt to find the diamonds.

Web Evaluation Criteria

So, here you are, at this potentially great site. Let's go though some ways you can determine if this site is one you can cite with confidence in your research. Keep in mind, ease of use of a Web site is an

Evaluating Web Sites Using
Five Criteria to Judge Web Site Content

Accuracy—How reliable is the information?

Authority—Who is the author and what are his or her credentials?

Objectivity—Does the Web site present a balanced or biased point of view?

Coverage—Is the information comprehensive enough for your needs?

Currency—Is the Web site up to date?

Use additional criteria to judge Web site content, including

- **Publisher, documentation, relevance, scope, audience, appropriateness of format,** and **navigation**
- Judging whether the site is made up of **primary (original) or secondary (interpretive) sources**
- Determining whether the information is **relevant** to your research

issue, but more important is learning how to determine the validity of data, facts, and statements for your use. The five traditional ways to verify a paper source can also be applied to your Web source: *accuracy, authority, objectivity, coverage,* and *currency.*

Content Evaluation

Accuracy.   Internet searches are not the same as searches of library databases because much of the information on the Web has not been edited, whereas information in databases has. It is your responsibility to make sure that the information you use in a school project is accurate. When you examine the content on a Web site or Web page, you can ask yourself a number of questions to determine whether the information is accurate.

1. Is the information reliable?
2. Do the facts from your other research contradict the facts you find on this Web page?
3. Do any misspellings and/or grammar mistakes indicate a hastily put together Web site that has not been checked for accuracy?
4. Is the content on the page verifiable through some other source? Can you find similar facts elsewhere (journals, books, or other online sources) to support the facts you see on this Web page?
5. Do you find links to other Web sites on a similar topic? If so, check those links to ascertain whether they back up the information you see on the Web page you are interested in using.
6. Is a bibliography of additional sources for research provided? Lack of a bibliography doesn't mean the page isn't accurate, but

having one allows you further investigation points to check the information.

7. Does the site of a research document or study explain how the data was collected and the type of research method used to interpret the data?

If you've found a site with information that seems too good to be true, it may be. You need to verify information that you read on the Web by crosschecking against other sources.

Authority.   An important question to ask when you are evaluating a Web site is, "Who is the author of the information?" Do you know whether the author is a recognized authority in his or her field? Biographical information, references to publications, degrees, qualifications, and organizational affiliations can help to indicate an author's authority. For example, if you are researching the topic of laser surgery citing a medical doctor would be better than citing a college student who has had laser surgery.

The organization sponsoring the site can also provide clues about whether the information is fact or opinion. Examine how the information was gathered and the research method used to prepare the study or report. Other questions to ask include:

1. Who is responsible for the content of the page? Although a webmaster's name is often listed, this person is not necessarily responsible for the content.

2. Is the author recognized in the subject area? Does this person cite any other publications he or she has authored?

3. Does the author list his or her background or credentials (e.g., Ph.D. degree, title such as professor, or other honorary or social distinction)?

4. Is there a way to contact the author? Does the author provide a phone number or email address?

5. If the page is mounted by an organization, is it a known, reputable one?

6. How long has the organization been in existence?

7. Does the URL for the Web page end in the extension .edu or .org? Such extensions indicate authority compared to dotcoms (.com), which are commercial enterprises. (For example, www.cancer.com takes you to an online drugstore that has a cancer information page; www.cancer.org is the American Cancer Society Web site.)

A good idea is to ask yourself whether the author or organization presenting the information on the Web is an authority on the subject. If the answer is no, this may not be a good source of information.

Objectivity.   Every author has a point of view, and some views are more controversial than others. Journalists try to be objective by providing both sides of a story. Academics attempt to persuade readers by presenting a logical argument, which cites other scholars' work. You need to look for two sided arguments in news and information sites. For academic papers, you need to determine how the paper fits within its discipline and whether the author is using controversial methods for reporting a conclusion.

Authoritative authors situate their work within a larger discipline. This background helps readers evaluate the author's knowledge on a particular subject. You should ascertain whether the author's approach is controversial and whether he or she acknowledges this. More important, is the information being presented as fact or opinion? Authors who argue for their position provide readers with other sources that support their arguments. If no sources are cited, the material may be an opinion piece rather than an objective presentation of information. The following questions can help you determine objectivity:

1. Is the purpose of the site clearly stated, either by the author or the organization authoring the site?
2. Does the site give a balanced viewpoint or present only one side?
3. Is the information directed toward a specific group of viewers?
4. Does the site contain advertising?
5. Does the copyright belong to a person or an organization?
6. Do you see anything to indicate who is funding the site?

Everyone has a point of view. This is important to remember when you are using Web resources. A question to keep asking yourself is, What is the bias or point of *view* being expressed here?

Coverage.   Coverage deals with the breadth and depth of information presented on a Web site. Stated another way, it is about how much information is presented and how detailed the information is. Looking at the site map or index can give you an idea about how much information is contained on a site. This isn't necessarily bad. Coverage is a criteria that is tied closely to *your* research requirement. For one assignment, a given Web site may be too general for your needs. For another assignment, that same site might be perfect. Some sites contain very little actual information because pages are filled with links to other sites. Coverage also relates to objectivity. You should ask the following questions about coverage:

1. Does the author present both sides of the story or is a piece of the story missing?

2. Is the information comprehensive enough for your needs?
3. Does the site cover too much, too generally?
4. Do you need more specific information than the site can provide?
5. Does the site have an objective approach?

In addition to examining what is covered on a Web site, equally revealing is what is not covered. Missing information can reveal a bias in the material. Keep in mind that you are evaluating the information on a Web site for your research requirements.

Currency.   Currency questions deal with the timeliness of information. However, currency is more important for some topics than for others. For example, currency is essential when you are looking for technology related topics and current events. In contrast, currency may not be relevant when you are doing research on Plato or Ancient Greece. In terms of Web sites, currency also pertains to whether the site is being kept up to date and links are being maintained. Sites on the Web are sometimes abandoned by their owners. When people move or change jobs, they may neglect to remove theft site from the company or university server. To test currency ask the following questions:

1. Does the site indicate when the content was created?
2. Does the site contain a last revised date? How old is the date? (In the early part of 2001, a university updated their Web site with a "last updated" date of 1901! This obviously was a Y2K problem, but it does point out the need to be observant of such things!)
3. Does the author state how often he or she revises the information? Some sites are on a monthly update cycle (e.g., a government statistics page).
4. Can you tell specifically what content was revised?
5. Is the information still useful for your topic? Even if the last update is old, the site might still be worthy of use *if* the content is still valid for your research.

Relevancy to Your Research: Primary versus Secondary Sources

Some research assignments require the use of primary (original) sources. Materials such as raw data, diaries, letters, manuscripts, and original accounts of events can be considered primary material. In most cases, these historical documents are no longer copyrighted. The Web is a great source for this type of resource.

Information that has been analyzed and previously interpreted is considered a secondary source. Sometimes secondary sources are more appropriate than primary sources. If, for example, you are asked to analyze a topic or to find an analysis of a topic, a secondary source of an analysis would be most appropriate. Ask yourself the following questions to determine whether the Web site is relevant to your research:

1. Is it a primary or secondary source?
2. Do you need a primary source?
3. Does the assignment require you to cite different types of sources? For example, are you supposed to use at least one book, one journal article, and one Web page?

You need to think critically, both visually and verbally, when evaluating Web sites. Because Web sites are designed as multimedia hypertexts, nonlinear texts, visual elements, and navigational tools are added to the evaluation process.

Help in Evaluating Web Sites.   One shortcut to finding high-quality Web sites is using subject directories and meta-sites, which select the Web sites they index by similar evaluation criteria to those just described. If you want to learn more about evaluating Web sites, many colleges and universities provide sites that help you evaluate Web resources. The following list contains some excellent examples of these evaluation sites:

- Evaluating Quality on the Net—Hope Tillman, Babson College
  www.hopetillman.com/findqual.html
- Critical Web Evaluation—Kurt W. Wagner, William Paterson University of New Jersey
  http://euphrates.wpunj.edu/faculty/wagnerk/
- Evalation Criteria—Susan Beck, New Mexico State University
  http://lib.nmsu.edu/instruction/evalcrit.html
- A Student's Guide to Research with the WWW
  www.slu.edu/departments/english/research/

Critical Evaluation Web Sites

WEB SITE AND URL	SOURCE
Critical Thinking in an Online World www.library.ucsb.edu/untangle/ jones.html	*Paper from "Untangling the Web" 1996*
Educom Review: Information www.educause.edu/pub/er/review/ reviewArticles/31231.html	*EDUCAUSE Literacy as a Liberal Art (1996 article)*

WEB SITE AND URL	SOURCE
Evaluating Web Sites www.lib.purdue.edu/InternetEval	*Purdue University Library*
Searching the Web www.lehigh.edu/helpdesk/ useweb.html	*Lehigh University*
Kathy Schrock's ABC's of Web Site Evaluation www.kathyschrock.net/abceval/	*Author's Web site*
Testing the Surf: Criteria for Evaluating Internet Information Sources http://info.lib.uh.edu/pr/v8/n3/ smit8n3.html	*University of Houston Libraries*
UCLA College Library Instruction: Thinking Critically about World Wide Web Resources www.library.ucla.edu/libraries/ college/help/critical/	*UCLA Library*
UG OOL: Judging Quality on the Internet www.open.uoguelph.ca/resources/ skills/judging.html	*University of Guelph*
Web Evaluation Criteria http://lib.nmsu.edu/instruction/ evalcrit.html	*New Mexico State University* *Library*
Web Page Credibility Checklist www.park.pvt.k12.md.us/academics/ research/credcheck.htm	*Park School of Baltimore*
Evaluating Web Sites for Educational Uses: Bibliography and Checklist www.unc.edu/cit/guides/irg-49.html	*University of North Carolina*
Evaluating Web Sites www.lesley.edu/library/guides/ research/evaluating_web.html	*Lesley University*

Tip: Can't seem to get a URL to work? If the URL doesn't begin with www, you may need to put the http:// in front of the URL. Usually, browsers can handle URLs that begin with www without the need to type in the "http://" but if you find you're having trouble, add the http://.

Documentation Guidelines for Online Sources

Your Citation for Exemplary Research

There's another detail left for us to handle—the formal citing of electronic sources in academic papers. The very factor that makes research on the Internet exciting is the same factor that makes referencing these sources challenging: their dynamic nature. A journal article exists, either in print or on microfilm, virtually forever. A document on the Internet can come, go, and change without warning. Because the purpose of citing sources is to allow another scholar to retrace your argument, a good citation allows a reader to obtain information from your primary sources, to the extent possible. This means you need to include not only information on when a source was posted on the Internet (if available) but also when you obtained the information.

The two arbiters of form for academic and scholarly writing are the Modern Language Association (MLA) and the American Psychological Association (APA); both organizations have established styles for citing electronic publications.

MLA Style

In the fifth edition of the *MLA Handbook for Writers of Research Papers,* the MLA recommends the following formats:

- **URLs:** URLs are enclosed in angle brackets (<>) and contain the access mode identifier, the formal name for such indicators as "http" or "ftp." If a URL must be split across two lines, break it only after a slash (/). Never introduce a hyphen at the end of the first line. The URL should include all the parts necessary to identify uniquely the file/document being cited.

    <http://www.csun.edu/~rtvfdept/home/index.html>

- **An online scholarly project or reference database:** A complete "online reference contains the title of the project or database (underlined); the name of the editor of the project or database (if given); electronic publication information, including version number (if relevant and if not part of the title), date of electronic publication or latest update, and name of any sponsoring institution or organization; date of access; and electronic address.

The Perseus Project. Ed. Gregory R. Crane.
    Mar. 1997. Department of Classics,
    Tufts University. 15 June 1998 <http://
    www.perseus.tufts.edu/>.

If you cannot find some of the information, then include the information that is available. The MLA also recommends that you print or download electronic documents, freezing them in time for future reference.

- **A document within a scholarly project or reference database:** It is much more common to use only a portion of a scholarly project or database. To cite an essay, poem, or other short work, begin this citation with the name of the author and the title of the work (in quotation marks). Then, include all the information used when citing a complete online scholarly project or reference database, however, make sure you use the URL of the specific work and not the address of the general site.

Cuthberg, Lori. "Moonwalk: Earthlings' Finest
  Hour." <u>Discovery Channel Online</u>. 1999.
  Discovery Channel. 25 Nov. 1999 <http://
  www.discovery.com/indep/newsfeatures/
  moonwalk/challenge.html>.

- **A professional or personal site:** Include the name of the person creating the site (reversed), followed by a period, the title of the site (underlined), or, if there is no title, a description such as Home page (such a description is neither placed in quotes nor underlined). Then, specify the name of any school, organization, or other institution affiliated with the site and follow it with your date of access and the URL of the page.

Packer, Andy. Home page. 1Apr. 1998 <http://
  www.suu.edu/~students/Packer.htm>.

Some electronic references are truly unique to the online domain. These include email, newsgroup postings, MUDs (multiuser domains) or MOOs (multiuser domains, object-oriented), and IRCs (Internet Relay Chats).

Email.   In citing email messages, begin with the writer's name (reversed) followed by a period, then the title of the message (if any) in quotations as it appears in the subject line. Next comes a description of the message, typically "Email to," and the recipient (e.g., "the author"), and finally the date of the message.

Davis, Jeffrey. "Web Writing Resources." Email
  to Nora Davis. 3 Jan. 2000.

Sommers, Laurice. "Re: College Admissions Practices." Email to the author. 12 Aug. 1998.

List Servers and Newsgroups.   In citing these references, begin with the author's name (reversed) followed by a period. Next include the title of the document (in quotes) from the subject line, followed by the words "Online posting" (not in quotes). Follow this with the date of posting. For list servers, include the date of access, the name of the list (if known), and the online address of the list's moderator or administrator. For newsgroups, follow "Online posting" with the date of posting, the date of access, and the name of the newsgroup, prefixed with "news:" and enclosed in angle brackets.

Applebaum, Dale. "Educational Variables." Online posting. 29 Jan. 1998. Higher Education Discussion Group. 30 Jan. 1993 <jlucidoj@unc.edu>.

Gostl, Jack. "Re: Mr. Levitan." Online posting. 13 June 1997. 20 June 1997 <news:alt.edu. bronxscience>.

MUDs, MOOs, and IRCs.   Begin with the name of the speaker(s) followed by a period. Follow with the description and date of the event, the forum in which the communication took place, the date of access, and the online address. If you accessed the MOO or MUD through telnet, your citation might appear as follows:

Guest. Personal interview. 13 Aug. 1998. <telnet://du.edu:8888>.

For more information on MLA documentation style for online sources, check out their Web site at http://www.mla.org/style/sources.htm.

APA Style

The newly revised *Publication Manual of the American Psychological Association* (5th ed.) now includes guidelines for Internet resources. The manual recommends that, at a minimum, a reference of an Internet source should provide a document title or description, a date (either the date of publication or update or the date of retrieval), and an address (in Internet terms, a uniform resource locator, or URL). Whenever possible, identify the authors of a document as well. It's important to remember that, unlike the MLA, the APA does not include temporary or transient sources (e.g., letters, phone calls, etc.) in its "References" page, preferring to handle them in the text. The general suggested format is as follows:

Online periodical:

Author, A. A., Author, B. B., & Author,
   C. C. (2000). Title of article. *Title of
   Periodical, xx*, xxxxx. Retrieved month, day,
   year, from source.

Online document:

Author, A. A. (2000). *Title of work*. Retrieved
   month, day, year, from source.

Some more specific examples are as follows:

FTP (File Transfer Protocol) Sites. To cite files available for downloading via FTP, give the author's name (if known), the publication date (if available and if different from the date accessed), the full title of the paper (capitalizing only the first word and proper nouns), the date of access, and the address of the FTP site along with the full path necessary to access the file.

Deutsch, P. (1991) Archie: An electronic
   directory service for the Internet. Retrieved
   January 25, 2000 from File Transfer Protocol:
   ftp://ftp.sura.net/pub/archie/docs/
   whatis.archie

WWW Sites (World Wide Web). To cite files available for viewing or downloading via the World Wide Web, give the author's name (if known), the year of publication (if known and if different from the date accessed), the full title of the article, and the title of the complete work (if applicable) in italics. Include any additional information (such as versions, editions, or revisions) in parentheses immediately following the title. Include the date of retrieval and full URL (the http address).

Burka, L. P. (1993). A hypertext history of
   multi-user dungeons. *MUDdex*. Retrieved
   January 13, 1997 from the World Wide Web:
   http://www.utopia.com/talent/lpb/muddex/essay/

Tilton, J. (1995). Composing good HTML (Vers.
   2.0.6). Retrieved December 1, 1996 from the
   World Wide Web: http://www.cs.cmu.edu/
   ~tilt/cgh/

Synchronous Communications (MOOs, MUDs, IRC, etc.). Give the name of the speaker(s), the complete date of the conversation being referenced in parentheses, and the title of the session (if applicable). Next, list the title of the site in italics, the protocol and address (if applicable), and any directions necessary to access the work. Last, list the date of access, followed by the retrieval information. Personal interviews do not need to be listed in the References, but do need to be included in parenthetic references in the text (see the APA *Publication Manual*).

Cross, J. (1996, February 27). Netoric's Tuesday "cafe: Why use MUDs in the writing classroom? *MediaMoo.* Retrieved March 1, 1996 from File Transfer Protocol: ftp://daedalus.com/pub/ ACW/NETORIC/catalog

Gopher Sites. List the author's name (if applicable), the year of publication, the title of the file or paper, and the title of the complete work (if applicable). Include any print publication information (if available) followed by the protocol (i.e., gopher://). List the date that the file was accessed and the path necessary to access the file.

Massachusetts Higher Education Coordinating Council. (1994). Using coordination and collaboration to address change. Retrieved July 16, 1999 from the World Wide Web: gopher://gopher.mass.edu:170/ 00gopher_root%3A%5B_hecc%5D_plan

Email, Listservs, and Newsgroups. Do not include personal email in the list of References. Although unretrievable communication such as email is not included in APA References, somewhat more public or accessible Internet postings from newsgroups or listservs may be included. See the APA *Publication Manual* for information on in-text citations.

Heilke, J. (1996, May 3). Webfolios. Alliance for Computers and Writing Discussion List. Retrieved December 31, 1996 from the World Wide Web: http://www.ttu.edu/lists/acw-l/ 9605/0040.html

Other authors and educators have proposed similar extensions to the APA style. You can find links to these pages at:

`www.psychwww.com/resource/apacrib.htm`

Remember, "frequently-referenced" does not equate to "correct" "or even "desirable." Check with your professor to see if your course or school has a preference for an extended APA style.

Research Tips for Psychology

Getting Started with Your Research Paper

The purpose of this section is to provide an overview of effective strategies for conducting subject specific literature searches and reviews using ResearchNavigator.com. Psychology is an extremely diverse discipline covering numerous subfields such as developmental, personality, and abnormal, as well as overlapping with other disciplines such as biology, sociology, and education. Such breadth of research topics provides a wealth of information, which is great when reviewing research or trying to write a paper because you are certainly going to find information in your area of interest. On the other hand, because psychology is such a diverse field, often there is too much information available on any given research topic. For this reason, and others, many students find it difficult to successfully narrow their research question and subsequent literature search.

For example, if one was interested in conducting a research report on *drug abuse*, the topic would likely be too broad. First, just consider how many abused drugs are available (e.g., cocaine, amphetamine, steroids, marijuana, nicotine, alcohol, heroin, and barbiturates just to name a few), certainly too many for a single research paper. Furthermore, there are far too many important research questions related to drug abuse to be addressed in a single paper. For example, one area of inquiry might include why people begin using drugs, which could include a developmental, personality, social, or biological perspective. Yet another area of inquiry might focus on the adverse consequences of long-term drug abuse, possibly examining its impact on health, family, work, or crime. Generally, the first step in developing a research paper is to articulate a focused research question and rationale. The research question and the rationale, basically the reason the question is important to address, will guide the way you conduct your literature review. Once these two initial steps are complete, conducting a thorough literature review will be much easier.

Although a lot of skill is required to effectively search through thousands of primary and secondary sources, like original research articles or review papers, the collection of information is rarely the primary objective to any assignment. Effective information gathering is simply a means to an end. Thus, the primary point in looking for scientific information is so it can be included in a cohesive and well articulated research paper.

It might seem a little ironic that with so much excellent research available, encompassing so many subjects, that providing a cursory review of a particular topic would be such a daunting task for so many students. However, this problem is certainly understandable considering few students have experience searching or reading profession scientific papers or research reports prior to college. Most students are naive to the scientific databases available, let alone how to efficiently use them. Fortunately, you have this guide as a resource, as well as ResearchNavigator.com, both of which are outstanding resources.

While skilled writing is inherently challenging, scientific writing, with so many caveats and nuances, provides additional challenges. Because there are so many components to good scientific writing, many students, especially those new to the task, can quickly feel overwhelmed. Understanding the basic arrangement and pattern of a scientific paper can go a long way in helping you plan, start, and complete a scientific paper.

Nearly all professional scientific papers follow a predictable format that can be relatively easy to duplicate. In terms of creating an easy analogy and visualization to follow, consider the shape of an hourglass. The hourglass shape is larger at the top and continually narrows toward the center; thereafter, it begins to expand again toward the base until it mirrors the top. Like the shape of an hourglass, scientific reports general start out discussing larger more general issues, followed by a systematic examination of data relevant to the specific research question.

As you move through your research paper, each paragraph should progressively and systematically be modified so that the larger more global ideas give way to more focused discussions, much like an hourglass. The introduction needs to provide a foundation for the more specific content that follows. After the introduction, subsequent paragraphs should focus on the specific variables of interest. For example, if you are interested in adolescent cocaine and methamphetamine abuse, then you need to transition from a survey of drug abuse, in general, to cocaine and methamphetamine abuse, and than followed by issues relevant to adolescence. Thereafter, a more detailed discussion on the specific issue, adolescent cocaine and methamphetamine abuse, would be appropriate. The reader should be drawn naturally to the value and significance of the research problem and the rationale for why your topic deserves further evaluation or consideration. In conclusion, research papers that predominately focus on the review of a particular topic generally start with larger issues and systematically focus on more specific aspects of the problem, while simultaneously emphasizing the importance of the topic.

While many research papers are considered complete after a thorough review of the literature, as you move through your college education, you may be asked to move past a review of a particular research question. You may be asked to develop your own ideas about a particular scientific problem; that is, you may be required to find the "gaps" in the scientific literature and generate new ideas concerning the next logical step in addressing the problem. In consideration of the hourglass analogy, this would be analogous to the bottom of the hourglass, the part that begins to expand. Generally, the end of the review paper is the just the beginning of this type of assignment. After a thorough review of the literature, you must generate a hypothesis statement. A hypothesis statement is a tentative proposal made to explain certain observations or facts that requires further research to be supported. After presenting the hypothesis statement, the goal is to provide information from other research papers or reports that indirectly support your hypothesis. This often takes the form of "if . . . then" statements. If related studies found positive results with a similar problem, then it is possible or likely that you will find such results given your hypothesis. Finally, the paper should conclude with large scale, global predictions like how many people could benefit or how much time and money could be saved, thus, emphasizing the value of your new idea.

The benefit in providing the hourglass analogy is so you can have an understanding on how to search the literature for relevant information for your research paper; that is, the hourglass metaphor provides a basis for systematically altering your literature searches to find the information you need for each part of the research paper. If you consider the analogy, it can be divided into nine parts starting with the top of the hourglass and moving inward: (1) Global, Large Scale Findings, (2) Connecting Ideas/Variables, (3) Significance, (4) Rationale or Justification, and the (5) Research Question. These five steps are generally part of a review paper. If you are required to introduce some of your own ideas, then you will have to complete the bottom of the hourglass: (6) Hypothesis Statement, (7) Unanswered Questions/Gaps, (8) Supporting Evidence, and (9) Global, Large Scale Value. Remember that, with the hourglass example that the search objective is always focused on the research question or expanding from it. Finding sources necessary for writing a good scientific paper will require many searches and turn up many sources; however, this guide should help you discern which types of resources will be most beneficial to your research.

Sample Searches

The following section will provide examples and search ideas and hints from ResearchNavigator.com, using the *ContentSelect Psychology* Database. For the purposes of this section, we are going to work through a series of searches related to "urban adolescent cocaine and methamphetamine abuse on health." The objective of the beginning of the paper is to convince the reader of the importance of the research topic or question. This often includes global, country, regional, state, and, perhaps local statistics, if applicable. Such information is used to demonstrate the impact of the problem on the population of interest. More specifically, the first part of the paper should discuss the impact of the problem on individual's health, work, and family and the economic impact of the problem in the world, country, and/or region of interest. The first section serves to convince the reader that the research question that is being addressed is important and worthy of their time and energy.

As noted previously, as you proceed through the paper the information should systematically focus and move the reader toward your specific research question. Depending on the length of your paper and number of sources, it may take several paragraphs or pages to effectively transition from the more global issues to your specific research question. Using our example, you will have to do several searches with each of the key words and combining key words.

In order to begin your series of searches, first consider what type of information you need. Using our hourglass model, it is best to begin with larger issues first. For example, a search on "cocaine" would yield 308 articles and a search on "methamphetamine" would yield a total of 133 articles. This is likely too many articles. One way to reduce the size of the available articles is to do a *Basic* search and change the search parameters to include only "full-text articles" (no abstracts). By changing the search parameters, the total number of articles for "cocaine" is now just 94 and for "methamphetamine is just 25. The articles are organized into groups of ten with brief summaries below each link, so it is easy to preview the articles before downloading them.

If you feel that you need more articles or want to include more topics related to cocaine and methamphetamine abuse, then you can go to *Basic* search and turn on the *expanders* (simply click on the boxes in the expander area). Conducting a literature search for "cocaine" with the expanders on yields 856 articles, while conducting a search for "methamphetamine" with the expanders on yields 215 articles. Effectively, having the expanders activated locates nearly every article that includes either cocaine or methamphetamine, some of which may be irrelevant.

In order to increase your probability of finding needed information during the initial search, you can also conduct more specific searches with the AND term such as "cocaine AND medical cost" or "cocaine AND crime." Similarly, searches can be conducted with a number of the key terms as well as the OR option such as "methamphetamine OR cocaine."

Once you complete a survey of the literature regarding general facts and statistics with cocaine and methamphetamine, a more focused discussion about teenage or adolescent drug abuse would be appropriate. Thereafter, the focus should shift to specific problems associated with cocaine and methamphetamine abuse in this population. However straightforward this might seem, conducting a search on "teenagers" results in 1402 articles, while conducting a search on "adolescent" produces 3765 results. Using the *Basic* search option to turn on the search expanders produces 2005 articles for "teenager" and 7171 articles for "adolescent." Obviously, thousands of articles are too many to efficiently read through, especially at only 10 articles per page. A more efficient approach, at this point, would be to combine search terms like "teenager AND cocaine (5 articles)" or teenager AND methamphetamine (13 articles)" as well as adolescent AND cocaine (16 articles)" or "adolescent AND methamphetamine (2 articles)." As noted before, if these or similar searches yield too many or too few results, you can adjust the search parameters, through the *Basic* search feature, to include either full text articles, which decreases the number of results, or to include similar and related terms, which increases the number of results.

As a general rule, the more focused your search is, the fewer articles you will find. For example, finding articles on drugs, cocaine, or methamphetamine as well as teenagers or adolescents will likely be numerous; however, as you begin to search for information more pertinent to your specific research question, the amount of available data and articles will likely decrease. However, even the best search techniques can result in articles that have little to do with your area of interest. Search engines follow rather simplistic search parameters, so be sure to evaluate the merit if each source.

If you are having difficulty finding appropriate terms for your search, included in the following section is a list of important terms in psychology broken down according to research area and/or topic. This list should provide an excellent source of terms, either used alone in combination, to begin your literature search. Because scientists seek to explain their findings in ever increasing detail, the amount of jargon, terminology, in science is also ever increasing and parallels scientific advances. Generally, the more specific the term, the more likely you are to locate articles of interest. For example, if you are interested in conducting a search on teenagers, then you could perform your search with "teenager," "puberty," or "adolescence." Although these terms are often thought of as synonyms, they may have different meanings in science. Similarly, if you are interested in conducting a search for medications used to treat depression, you could perform a search using "Prozac," "Fluoxetine," or "Selective Serotonin Reuptake Inhibitors." EBSCO's *ContentSelect* for Psychology is helpful in this regard because it provides a list of recommended key words for every search.

Important Subject Specific Journals and Word Bank

Listed below are several well-known research publications and journals for each of the major divisions within psychology included in the *ContentSelect Academic Journal List*. Also included are a number of key words that will be helpful in starting your literature review and research paper. In addition to the topic list and word bank below, ResearchNavigator.com also provides helpful recommendations for expanding or narrowing your search. If your research topic includes overlapping areas of interests, then all you need to do is combine two or more key words in your search; alternately, you could follow the recommendations from ResearchNavigator.com to modify your search through the use of similar or related terms. For example, conducting a search on *cocaine* could be expanded by including *cocaine* OR *drug abuse, substance abuse,* or *addiction* or it could be narrowed by including *cocaine* AND *treatment, consequences,* or

crime. Finally, the list below is not exhaustive. ResearchNavigator.
com provides many more journals, websites, and word banks that
will most definitely help you complete your research paper.

JOURNALS	KEY TERMS	
Current Psychology	**The Science of Psychology**	
Journal of General Psychology	Scientific method	Cognitive science
Psychological Bulletin	Behavior	Health science
	Individual	Organismic variables
	Mental processes	Dispositional variables
	Levels of analysis	Environmental variables
	Social science	Situational variables
	Biological science	
Journal of Experimental Psychology/ General	**Research Methods in Psychology**	
	Theory	Double-blind control
Journal of Applied Statistics	Hypothesis	Placebo control
Understanding Statistics	Operational definition	Self-Report measures
	Independent variable	Subject sampling
	Dependent variable	Experimental design
	Confounding variable	
Behavioral Neuroscience	**Biological Basis of Behavior**	
International Journal of Neuroscience	Heredity	Cerebrum
Journal of Psychiatry & Neuroscience	Genetics	Cerebral cortex
	Neuroscience	The Endocrine System
	Central nervous system (CNS)	Peripheral nervous system (PNS)
	Brain stem	Neuron
	Limbic system	Neurotransmitters
Journal of Constructivist Psychology	**Sensation and Perception**	
Journal of Experimental Psychology/ Human Perception & Performance	Psychophysics	Kinesthetic Senses
	Transduction	Pain and Nociception
Visual Cognition	Sensory receptors	Illusions
	Visual System	Gestalt psychology
	Hearing	Selective Attention
	Smell	Bottom-Up Processes
	Taste	Top-Down Processes
	Touch and Skin Senses	Object Recognition
American Journal on Addictions	**Mind, Consciousness, and Alternate States**	
Mind, Culture & Activity	Self-awareness	Narcolepsy
Scientific American Mind	Repressed memories	Sleep Apnea
	Unconscious	Lucid Dreaming
	Sleep	Hypnosis
	Dreams	Mind-Altering Drugs
	Circadian Rhythms	Depressants
	Rapid eye movements (REM)	Hallucinogens or psychedelics
	Sleep Disorder	Stimulants
	Insomnia	Addiction and dependence

Journal of Comparative Psychology
Journal of Experimental Psychology/
Animal Behavior Processes
Journal of Experimental Psychology/
Learning, Memory & Cognition

Learning
Conditioning
Learning-performance distinction
Classical Conditioning
Acquisition
Extinction
Spontaneous recovery
Pychoneuroimmunology
Operant Conditioning
The Law of Effect
Experimental Analysis of Behavior
Positive and negative reinforcers
Positive and negative punishment
Schedules of Reinforcement
Animal Cognition
Observational Learning

Memory
Clinical Neuropathology
Journal of Alzheimer's Disease

Memory
Implicit memory	Sensory Memory
Explicit memory	Iconic Memory
Declarative memory	Echoic Memory
Procedural memory	Long-Term Memory
Encoding	Retrieval Cues
Storage	Forget
Retrieval	Amnesia and Dementia
Short-Term Memory (STM) and Working Memory	Context and Encoding Cues

Cognitive Psychology
European Journal of Cognitive Psychology
Thinking & Reasoning

Cognitive Processes
Serial processes	Algorithm
Parallel processes	Heuristics
Controlled processes	Deductive Reasoning
Automatic processes	Inductive Reasoning
Language	Judgment
Visual Cognition	Decision making
Problem Solving	Decision aversion

Creativity Research Journal
Journal of Intellectual &
Developmental Disability
Psychological Assessment

Intelligence
Standardization	Wechsler Scale
Norm Curve	Heritability
Content Validity	Giftedness and Genius
Predictive Validity	Mental Retardation
Stanford-Binet Scale	Creativity

Eating Disorders
Sexual Addiction & Compulsivity
Work & Stress

Motivation and Emotion
Goal-Directed-Behavior	Maslow's Hierarchy
Drive Theory	Self-Actualization
Homeostasis	Hunger
Arousal	Obesity
Expectancy Theory	Anorexia Nervosa
Yerkes-Dodson Law	Bulimia Nervosa
Intrinsic Motivation	Sexual Response Cycle
Extrinsic Motivation	

Child Development
Developmental Psychology
Early Years: Journal of International Research & Development

Child Development

Nature vs. Nurture	Jean Piaget
Zygote	Moral Reasoning
Embryo	Attachment
Fetus	Bonding
Teratogen	Temperament
Reflex	Vygotsky's Sociocultural Theory

Adolescent Psychiatry
Adultspan: Theory Research & Practice
International Journal of Aging & Human Development

Adolescent and Adulthood

Puberty	Fitness
Imaginary Audience	Ageism
Personal Fable	Dementia
Gender Identity	Alzheimer's Disease
Androgyny	Hospice
Menopause	Secondary Sex Characteristics

Educational & Psychological Measurement
Identity
Journal of Personality & Social Psychology

Personality and Assessment

Freud	Self
Psychoanalysis	Self-Efficacy
Defense Mechanisms	MMPI
Neo-Freudism	Projective Test
Jung	Borderline
Fulfillment	Narcissism
Thematic Apperception Test	

Journal of Personality & Social Psychology
Journal of Social Psychology
Studies in Cultures, Organizations & Societies

Social Psychology

Attitude	Conformity
Cognitive Dissonance	Social Facilitation
Self-Perception Theory	Social Loafing
Reactance Theory	Group Polarization
Impression Formation	Groupthink
Attribution	Deindividualization
Self-Serving Bias	Aggression
Stereotypes	Prosocial Behavior
Social Categorization	and Altruism

Anxiety, Stress & Coping
International Journal of Behavioral Medicine
Psychology & Health

Stress and Health Psychology

Anxiety	Burnout
Frustration	Type A vs. Type B
Conflict	Coping
Pressure and Stress	Resilience
Posttraumatic Stress Disorder	Psychoneuroimmunology
	Stress Management

Journal of Abnormal Psychology
Journal of Counseling Psychology
International Journal of Clinical Pharmacology & Therapeutics

Psychological Disorders and Treatment

Anxiety	Bipolar Disorder
Phobia	Schizophrenia
Somatoform Disorders	Therapy
Dissociative Disorders	Placebo Effect
Obsessive-Compulsive Disorder	Systematic Densitization
Personality Disorders	Psychosurgery
Mood Disorders	Drug Therapy
Depression	

Journal of Applied Psychology
Journal of Forensic Psychiatry
& Psychology
Organization Science: A Journal
of the Institute of Management
Sciences

Applied Psychology
Industrial/Organizational Psychology
Equity Theory
Leadership
Human Factors
Ergonomics
Forensic Psychology
Educational Psychology
Sport Psychology

PART 4

Online Resources

Internet Sites Useful in Psychology

Introduction, Research, and History of Psychology

Glossary of Online Psychiatry

http://www.priory.com/gloss.htm

Alphabetical list of hundreds of psychological/psychiatric terms and their definitions.

Psychwatch

http://www.psychwatch.com/index.htm

Psychwatch is a weekly email newsletter detailing events and Internet-related developments in the mental health field. You can have their newsletter emailed to you weekly. This is a fairly effortless way to keep with what is going on in mental health.

A Guide to Psychology and Its Practice

http://members.aol.com/avpsyrich/

This site provides a very extensive array of information about the practice or application of psychology, including information about insurance to opening a practice.

Irvine Health Foundation Lecture Series

http://www.ihf.org/

This site provides full-text articles from some of the most renowned psychologists in the world.

Psychology Departments on the Web

http://www.psychwww.com/resource/deptlist.htm

This very extensive listing of all psychology departments on the Internet is a must for any student making decision about which program to attend.

Gallup Polls

http://www.gallup.com/

This site features public releases, special reports on key social and business-related issues, and Gallup Polls, a major source for public opinion data since 1935.

Educational Testing Service

http://www.ets.org/

This is the Educational Testing Service home page, with information for parents and students, educator-researchers and policymakers.

Code of Conduct

http://www.apa.org/ethics/code.html

This American Psychological Association site deals with ethical principles of psychologists and defines the code of conduct.

Statistics on the Web

http://www.spss.com

Statistics on the World Wide Web may be found at this site.

Psychological Research on the Net

http://psych.hanover.edu/APS/exponnet.html

Links to known experiments on the Internet that are psychologically related are organized by general topic areas with the topic areas listed alphabetically.

Major Areas of Psychology

http://www.psychwww.com/careers/specialt.htm

Explanations of ten different specialty areas in psychology—clinical, counseling, developmental, educational, experimental, health, industrial/organizational, physiological, school, and social psychology—are found at this site.

Careers in Psychology

http://www.rider.edu/users/suler/gradschl.html

This site offers a detailed discussion of what one can do with a degree in psychology, the types of subfields, and how to get into graduate school.

Today in the History of Psychology

http://www.cwu.edu/~warren/today.html

This interactive site allows the user to pick a date and see what happened in psychology on that date.

Biological Psychology

Brain and Mind Magazine

http://www.cerebromente.org.br/

A general public magazine on neuroscience. It is interesting and informative.

Science Direct

http://www.sciencedirect.com/science/journal/03010511

Publishes original scientific papers on the biological aspects of psychological states and processes.

A Primer of Imaging in Psychiatry

http://www.musc.edu/fnrd/primer_index.htm

This site provides a wealth of information helpful to understand the distinction between brain structure and function and to realize the limitations of overinterpreting functional brain scans.

Traumatic Brain Injury Survival Guide

http://www.tbiguide.com

Dr. Glen Johnson's traumatic brain injury survival guide. This site provides a free text on brain injury for general audiences.

"Splitting the Human Brain"

http://www.indiana.edu/~pietsch/split-brain.html

By Paul Pietsch. An interesting article on detailing split-brain surgery and the consequences.

Faculty for Undergraduate Neuroscience

http://www.funfaculty.org/

This is a society dedicated to teaching neuroscience at the undergraduate level.

The Sheep Brain Dissection Guide

http://academic.uofs.edu/department/psych/sheep/

A Manual of Sheep Brain Dissections developed by Robert Wheeler et al. at the University of Scranton.

Neurosciences on the Net

http://www.neuroguide.com/index.html

A searchable and easy to browse index of neuroscience resources available on the Internet including such topics as: Neurobiology, neurology, neurosurgery, psychiatry, psychology, cognitive science sites and information on human neurological diseases.

Two Brains are Better than One

http://whyfiles.org/026fear/physio1.html

The NSF claims that we have a second information processing system located around our stomachs! This article and its links provide evidence suggesting that our enteric system (i.e., gut) is capable of "thinking".

Drugs, Brains, and Behavior

http://www.rci.rutgers.edu/~lwh/drugs/

Timmons & Hamilton provide a complete online textbook on psycho-pharmacology. In addition to the text, there are other valuable resources like a complete bibliography, definitions, and links to other resources.

Virtual Hospital: The Human Brain

http://www.vh.org/Providers/Textbooks/
BrainAnatomy/BrainAnatomy.html

The Department of Anatomy and Cell Biology at the University of Iowa designed this very user friendly and informative site about brain function and pathology (i.e., disease). "This electronic publication is intended to serve students of all the health and biological sciences who are seeking to understand the organization and functions of the human nervous system." The site provides some truly incredible images and explanations of the brain.

Basic Neural Processes Tutorials

http://psych.hanover.edu/Krantz/neurotut.html

This is a short tutorial of the basics of neural processing.

Neuropsychology Central

http://www.neuropsychologycentral.com/

An extremely large and diverse site that contains links to many other sites, including assessment, treatment, organizations, image sites and medical consideration, this is one of the most complete sites on the Net. It even includes music.

Brain Imaging

http://www.bic.mni.mcgill.ca/demos/

These are interesting examples of brain imaging techniques. The brain imaging demos at this site require a graphics browser.

Neuroscience

http://faculty.washington.edu/chudler/ehceduc.html

This extremely detailed site consists of links for education and is large enough to spend several days exploring. It is must for anyone interested in the neuroscience.

The Whole Brain Atlas

http://www.med.harvard.edu/AANLIB/home.html

A complete reference to the brain, this site has information, images, and QuickTime movies all related to the brain. Included is a discussion on the pathology of Alzheimer's disease.

The Visible Human Project

http://www.nlm.nih.gov/research/visible/
visible_human.html

The Visible Human Project is creating complete, anatomically detailed, three-dimensional representations of the male and female human bodies.

Human Genome Project

http://www.ornl.gov/TechResources/Human_Genome/
home.html

This home page is maintained by the Human Genome Management Information System (HGMIS) for the U.S. Department of Energy Human Genome Program. Explore this site for material about the history, progress, research, and resources of the Human Genome Project.

Neuroscience

http://neuro.med.cornell.edu/VL/

This World Wide Web Virtual Library is supported by The Department of Neurology and Neuroscience at Cornell University Medical College.

McConnell Brain Imaging Center

http://www.bic.mni.mcgill.ca/

The McConnell Brain Imaging Center (BIC) is one of the largest scientific communities in North America dedicated solely to research imaging of the human brain.

Sensation and Perception

Illusions Gallery

http://dragon.uml.edu/psych/illusion.html

A collection of visual illusions with explanations and tutorials.

Webvision: The Neural Organization of the Vertebrate Retina

http://webvision.med.utah.edu/

This site provides a very detailed and up-to-date resource on the retina.

Psychological Tutorials and Demonstrations from Hanover College

http://psych.hanover.edu/Krantz/tutor.html

A small collection of tutorials and demonstrations in sensation and perception.

All Psych Online

http://www.Allpsych.com/psychology101/
sensation_perception.html

Although intimately related, sensation and perception play two complimentary but different roles in how we interpret our world. This site helps in unraveling these differences.

Resources in Psychology: Sensation and Perception

http://www.indiana.edu/~iuepsyc/topics/s_p.htm

This site provides several exhibits that examine sensation and perception.

Let's Play Jeopardy!

http://www.uni.edu/walsh/jeopardy.html

Sensation and perception jeopardy.

Sensation and Perception

http://www.skidmore.edu/~hfoley/perception.htm

A wealth of material available for sensation and perception

Acoustical Society of America

http://asa.aip.org/

A scientific society dedicated to expanding our knowledge base in acuistics.

Encyclopedia of Psychology

http://www.psychology.org/links/Environment_
Behavior_Relationships/Sensation_and_Perception/

Resources on sensation and perception in a question/answer format.

Monell Chemical Senses Center

http://www.monell.org/sensation.htm

Scientific institute for multidisciplinary research on taste, smell, and chemosensory irritation.

Brain Briefings: Pheromones

http://www.sfn.org/briefings/pheromones.html

This site is provided by the Society for Neuroscience and explains human pheromone perception.

Visual Illusions and Illustrations

http://dogfeathers.com/java/necker.html

This highly visual and interactive site provides examples of several visual illusions (e.g., the necker cube and the Fechner color illusion) as well as illustrates a couple of visual perception phenomenon (e.g., stereoscopic animated hypercube).

Eye Anatomy

http://www.stlukeseye.com/anatomy.htm

St. Luke's Cataract & Laser Institute has a lot of resources on their site related to visual anatomy and disease.

Subliminal Perception

http://www.yahoo.com/Science/Cognitive_Science/
Unconscious_Cognition/Subliminal_Perception/

A discussion of backward masking, hypnosis, and subliminal advertising can be found at this site.

Exploratorium

http://www.exploratorium.edu/imagery/exhibits.html

This site contains digital versions of Exploratorium exhibits. It is important understand that these versions in most cases are not adequate replacements for the real experiences that you will have if you are able to visit the Exploratorium in San Francisco. Most of these exhibits are electronic versions from the museum floor; a few are unique.

Illusionworks

http://www.illusionworks.com/

This is one the most comprehensive collections of optical and sensory illusions on the Internet.

Kubovy Perception Lab University of Virginia Department of Psychology

http://minerva.acc.virginia.edu/~mklab/

This site is a working laboratory studying topics like Gestalt detection, symmetry perception, picture perception, skin reading, and rhythm and time perception.

University of California at Santa Cruz Perceptual Science Laboratory

http://mambo.ucsc.edu/

The Perceptual Science Laboratory is engaged in a variety of experimental and theoretical inquiries in perception and cognition. A major research area concerns speech perception by ear, eye, and facial animation.

The Joy of Visual Perception: A Web Book

http://www.yorku.ca/eye/

This is an interactive book with links.

States of Consciousness

States of Consciousness

http://www.psychwww.com/asc/asc.html

References to different states of consciousness.

Altered States of Consciousness

http://www.en.wikipedia.org/wiki/altered_state_of_consciousness

A page dedicated to information on altered states of consciousness.

AmeobaWeb

http://www.vanguard.edu/faculty/ddegelman/
amoebaweb/index.aspx?doc_id=875

Sleep and dreaming, hypnosis, disorders; studying states of consciousness

The Association for the Scientific Study of Consciousness

http://assc.caltech.edu/index.htm

The ASSC promotes research within cognitive science, neuroscience, philosophy, and other relevant disciplines in the sciences and humanities, directed toward understanding the nature, function, and underlying mechanisms of consciousness.

Neuroscience of Psychoactive Substance Use and Dependence

http://www.who.int/substance_abuse/publications/
psychoactives/en/

This site provides a link to the World Health Organization report on "Neuroscience of Psychoactive Substance Use and Dependence." This text provides an authoritative summary of current knowledge of the biological basis of substance use behaviors, including their relationship with environmental factors. The report focuses on a wide range of psychoactive substances, including tobacco, alcohol and illicit drugs."

Near Death Experiences

http://www.iands.org/

This site, provided by the International Association for Near-Death Studies, Inc., is concerned with near-death experiences (NDE). The NDA states that such experiences are some of the most powerful emotional and psychological events known. This site is provided as a public service to give reliable information about near-death experiences, along with resources for more information and support.

New Clues to Why We Dream

http://www.psychoanalysis.org.uk/dreaming.htm

An article on dreaming by from the British Psychoanalytic Society. The article addresses the science of dreaming both in terms of the historical perspective (i.e., Freud) and the current perspective (i.e., neurophysiological).

Introduction to Club Drugs

http://www.nida.nih.gov/DrugPages/Clubdrugs.html

Clubs Drugs presented by this site include Alcohol, LSD (Acid), MDMA (Ecstasy), GHB, GBL, Ketamine (Special-K), Fentanyl, Rohypnol, amphetamines and methamphetamine. Information concerning their toxicity, street names, and primary euphoric effects are addressed.

What is Sleep . . . and why do we do it?

http://faculty.washington.edu/chudler/sleep.html

This site provides a basic overview of sleep, how it is measured, and what it is thought to accomplish.

Association for the Scientific Study of Consciousness

http://assc.caltech.edu/

"ASSC promotes research within cognitive science, neuroscience, philosophy, and other relevant disciplines in the sciences and humanities, directed toward understanding the nature, function, and underlying mechanisms of consciousness."

Sleep Disorders

http://www.sleepnet.com/disorder.htm

All of the common sleep disorders are discussed at this site.

Dreams

http://www.dreamgate.com/dream/resources/online97.htm

A massive site that contains Mail List, Usenet Newsgroups, and Web sites by Category: Dream Sharing, Magazines and Journals, Information, Education and Organizations, Personal Dream Journals, Religion, Spirituality and Healing (and Shamanism), Lucid Dreaming, Psi, Paranormal, Telepathic Dreaming, Dream Science and Research, Dreams and Anthropology, Dream Bibliography Collections, Dream Art, Dream Software, Jung and Dreams, Freud and Dreams, Books and Articles Online, and Lists of Links.

Memory and Learning

Frequently Asked Questions

http://www.supermemo.com/help/faq/memory.htm

FAQ on memory and learning answered by Dr. Wozniak.

Learning Techniques

http://www.web-us.com/memory/default.htm

Memory learning techniques, improving memory skills.

The Brain from Top to Bottom

http://www.thebrain.mcgill.ca/flash/d/d_07/
d_07_p/d_07_p_tra/d_07_p_tra.html

A useful description on the differences between learning and memory with helpful diagrams and tables.

Prenatal Memory and Learning

http://www.birthpsychology.com/lifebefore/
earlymem.html

A very interesting article on prenatal memory.

Memory Boosting, Memory Suppression

http://www.bioethics.gov/topics/memory_index.html

A chapter from the President's Council on Bioethics regarding memory boosting and memory suppression.

The Journal of Experimental Psychology: Learning, Memory, and Cognition

http://www.apa.org/journals/xlm/

This journal "publishes original experimental studies on basic processes of cognition, learning, memory, imagery, concept formation, problem solving, decision making, thinking, reading, and language processing."

Encyclopedia of Psychology

http://www.psychology.org/links/Environment_
Behavior_Relationships/Memory/

Several important articles on memory relevant to the field of psychology.

Interactive Classical Conditioning

http://www.uwm.edu/~johnchay/cc.htm

This site provides an interactive module that illustrates the basic concepts of Pavlovian conditioning.

Interactive Operant Conditioning

http://www.uwm.edu/~johnchay/oc.htm

This site provides a very informative and highly graphical description of operant conditioning.

Glossary of Conditioning Terms

http://www.psychology.uiowa.edu/Faculty/
Wasserman/Glossary/index%20set.html

This is an interactive glossary of terms most often used in learning courses.

Common Cents

http://www.exploratorium.edu/memory/index.html

This site presents experiments in memory from the Exploratorium in San Francisco on memory for United States pennies.

Positive Reinforcement: Overview of Behavioral Psychology

http://chiron.valdosta.edu/whuitt/col/behsys/
behsys.html

This site discusses theories and defines terms in the behavioral perspective of learning.

Cognition and Intelligence

Cognitive Science

http://plato.stanford.edu/entries/
cognitive-science/

Cognitive science is the interdisciplinary study of mind and intelligence, embracing philosophy, psychology, artificial intelligence, and neuroscience.

Piaget's Theory of Cognitive Development

http://chiron.valdosta.edu/whuitt/col/cogsys/
piaget.html

An overview of Piaget's theory of cognitive development.

The Animal Cognition Web

http://www.pigeon.psy.tufts.edu/psych26/

Developed by Dr. Robert Cook, this site provides basic experimental results from cognition and intelligence testing in animals.

Intelligence Testing

http://psychclassics.yorku.ca/topic.htm#iq

This site provides an interactive review of the history of intelligence testing.

The Jean Piaget Society

http://www.piaget.org/

Established in 1970, this society has an international, interdisciplinary membership of scholars, teachers and researchers interested in exploring the nature of the developmental construction of human knowledge. The Society was named in honor of the Swiss developmentalist, Jean Piaget, who made major theoretical and empirical contributions to our understanding of the origins and evolution of knowledge.

History of Cognitive Psychology

http://www.muskingum.edu/~psych/psycweb/history/
cognitiv.htm

This site provides an overview of the history of cognitive psychology.

A1 Topics

http://www.aaai.org/AITopics/

A special Web site provided by the American Association for Artificial Intelligence (AAAI) for students, teachers, journalists, and everyone who would like to explore *what artificial intelligence is,* and *what AI scientists do.*

Can Animals Use Language

http://www.gsu.edu/~wwwlrc/index.html

The Language Research Center (LRC) is a world renown primate research facility in Atlanta, Georgia, associated with Georgia State University specializing in language research with an emphasis on work with bonobos (*Pan paniscus*) and chimpanzees (*Pan troglodytes*).

Language Problems: Aphasia

http://www.aphasia.org/

The National Aphasia Association is a nonprofit organization that promotes public education, research, rehabilitation, and support services to assist people with aphasia and their families.

The Center for Neural Basis of Cognition

http://www.cnbc.cmu.edu/

Many links to other sites on science of cognition may be found at this site.

Literature, Cognition, and the Brain

http://www2.bc.edu/~richarad/lcb/home.html

This Web page features research at the intersection of literary studies, cognitive theory, and neuroscience.

IQ Tests

http://www.2h.com/Tests/iqtrad.phtml

Large number of IQ tests, puzzles, and practice items all in the area of intelligence testing may be found at this site.

Test of Intelligence

http://www.geocities.com/CapitolHill/1641/iqown.html

This site offers a traditional test of intelligence, with answers provided.

Motivation and Emotion

All Psych Online

http://allpsych.com/psychology101/motivation_
emotion.html

Lecture notes and general information about motivational psychology including various theories related to motivation and emotion.

Motivation and Emotion

http://www.alleydog.com/101notes/mot-emot.html

An introductory level presentation on the topic of motivation and emotion.

Mood Control

http://www.bioethics.gov/topics/happiness_index.html

A chapter from The President's Council on Bioethics that discusses the ethical problems involved in using drugs that manipulate motivation and mood.

Jealousy Self Assessment

http://www.psychtests.com/tests/alltests.html

This site provides several interactive tests on jealousy. It might be interesting to compare the results across gender, although it shouldn't be taken too seriously. This test might serve as a good critical thinking exercise for students.

Genderbender

http://www.utdallas.edu/~waligore/digital/garvey.html

This site provides and interactive test on one's perception of their own sex roles. It is based on the Bem sex role inventory. It should be an interesting way to get a discussion started on sex-typing and stereotypes.

Measuring Emotional Quotients

http://eqi.org/

The information on this site is organized into two basic groups: Academic—A resource for those interested in serious scientific and academic research in the field of emotions and emotional intelligence. Everything else—Contains practical information on what I call EQ, which I define as the development of one's innate emotional intelligence. Also contains a variety of personal growth and related writings and resources.

Motivation

http://choo.fis.utoronto.ca/FIS/Courses/LIS1230/
LIS1230sharma/motive4.htm

A discussion of several theories of motivation may be found at this site.

Go Ask Alice

http://www.goaskalice.columbia.edu/

This site offers discussions of real life sexual motivations.

Anger

http://www.apa.org/pubinfo/anger.html

Anger is an emotional state that varies in intensity from mild irritation to intense fury and rage. Like other emotions, it is accompanied by physiological and biological changes. This site explores the varied aspects of the emotion anger.

Child and Adolescent Development

Drugs, Children, and Behavior Control

http://www.bioethics.gov/topics/drugs_index.html

A chapter from The President's Council on Bioethics that discusses the impact of drugs, children, and behavior; for example, the chapter discusses the ethical challenges in using prescription stimulants in children.

Children

http://www.bioethics.gov/topics/children.html

A chapter from The President's Council on Bioethics that discusses the ethical implications of a variety of childhood problems like pre-natal screening, ethical caregiving, clinical research, and moral obligation for treating children in America.

Mental Health

http://mentalhelp.net/poc/center_index.php?id=28

This site provides a wealth of practical information on child and adolescent development including abnormal development.

Child and Adolescent Health and Development

http://www.who.int/child-adolescent-health/

World Health Organization site dedicated to infant, child, and adolescent development. The Department of Child and Adolescent Health and Development (CAH) is responsible for interventions concerning health, growth, and development for the age group of 0–19 years.

Adolescent Growth and Development

http://www.ext.vt.edu/pubs/family/350-850/
350-850.html

This site provides a basic overview of important changes that take place during puberty.

Normal Adolescent Development

http://www.aacap.org/publications/factsfam/
develop.htm

The site provides information that should help parents understand adolescent of development from a biopsychosocial standpoint.

The Visible Embryo

http://www.visembryo.com/

The Visible Embryo is a comprehensive resource of information on human development from conception to birth, designed for both medical student and interested lay people. This site offers a detailed pictorial account of normal and abnormal development.

Fetal Development

http://www.w-cpc.org/fetal.html

This site provides a systematic overview of fetal development along with numerous pictures.

Fetal Psychology

http://www.leaderu.com/orgs/tul/psychtoday9809.html

This article presents some very interesting findings in the area of fetal psychology.

Attention Deficit Disorder

http://www.ncpamd.com/adhd.htm

This site provides an extensive list of resources related to the diagnosis, prognosis, and treatment of ADHD.

Dyslexia Center

http://www.dyslexiacenter.com/

This is another site dedicated to understanding dyslexia.

America Reads

http://www.ed.gov/inits/americareads/nichd.html

The America Reads Challenge recognizes the supreme importance of an early and successful start to learning to read. Providing children with the right literacy and reading experiences in the early years is likely to set the stage for successful reading and citizenship in later years. To determine the literacy, language, and reading experiences that are important for young readers, we rely on the substantial research that has been conducted in beginning reading by researchers all over the world, and particularly by researchers at Federally sponsored agencies in the United States.

Whole-Language versus Phonics

http://www.education-world.com/a_curr/curr029.shtml

Whole Language and Phonics: Can They Work Together? This site provides an article addressing the debate between whole-language and phonics.

Reading Instruction

http://www.tampareads.com/phonics/phonics-articles.htm

Index to articles on two different reading methods—click link to see article.

Adolescent Development

http://www.yale.edu/ynhti/curriculum/units/
1991/5/91.05.07.x.html

This site discusses the physiological and psychological development of the adolescent.

Pregnancy and Early Care

http://www.parentsplace.com/pregnancy

This extensive site includes many discussions and links on the topics of pregnancy and early care for infants.

Young Children

http://www.earlychildhood.com/

The source of information for all who share an interest in improving the education and general life experience of young children, this is a place for getting advice from experts in the early childhood field, expanding your collection of creative projects, and sharing ideas and questions with the early childhood community.

Classic Theories of Child Development

http://childstudy.net/cdw.html

This large site includes tutorials on theory (a discussion of the classic theories of child development), and a key word search engine.

The Parent's Page

http://www.moonlily.com/parents

An extensive listing of traditional and nontraditional birthing, parenting, and pregnancy issues can be found at this site.

Midwifery, Pregnancy, Birth, and Breast-feeding

http://www.moonlily.com/obc

Links and articles on midwifery, pregnancy, birth, and breast-feeding are available at this site.

Piaget

http://www.piaget.org/biography/biog.html

This site is a short biography of Jean Piaget.

Language Development

http://www.parentingme.com/language.htm

This is a site dedicated to the understanding of language development.

Adult Development
Age-Retardation (Life Extension)

http://www.bioethics.gov/topics/ageless_bodies_
index.html

A chapter from the President's Council on Bioethics regarding using medical procedures and medication to slow the aging process and extend life.

Aging and End-of-Life

http://www.bioethics.gov/topics/end_of_life_
index.html

A chapter from the President's Council on Bioethics regarding caregiving, death, and dying.

The American Psychological Association

http://apadiv20.phhp.ufl.edu/

This division of the American Psychological Association is dedicated to studying the Psychology of Adult Development and Aging.

Society for Research in Adult Development

http://www.adultdevelopment.org/

"The international membership of the Society for Research in Adult Development (SRAD) includes people from all disciplines who are interested in positive adult development. Positive adult development refers to development starting in late adolescence and continuing through life. The focus is on expanded capabilities and changes that improve the quality of life."

Social Psychology Network

http://www.socialpsychology.org/person.htm

This site provides a number of links related to personality theory and research, personality assessment, online personality tests, intelligence testing, and more.

Personality Psychology

http://en.wikipedia.org/wiki/Personality_
psychology

One of the issues in adult development is the development of the personality. Personality psychology is a branch of psychology which studies personality and individual differences. This site explores the topic of personality development.

Great Ideas in Personality

http://www.personalityresearch.org

This Web site deals with scientific research programs in personality psychology. They are offered as candidates for the title "great ideas"; whether they are indeed great remains an open question.

Personality Psychology

http://www.thepersonalitysystem.org/

This site provides an introduction to personality and personality.

National Center for Fathering

http://www.fathers.com/

This is a site dedicated to educating the public about the importance of fathers as well as providing practical resources for fathers.

The National Fatherhood Initiative

http://www.fatherhood.org/

The mission of the National Fatherhood Initiative (NFI) is to improve the well-being of children by increasing the number of children growing up with loving, committed and responsible fathers.

Marriage Builders

http://www.marriagebuilders.com/

In this Marriage Builders site, you will be introduced to some of the best ways to overcome marital conflicts and some of the quickest ways to restore love.

Journal of Family Psychology

http://www.apa.org/journals/fam.html

This APA sponsored journal on the family provides numerous full-text journals on issues relevant to families.

Mental and Physical Health Effects on Divorced People

http://www.divorcereform.org/health.html

Many resources and statistics concerning the influence of divorce on physical and mental health.

The Buck Institute on Aging

http://www.buckinstitute.org/

The mission at the Buck Institute, an independent, nonprofit research center, is to increase the healthy years of each individual's life through research and education on the aging process and age-associated diseases.

The Health and Retirement Study

http://www.umich.edu/~hrswww/

The main purpose of this site is to present survey data that will inform researchers and policymakers about elderly populations particularly concerning retirement.

Huffington Center on Aging

http://www.hcoa.org/

These pages will provide you with an overview of the research efforts, educational initiatives, and training programs of the center as well as affiliated clinical services and training activities administered by the center.

Human Nutrition Research Center on Aging

http://www.hnrc.tufts.edu/

The overall mission of the HNRC is to explore the relationship between nutrition and good health and to determine the nutritional and dietary requirements of the maturing and elderly population. The interaction between nutrition and the onset and progression of aging and associated degenerative conditions is of special concern.

National Institute on Aging (NIA)

http://www.nia.nih.gov

The National Institute on Aging (NIA) is one of the National Institutes of Health, the principal biomedical research agency of the United States Government. The NIA promotes healthy aging by conducting and supporting biomedical, social, and behavioral research and public education.

Administration on Aging

http://www.aoa.dhhs.gov/

This Department of Health and Human Services site on the Administration on Aging offers extensive links to government services and other sites. It is a good site to explore the graying of America.

Personality

Early Childhood Behavior and Temperament Predict Later Substance Use

http://www.nida.nih.gov/NIDA_Notes/NNVOL10N1/
Earlychild.html

By the first grade, or earlier, children show temperament and behavior traits that are powerful indicators of their inclination to use and abuse drugs in their teenage and adult years. Researchers have identified not only common childhood risk factors and behaviors that predict drug abuse potential but also protective factors that shield some children from influences to use drugs.

What Is a Personality/Social Psychologist?

http://www.spsp.org/what.htm

The Society for Personality and Social Psychology (SPSP) was founded in 1974 as Division 8 of the American Psychological Association. Today, SPSP includes both APA members and nonmembers in a wide array of subfields.

Encyclopedia of Mental Health: Shyness

http://www.shyness.com/encyclopedia.html

The Palo Alto Shyness Clinic provides a full-text review on the science of shyness. Topics like prevalence and diagnosis are covered, as are topics like the biology of shyness. The article is written by one of the foremost experts in the field of shyness.

Great Ideas in Personality

http://www.personalityresearch.org/

This Web site deals with scientific research programs in personality. They are offered as candidates for the title "great ideas"; whether they are indeed great remains an open question.

Carl Rogers

http://psy1.clarion.edu/jms/Rogers.html

This site discusses Carl Rogers and his views on the therapeutic relationship.

Personality Tests

http://www.2h.com/Tests/personality.phtml

This site contain a large selection of personality tests that you can take on the Internet. Including test of anxiety, self esteem, attention deficient and type A personality.

Do You Have a Type A Personality?

http://www.queendom.com/tests/personality/
type_a_personality_access.html

An online personality test, containing seventeen items, which attempts to differentiate between A- and B-type personalities.

Classical Adlerian Psychology

http://ourworld.compuserve.com/homepages/
hstein/homepage.htm

Classical Adlerian psychology is a values-based, fully-integrated theory of personality, model of psychopathology, philosophy of living, strategy for preventative education, and techniques of psychotherapy.

The Keirsey Temperament Sorter

http://www.keirsey.com/cgi-bin/keirsey/newkts.cgi

The Keirsey Temperament Sorter by David Keirsey is a personality test which scores results according to the Myers-Briggs system (the actual Myers-Briggs test is a professional instrument and may only be administered by a licensed practitioner).

Stress and Health

Stress: Coping with Everyday Problems

http://www.nmha.org/infoctr/factsheets/41.cfm

A fact sheet provided by the National Mental Health Association on stress and coping with everyday problems.

Stress at Work

http://www.cdc.gov/niosh/stresswk.html

This booklet, provided by the Center for Disease Control, highlights knowledge about the causes of stress at work and outlines steps that can be taken to prevent job stress.

Stress Management

http://www.lifepositive.com/Mind/psychology/
stress/stress-management.asp

This site explores the link between stress and health as well as how to effectively manage stress-related problems.

The Truth About Sexually Transmitted Diseases

http://www.unspeakable.com/

A frank, accurate, and unembarrassed guide to the prevention and treatment of sexually transmitted diseases sponsored by Pfizer Pharmaceuticals.

Stress Management: A Review of Principles

http://www.unl.edu/stress/mgmt

This document presents the core concepts of stress management education. It includes everything from defining stress to detailing the adverse consequences on one physical and mental state.

Health Risk Assessment

http://www.youfirst.com/index.asp

This questionnaire uses information provided by you regarding diet, exercise, stress, drug and alcohol usage, body size, blood pressure levels, and family history information to generate a health report. The health report is very comprehensive, personalized, and confidential. Throughout the personalized report, you are given your current health status on a number of variables, as well as information on your potential health status.

The American Institute on Stress

`http://www.stress.org/`

This site is dedicated to advancing the knowledge base in the role of stress in health and disease. This site also serves as a national clearinghouse on stress-related information.

Sidran Traumatic Stress Foundation

`http://www.sidran.org/`

Sidran Traumatic Stress Foundation is a nonprofit charitable organization devoted to education, advocacy, and research to benefit people who are suffering from injuries of traumatic stress.

Crises, Grief, and Healing

`http://www.webhealing.com/`

A site dedicated to helping people understand and recovery from strong emotional loss.

Go Ask Alice

`http://www.goaskalice.columbia.edu/`

This site contains the Health Education and Wellness program of the Columbia University Health Service. This site is committed to helping individuals make choices that will contribute to their personal health and happiness, and to the well-being of others.

The Longevity Game

`http://www.northwesternmutual.com/games/longevity/`

This game determines how long one can expect to live based on one's current life style. This site is also listed as an activity.

Social Anxiety Test

`http://www.queendom.com/tests/health/social_anxiety_r_access.html`

An online social anxiety test containing twenty-five items is offered at this site.

What is Stress?

http://www.ivf.com/stress.html

This site describes stress as the "wear and tear" our bodies experience as we adjust to our continually changing environment; it has physical and emotional effects on us and can create positive or negative feelings. Techniques for stress management and reductions are discussed.

The National Clearinghouse for Alcohol and Drug Information

http://www.health.org/

This site offers links to prevention and treatment of substance abuse. PREVLINE offers electronic access to searchable databases and substance abuse prevention materials that pertain to alcohol, tobacco, and drugs.

Abnormal Psychology

Psychiatry 24x7

http://www.psychiatry24x7.com/

An informative website on mental illness sponsored by the European Advisory Board.

The Journal of Abnormal Psychology

http://www.apa.org/journals/abn/

The *Journal of Abnormal Psychology* publishes articles on basic research and theory in the broad field of abnormal behavior, its determinants, and its correlates.

Mental Health

http://www.mentalhealth.com/p20-grp.html

A detailed description of common mental disorders based on the European and American models of abnormality.

Merck

http://www.merck.com/

A comprehensive guide to medications provided by Merck, which is considered one of the most used resources around the world.

Suicide Awareness Voices Organization

http://www.save.org/

"SAVE's Mission is to prevent suicide through public awareness and education, eliminate stigma and serve as a resource to those touched by suicide."

Depression and Bipolar Support Alliance

http://www.dbsalliance.org/index.html

This Web site is aimed at helping patients and their loved ones receive a wide range of information and support as they seek to gain a greater understanding of depression and bipolar disorder.

Mental Health: A Report of the Surgeon General

http://www.surgeongeneral.gov/library/
mentalhealth/chapter2/sec2.html

The Surgeon General's office has developed a site that provides an overview of mental health problems, their causes, and treatment.

When Your Parent has a Mental Illness

http://www.couns.uiuc.edu/brochures/parents.htm

This site provides advice for children who have a parent with a mental illness.

"Defining mental illness: An interview with a Mayo Clinic specialist"

http://www.mayoclinic.com/health/mental-illness/
HQ01079

See what a medical expert says about the types of mental illness, the role of brain chemistry, medication use, the effects of stress, and more."

Schizophrenia in Children

http://aacap.org/page.ww?section=Facts+for+
Families&name=Schizophrenia+In+Children

An overview of schizophrenia and children provided by the American Academy of Child and Adolescent Psychiatry.

The Antipsychiatry Coalition

http://www.antipsychiatry.org/index.htm

"The Antipsychiatry Coalition is a nonprofit volunteer group consisting of people who feel we have been harmed by psychiatry—and of our supporters. We created this Web site to warn you of the harm routinely inflicted on those who receive psychiatric "treatment" and to promote the democratic ideal of liberty for all law-abiding people that has been abandoned in the U.S.A., Canada, and other supposedly democratic nations."

"Serious Mental Illness and Its Co-Occurrence with Substance Use Disorders"

http://oas.samhsa.gov/CoD/CoD.htm

An article developed by the Department of Health and Human Services, Substance Abuse and Mental Health Services Administration, Office of Applied Studies

CounselingNet

http://www.counselingnet.com/

Online Counseling Psychology and Information For Anxiety, Depression, Stress, Relationships, Marriage, Addictions, Sexual Problems, Career and Personal Problems, Divorce, and Custody.

APA DSM-IV Diagnostic Classification

http://www.behavenet.com/capsules/disorders/
dsm4classification.htm

Near exhaustive listing of mental disorders grouped according to their *DSM-IV* classification.

The Center for Eating Disorders

http://www.eating-disorders.com/

Sponsored by St. Joseph Medical Center, this site provides information concerning the diagnosis, treatment, and medical consequences of eating disorders.

Internet Therapy

http://www.metanoia.org/imhs/

What is your opinion on psychologists conducting therapy or counseling online? "Now you can meet with a psychotherapist for private counseling or advice, from the privacy of your own computer. Using the Internet, professional counselors are forming effective helping relationships with people like you."

Drug and Alcohol Treatment and Prevention Global Network

`http://www.drugnet.net/metaview.htm`

Perhaps one of the most exhaustive sites on the Internet related to drug abuse and addiction. This site provides links to drug abuse and addiction resources all over the United States and world.

Mental Health InfoSource

`http://www.mhsource.com/`

This site is designed primarily for mental health professions. Numerous professional resources are located on this site. Additionally, there are links to specific psychological disorders, their cause, diagnosis, and treatment.

Center for the Study of Autism

`http://www.autism.org/`

The Center provides information about autism to parents and professionals, and conducts research on the efficacy of various therapeutic interventions.

Psychopharmacology Links

`http://www.ncpamd.com/psychopharm.htm`

Northern County Psychiatric Associates Psychiatric Services for Children, Adolescents, Adults and Families has assembled a comprehensive list of psychopharmacology resources. Most drug classes are included in this list as are numerous links to other psychopharmacology resources.

The Phobia List

`http://phobialist.com`

This site includes a complete listing of phobias.

National Anxiety Foundation

`http://lexington-on-line.com/naf.html`

This site contains many links of the topic of anxiety disorders.

The Efficacy of Psychotherapy

http://www.apa.org/practice/peff.html

This site discusses the benefits of psychotherapy in 475 controlled studies, using only studies of patients seeking treatment for neuroses, true phobias, and emotional-somatic complaints. Statistical analysis of the data are discussed.

Eating Disorder

http://www.edap.org/

This home page provides some basic information about Eating Disorders, awareness, prevention, and eating disorders in general.

Sleep Disorders

http://www.sleepnet.com/disorder.htm

This site contains everything you wanted to know about sleep disorders but were too tired to ask.

BPD Central

http://www.bpdcentral.com/

Borderline Personality Disorder (BPD) is a major disorder in the personality disorders and anyone knowing someone so diagnosed should view this site, which offers listings of links for BPD.

MentalHealth.Com

http://www.mentalhealth.com/p.html

Internet Mental Health, a free encyclopedia of mental health information. The goal of Internet Mental Health is to promote improved understanding, diagnosis, and treatment of mental illness throughout the world.

DSM Criteria

http://www.apa.org/science/lib.html

This extensive APA site consists of terms and definitions of *DSM* criteria and describes all of what is currently considered to be abnormal behavior by the American Psychiatric Association.

Social Psychology

Social Psychology Network

http://www.socialpsychology.org/

"Welcome to Social Psychology Network, the largest social psychology database on the Internet. In these pages, you'll find more than 13,000 links related to psychology."

Social Psychology

http://www.trinity.edu/~mkearl/socpsy.html

A tour through social psychology from the nature–nurture debate through to the psychology of urbanization.

Current Research in Social Psychology

http://www.uiowa.edu/~grpproc/crisp/crisp.html

Current Research in Social Psychology (CRISP) is a peer reviewed, electronic journal covering all aspects of social psychology. Publication is sponsored by the Center for the Study of Group Processes at the University of Iowa which provides free access to its contents.

Cultic Studies Review

http://www.culticstudiesreview.org/

"Information on cults, psychological manipulation, psychological abuse, spiritual abuse, brainwashing, mind control, thought reform, abusive churches, extremism, totalistic groups, authoritarian groups, new religious movements, exit counseling, recovery, and practical suggestions."

The Persuaders

http://www.pbs.org/wgbh/pages/frontline/shows/persuaders/

"In 'The Persuaders,' FRONTLINE explores how the cultures of marketing and advertising have come to influence not only what Americans buy, but also how they view themselves and the world around them. The 90-minute documentary draws on a range of experts and observers of the advertising/marketing world, to examine how, in the words of one on-camera commentator, 'the principal of democracy yields to the practice of demography,' as highly customized messages are delivered to a smaller segment of the market."

Social Cognition Paper Archive and Information Center

http://www.indiana.edu/~soccog/scarch.html

Archive of research papers and researchers in social cognition, a scientific subfield of social psychology.

Society for Judgment and Decision Making

http://www.sjdm.org/

"The Society for Judgment and Decision Making is an interdisciplinary academic organization dedicated to the study of normative, descriptive, and prescriptive theories of decision. Its members include psychologists, economists, organizational researchers, decision analysts, and other decision researchers. The Society's primary event is its Annual Meeting at which Society members present their research. It also publishes the journal *Judgment and Decision Making*."

Social Psychology Links of Interest

http://www.usi.edu/libarts/socio/socpsy/SOCPSY.HTM

This page contains a multitude of Social Psychology links of interest from the Sociology Department at the University of Southern Indiana.

Social Psychology

http://www.cogprints.org/view/subjects/soc-psy.html

This site provides a list of some of the most important research papers in social psychology.

Influence at Work: The Psychology of Persuasion

http://www.influenceatwork.com/

"Influence is a rapidly expanding field of psychological inquiry devoted to discovering the principles that determine beliefs, create attitudes, and move people to action. In other words, influence examines the process that causes humans to change."

Stanford Prison Experiment

http://www.prisonexp.org/

This site provides an overview of the now famous experiment by Philip G. Zimbardo entitled the "Stanford Prison Experiment." In addition to learning all about the experiment through various texts, this site also provides a slide tour describing the experiment and uncovering what it tells us about the nature of Human Nature.

The Society of Experimental Social Psychology

http://www.sesp.org/

The Society of Experimental Social Psychology (SESP) is a scientific organization dedicated to the advancement of social psychology.

Cults and Psychological Manipulation

http://www.csj.org/

AFF, the leading professional organization concerned about cults and psychological manipulation, was founded 20 years ago in 1979. AFF is known for its professionalism, for building its practical educational services for families, former group members, helping professionals, educators, and young people on a base of scholarly study and research.

National Television Violence Study

http://www.reseau-medias.ca/eng/med/home/
resource/ntvs.htm

This study is the most elaborate and comprehensive assessment ever conducted of the context in which violence appears on TV.

Locus of Control Test

http://www.queendom.com/tests/personality/
lc_access.html

This test assesses your locus of control orientation and your attributional style with forty-two items. A locus of control orientation is a belief about whether the outcomes of our actions are contingent on what we do (internal control orientation) or events outside our personal control (external control orientation).

Social Psychology Network

http://www.socialpsychology.org/

This page contains links to the major topics in social psychology. It is a very good starting place for any new student to the field of social psychology.

Applied Psychology

Memory and Reality

http://www.fmsfonline.org/

The purpose of the FMSF is to seek the reasons for the spread of False Memory Syndrome; to work for the prevention of new cases of False Memory Syndrome; and to aid the victims, both primary and secondary, of False Memory Syndrome.

Forensic Psychiatry Online

http://www.priory.com/forpsy.htm

"A collection of papers and articles regarding forensic psychiatry."

Some Exciting Areas in Applied Psychology

http://www.wcupa.edu/_ACADEMICS/sch_cas.psy/career.htm

Detailed information, such as pros and cons, skills needed, and educational resources, regarding careers in applied psychology.

The Journal of Applied Psychology

http://www.apa.org/journals/apl

The *Journal of Applied Psychology* emphasizes the publication of original investigations that contribute new knowledge and understanding to fields of applied psychology.

Applied Psychology: An International Review

http://www.blackwellpublishing.com/journal.asp?ref=0269-994X

The official journal of the International Association of Applied Psychology (IAAP), and the oldest worldwide association of scholars and practitioners of the discipline of psychology (founded in 1920).

Applied Psychology in Criminal Justice

http://www.apcj.org/

Applied Psychology in Criminal Justice is an interdisciplinary, peer reviewed, academic journal that examines the intersection of psychology and criminal justice

The Metropolitan New York Association for Applied Psychology

http://www.metroapppsych.com/

METRO was founded in 1939 as a not-for-profit professional association. We are the oldest and largest local professional association of applied psychologists in the U.S.

School Psychology Resources for Psychologists, Parents, and Educators

http://www.bcpl.net/~sandyste/school_psych.html

Research learning disabilities, ADHD, functional behavioral assessment, autism, adolescence, parenting, psychological assessment, special education, mental retardation, mental health, and more.

International Society of Political Psychology

http://ispp.org/

The purpose of this site is to facilitate communication across disciplinary, geographic and political boundaries among scholars, concerned individuals in government and public posts, the communications media, and elsewhere who have a scientific interest in the relationship between politics and psychological processes.

Traffic Psychology

http://www.soc.hawaii.edu/leonj/leonj/leonpsy/traffic/tpintro.html

Traffic psychology refers to the knowledge one acquires about how to use behavioral principles to modify one's own style of conduct in traffic situations including driving, bicycling, walking, and other forms of locomotion in shared spaces. A common activity in traffic psychology is to attempt to modify one's old driving persona to a new and better driving persona.

Psychology of Religion Pages

http://www.psywww.com/psyrelig/

This is a general introduction to the psychology of religion, for example, as scientists in Division 36 of the American Psychological Association study it. Here you will find a description of what psychologists have learned about how religion influences people's lives.

Human Factors and the FAA

http://www.hf.faa.gov/

This site provides the aviation community and other interested users with information about human factors research and applications under the auspices of the National Plan for Civil Aviation Human Factors

I/O Survival Guide

http://allserv.rug.ac.be/~flievens/guide.htm

This guide provides a plethora of Internet sites valuable to the understanding of the field of industrial and organizational psychology.

Zeno's Forensic Page

http://forensic.to/forensic.html

This is a large site with many links in the area of forensic psychology.

CUErgo

http://ergo.human.cornell.edu/

Cornell's Human Factors and Ergonomics Program focuses on ways to improve comfort, performance, and health through the ergonomic design of products and environments.

Human Factors at NASA

http://human-factors.arc.nasa.gov/

The NASA mission for this section is to develop a world-class center for human factors research, and to promote the broadest possible application of this research.

Other Online Resources

Allyn & Bacon Psychology Web Site

www.ablongman.com/psychology

This Web site provides an overview of Allyn and Bacon Psychology texts and their corresponding supplements. Web links provide content to review, enrich, and expand upon information in an accompanying Allyn and Bacon Psychology text.

NOTES

NOTES

NOTES

NOTES

NOTES

NOTES

NOTES

NOTES

NOTES

NOTES

With Music and Justice for All

WITH MUSIC AND JUSTICE FOR ALL

Some Southerners and Their Passions

Frye Gaillard

VANDERBILT UNIVERSITY PRESS • NASHVILLE

Published by Vanderbilt University Press
First Edition 2008

12 11 10 09 08   1 2 3 4 5

This book is printed on acid-free paper
made from 50% post consumer recycled paper.
Manufactured in the United States of America
Cover design: Bruce Gore
Text design: Dariel Mayer

Library of Congress Cataloging-in-Publication Data
Gaillard, Frye, 1946 –
With music and justice for all : some southerners
and their passions / Frye Gaillard. — 1st ed.
        p. cm.
ISBN 978-0-8265-1588-9 (cloth : alk. paper)
1. Southern States—Civilization.
2. Southern States—Biography. I. Title.
F209.G25 2008
975'.043—dc22
                    2007033183

To the memory of Judge Walter Gaillard,
with gratitude for his legacy of fairness

Contents

Part III

Soundtracks

Part IV

Characters

Preface

This book is a collection of work that I have done over some thirty-five years. During that time, I have been lucky enough to write about the South—a combination of journalism and memoir, with a dash of history thrown in here and there. I continue to believe that the larger-than-life figures of our age—from Johnny Cash to Jimmy Carter, Billy Graham to the leaders of the civil rights movement; even John T. Scopes, whom I met briefly in 1970—put a revealing face on the era we have lived through. In a sense, the book represents the evolution of one writer's career, but more than that it is intended to be a portrait of a place, or at least a collection of verbal snapshots.

There are stories here from the realms of religion, music, civil rights, and social change, and in addition to the smattering of well-known names—Emmylou Harris, James Baldwin, Robert F. Kennedy—there are people some readers will not recognize. Perry Wallace, for example, was the first black basketball player in the Southeastern Conference, a young Jackie Robinson, many people said, who came to Vanderbilt in the 1960s and carried himself with dignity and grace. Will Campbell was and is a renegade Baptist preacher, author, and human rights activist who has taken delight in shaking up the flock. And Robert Howard Allen is a Tennessee poet who had never set foot in the doors of a school until he went off to college at the age of thirty-two.

These are people whose stories I am honored to tell. Many of the pieces assembled in these pages appeared in different form in other places—in newspapers, magazines, and occasionally other books. Most are recast here with new introductions to set them in context. I am grateful to the editors I have worked with, GayNelle Doll and Ken Schexnayder at *Vanderbilt Magazine*, Bonnie Ertelt at the *Peabody Reflector*, John Grooms at *Creative Loafing*, Ed Williams and Jerry Shinn at the *Charlotte Observer*, Erwin Knoll at the *Progressive*,

Marc Smirnoff at the *Oxford American*, John Sledge at the *Mobile Register*, Michael Bane at *Country Music* magazine, Jeanie Thompson and Jay Lamar at *First Draft* magazine, Jerry Bledsoe at Down Home Press, Carolyn Sakowski at John F. Blair, Publisher, Randall Williams at NewSouth Books, Dan Ross at the University of Alabama Press, Nicole Mitchell at the University of Georgia Press, Julie Garriott at St. Martin's Press, and M. Scott Douglass at Main Street Rag Publishing Company. These and others who will know who they are have helped to improve my writing through the years. I hope the results do justice to the men and women whose stories I tell, for all of them deserve a writer's best.

—Frye Gaillard

Introduction

The Heart of Dixie

The human heart in conflict with itself . . . only that is
worth writing about, worth the agony and the sweat.
—William Faulkner

There are memories now of the Alabama summers and a farm
in rural Montgomery County, a rolling piece of Black Belt
prairie where the Muskogee people hunted buffalo and deer. In the
1950s it was a tamer place as I came to know it—nearly two thousand acres near the Lowndes County line, where the white-faced
cattle grazed on the hills and every so often there were stands of
pine that slowly gave way to blackwater swamps. As a boy I roamed
every inch of the place, learning to ride with the help of old Mack,
a swaybacked bay nearly thirty years old. He was an animal wise
in the ways of young children, gentle and sure, not much given to
stubbornness or fright. We scouted the range for outlaws and Indians
until one fine day, on the strength of his teaching, our cowboy games
gave way to the real thing.

The work was hard—long days in the sun chasing steers or
cutting hay, sometimes castrating the newborn calves. But with my
uncles and cousins and the other hands on the place, we managed to
find a little time for adventure.

One hot afternoon after a morning in the fields we went to fish
at a pond behind the house. On the distant bank we saw an old
canoe—a dugout that my uncle had carved from a tree. There had
been a storm the night before, and the boat had obviously blown
loose from its moorings.

It lay upside down in the mud, waterlogged and in need of repair. I agreed to paddle it back across the lake so we could pull it out
at the dock. At worst, I thought the canoe would sink and I would
simply swim ashore. But as I moved out sluggishly toward the middle
of the water, I realized it was not going to be that easy. The canoe

listed badly to the starboard side, and no matter how I paddled, it tended to veer in that direction.

I was cursing it silently when all of a sudden, to my absolute horror, a rifle shot rang out from the shore. The bullet hit the water not a foot from the boat.

"My God!" I screamed. "Have you gone crazy?"

"Just keep paddling," my uncle replied, taking new aim. I thought of diving for the safety of the water as a second shot thudded into the side of the canoe. But then I saw my uncle's target—or multiple targets, to be more precise—for I had apparently paddled through a nest of water moccasins, and they were swimming purposefully in the direction of the boat. One, in fact, was slithering inside when the second rifle bullet split him in two. It was a situation so appalling, so completely terrifying and absurd, that I had trouble for a moment believing it was real.

I paddled furiously for the next several minutes, which seemed like days, while my uncle continued to fire away at the snakes.

Finally, just as I thought I might have it made, the canoe ran aground thirty feet from the shore. Swept away by a new wave of panic, I jumped out and ran, my feet barely breaking the surface of the lake.

For years after that, my uncle told the story, and it became enshrined as a piece of family lore—the day a mere mortal walked on the water.

And so the summers unrolled through the years, with each adventure a little more grand, until boyhood suddenly ended with a jolt. Before I really knew what was happening, I was compelled to deal with a set of contradictions—the rich ambiguities of the human condition—that left little doubt that I would be a writer.

Those were dark and dangerous times in Alabama, as they were in much of the American South, for there was a revolution under way, and many of us in the 1950s were not at all sure we were on the winning side. The way we understood it at the time, the whole thing started in the city of Montgomery, when a black middle-class preacher named Martin Luther King Jr. made a speech to a rally at a Montgomery church. King was only twenty-six years old, fresh out of graduate school in Boston—a young upstart, many white people said, who wanted to tear things apart.

We had no way of knowing when we first heard about it that on

December 5, 1955, just before his speech, King was so overcome by his doubts, his sense of inadequacy for the task that lay ahead, that he put his trembling pen aside and prayed that God would help him find the words. Such images were invisible to white Alabamians. What we saw instead was an insurrection, reaching far beyond the modest demands of the bus boycott taking shape in Montgomery. Embedded in the majestic sweep of King's sermon were intimations of a shredded status quo—a radical recasting of the southern way of life, with blacks leading the way on the road to redemption. And the most disconcerting thing about it was this: Despite his secret fears on the same afternoon, Martin Luther King seemed to be so sure. "We are not wrong tonight," he proclaimed.

"If we are wrong, the Supreme Court of this nation is wrong. If we are wrong, the Constitution of the United States is wrong. If we are wrong, God Almighty is wrong. . . . If we are wrong, justice is a lie."

I still remember the response of my family—their rage at the impudence of this young black preacher, who may have been raised in the state of Georgia but had picked up some funny ideas in Boston. As a child, I didn't know what to think, but then I saw him one day in Birmingham. I believe it was the spring of 1963. I had come to the city on a high school trip, and King was there as the civil rights movement was rushing toward a peak. He was afraid of Birmingham in a way. He thought it was the place where he might be killed, for this was the city of Eugene "Bull" Connor, the infamous commissioner of public safety who regarded brutality as a necessary tool. But for the civil rights movement that was the point. King and the others intended to show that segregation in the South had never been benign—that it was not simply custom or polite separation, as many white southerners preferred to pretend, but an ugly stain, violent at its core. They hoped Bull Connor would not disappoint them.

The skirmishing began in April 1963, just before Easter Sunday. I happened to be there as King was arrested, and at the moment it didn't seem particularly historic. The crowd of marchers was small, and by the time I wandered onto the scene, a bewildered bystander, it was almost over. Somebody told me there had been some demonstrations at a lunch counter, and then the march, but the police now had it under control. They were hauling King away to a paddy wagon, and even to the whites who had learned to hate him, he didn't seem especially threatening anymore. He was a smallish man in blue overalls, with an expression that betrayed neither anger nor fear but a stoicism that seemed to shade into sadness.

The sympathy I felt for him came in a flash, almost involuntary at first. I don't remember thinking of segregation or civil rights but simply that I knew who the underdog was—the victim of a cruelty that grew more vivid in the next few days as the snarling Bull Connor turned loose his dogs and aimed his fire hoses at the crowds of demonstrators. It was not always that simple and pat, for there were blacks who showered the policemen with rocks. But Connor and his troopers made no distinction between those who were violent and those who were not. The images flashing across the country were awful—German shepherds tearing at a teenager's flesh while another person was knocked from his feet by a hose and blown along the ground like a piece of tissue paper.

It was exactly what Martin Luther King had hoped for—a demonstration of the violence at the heart of segregation—and yet he brooded about it in private. Some years later I interviewed his daughter, Yolanda King, who remembered her father's anguish when Birmingham's white citizens blamed the problems on him. Even the most moderate ministers in the city issued a statement condemning the protests, charging that King's nonviolence was a mockery at its core, for violence, after all, was precisely the point, the drama that kept the movement in the headlines.

King recognized the grain of truth, especially in September 1963, when dynamite exploded at a Birmingham church. It was 10:29 on a Sunday morning, and the crowds were beginning to gather for worship. Four teenaged girls—Carole Robertson, Addie Mae Collins, Cynthia Wesley, and Denise McNair—were especially excited on this particularly morning, a late summer's day with the sound of church bells and the singing of birds. They were junior high school students who had been invited to participate in the service for adults. They had gone to the ground-floor restroom to primp when the bomb went off and ripped through the wall, killing all four in a cascade of bricks. Dr. King was in Atlanta when the phone call came, bringing with it the grisly details—four murdered girls who were killed for one reason: Their church had been a base of operations for his movement.

The members of his family had never seen him so depressed.

This was segregation laid bare, but he had never quite dreamed there would be such a price—the blood of four children barely older than his own. Was it really his fault? The irony of the question was nearly more than he could bear, but whatever the answer, he also knew there was no turning back. He was the personification of the movement by now. A few weeks earlier, in the most triumphant moment of his life, he had spoken to a remarkable march on Washington, delivering the most powerful address that many of the people in the crowd had ever heard. It didn't start out that way. He was plodding at first through the printed text, almost reading, when he got caught up in the excitement of the day. The crowd was huge, maybe two hundred thousand people, a fourth of them white, spreading out from the base of the Lincoln Memorial. As he moved through the text, gazing out across the mass of jubilant faces, he remembered a passage he hadn't thought to include. He had used it before, and it had gone over well in Birmingham and Detroit, "and I just felt," he told his biographer, David Garrow, "that I wanted to use it here." So he pushed his printed text aside and simply let the words pour out in a rush:

> I say to you today, my friends, even though we face the difficulties of today and tomorrow, I still have a dream. It is a dream deeply rooted in the American dream. I have a dream that one day this nation will rise up and live out the true meaning of its creed—we hold these truths to be self-evident, that all men are created equal.
>
> I have a dream that one day on the red hills of Georgia, the sons of former slaves and the sons of former slave-owners will be able to sit down together at the table of brotherhood. . . . I have a dream today!

It was a vision that became his gift to the country, an antidote to the tragedies of Birmingham and other places. And for some of us growing up in those times, it became an image that we couldn't put aside.

For me, however, the final conversion on the issue of race, the moment I knew there was no going back, came a few years later at Vanderbilt University. I was a history major, class of '68, which happened to be the first at that particular institution that contained a smattering of black undergraduates. The first group was impressive, some of the brightest young people I had known, and I found it hard to explain to the student down the hall, making A's in calculus while I was fervently praying for a D, why his race was inherently inferior to mine.

The epiphany, however, came later in the year, when George Wallace arrived to speak on the campus. In 1964 the governor of Alabama made a run for the presidency, and although he came up short, the people back home were proud of his spunk. There was a theory circulating among the members of my family that Wallace was not really talking about race—that even his stand in the schoolhouse door, a symbolic barrier to two black students who had been admitted to the University of Alabama, was simply a principled defense of states' rights. In retrospect, it was pure nonsense, but at the time it was a theory that I wanted to accept—a gesture of loyalty, I suppose, to the family. Wallace, however, made the truth very clear.

On the day of his speech, there were blacks in the crowd—a handful of students from Fisk University, well-mannered and brave, who had made the trip across town to see whether he was really as bad as they had heard. One girl rose to ask him a question, a tremble in her voice, and Wallace interrupted her question in the middle.

"What's that, honey? You'll have to speak up."

She tried again, and Wallace again cut her off with a sneer, the sarcasm dripping from the edges of his voice. "You're mighty pretty, honey, go ahead with your question."

Many years later, George Wallace would change. Long after the murder of Martin Luther King, after he, too, had been crippled by a would-be assassin, Wallace paid a visit to King's church in Montgomery. Ray Jenkins, one of Alabama's great journalists, described the remarkable moment in the little brick chapel, barely a block from the Alabama state capitol, where Jefferson Davis had taken his oath and "Dixie" had been chosen as the battle anthem of the South. Wallace, still governor but confined to a wheelchair, spoke of the redemptive power of suffering and the ability of God to change a man's heart. As he was wheeled down the aisle at the end of the sermon, the choir sang "The Battle Hymn of the Republic," and the people wept and a hundred black hands reached out to touch him.

But all of that was well hidden in the future, and what we saw at Vanderbilt in 1965 was a demonstration of spite, the racism elemental and pure. And all we could feel, my friends from Alabama and I, was a deep sense of shame that this man was one of us.

Visits home were harder after that. I remember one particular occasion when I was lecturing the family on the latest outrage. There had been a killing up the road in Lowndes County. A civil rights worker named Jonathan Daniels, a white Episcopal priest from Massachusetts who had come south on a voter registration campaign, was murdered in the sleepy little town of Hayneville. He was torn apart by a shotgun blast, and there were a couple of witnesses, both of them black. But the killer's lawyer made a simple defense: Jonathan Daniels, he said, was a rabble-rouser from the North who had gotten pretty much what he deserved. His death was a warning, a declaration of war against those who would tamper with the southern way of life, and it was the jury's duty to let the killer go free.

The jury agreed. The twelve white people quickly voted to acquit, and I told the members of my family at the time that it made me ashamed to be from Alabama. I was sitting in a small rocking chair as I spoke, lounging back comfortably, when an uncle from my mother's side of the family decided suddenly that he had heard enough. He bolted angrily across the room and with both hands braced on the arms of the chair—his face only a couple of inches from mine—he called me a traitor to my family and the South. I called him a race-baiting son of a bitch, then pushed him aside and stalked from the house.

For me, at least, it was a moment of hurt. I was fond of my uncle and knew him as a good and decent man. He was a courageous veteran of World War II, having survived the fighting in the Ardennes Forest—the Battle of the Bulge, the Americans called it—when the German army rallied for one last assault. The struggle for a while was nearly hand-to-hand, scarring the survivors with memories that were often too vivid to recount. My uncle certainly never talked about it much, but he brooded sometimes in a world of his own as he puttered around his Montgomery farm, the site of many of my boyhood adventures. He was shaped, I think, by the spirit of the place, which was worked in the 1950s and 1960s by a group of black people who lived in small and unpainted cabins without electricity or indoor plumbing. A few of them turned their jobs into art—cooking, training horses, performing with consummate pride and skill the functions that were necessary to the farm. Others, however, merely tried to get by, putting in their time until nightfall finally brought a reprieve. Those of us not part of that life never knew very much about the nights—what mysteries lay concealed in the black people's cabins—though a small boy could lie in his bed and wonder.

That was particularly true on the night that Savannah came screaming to the house. "Mr. Ned!" she cried. "Mr. Ned, Mr. Ned! You gotta help me, Mr. Ned. The man's gonna kill me." Savannah was a cook who worked at the farm, and she was fighting that night with a man at her cabin. We never knew why. An infidelity perhaps? Attention withheld? Those were some of the points of speculation, but whatever the case, Savannah was drunk and afraid for her life and she had fled across the fields to the only haven she knew.

"I'm staying here with my white folks!" she screamed. Out in the car, the man yelled back, threatening more harm if she didn't come out. My uncle surveyed the whole scene calmly, then shook his head and strolled toward the car.

"We don't need any trouble," he announced. "You better move on." And he knew when he said it that the man would obey.

My uncle's conception of the issue of race was shaped, of course, by moments such as that, while mine was shaped by the civil rights movement. The gap between us should have come as no surprise.

But on an April afternoon in 1966, I was back at college and thinking about those family estrangements when a professor of mine, who knew of my budding ambition to be a writer, handed me an essay by William Faulkner. It was a speech that Faulkner had delivered in the fifties, when he was accepting the Nobel Prize for literature. He had been asked, apparently, to define good writing, and this, in part, is what he said:

> The young man or woman writing today has forgotten the problems of the human heart in conflict with itself which alone can make good writing because only that is worth writing about, worth the agony and the sweat. He must learn them again, . . . leaving no room in his workshop for anything but the old verities and truths of the heart, the old universal truths lacking which any story is ephemeral and doomed—love and honor and pity and pride and compassion and sacrifice. . . .
> The poet's, the writer's duty is to write about these things. It is his privilege to help man endure by lifting his heart. . . .

The poet's voice need not merely be the record of man, it can be one of the props, the pillars to help him endure and prevail.

As I read those words, I suppose I was stirred by the poetic elegance, and even more by the message—the notion that the only fit subject for a writer is the human heart in conflict with itself. As a young man coming of age in Alabama, I thought I knew what Faulkner had in mind, for the conflict seemed to be everywhere, not only in the hearts of individual people, but also in the collective heart and soul of our place.

It was easy enough in the 1960s for a journalist to find himself drawn to that story, and there was something about the vantage point of Alabama. There were those horrible moments like the day in May 1961 when the Freedom Riders came through and the Montgomery police made a bargain with the Klan. In his remarkable book *The Children*, David Halberstam offers a chilling account of that agreement: We'll give you fifteen minutes, the police officials said. Whatever you want to do to these people, make sure it happens within that time. And the Klan, of course, accomplished much of what it set out to do.

In interviews with Halberstam, and some of the rest of us, too, John Lewis remembered the late-morning stillness as the bus pulled into the Greyhound station, an eerie quiet, stark, unnatural, holding the promise of the violence just ahead. Lewis was the senior member of the group, not in age but in the level of his commitment to the civil rights movement. He was a young Alabamian who was a student in Nashville and had been a leader in the sit-ins. He had established a reputation for his courage, and it was tested that day on the streets of Montgomery as the crowd of white people closed in around them, armed with clubs and pieces of pipe.

"Stand together. Don't run," Lewis called to the others as the beatings began, and for the next several minutes he assumed he would die. But then a couple of shots rang out as Alabama's commissioner of public safety, Floyd Mann, who had heard about the Faustian bargain with the Klan, fired his pistol into the air and declared emphatically enough for everyone to hear: "There will be no killing here today."

For many of us in the years after that, it was satisfying to write about the heroes—John Lewis, Floyd Mann, and all of the others—

and it was easy to write about the villains in the Klan. But there were also the thousands of people in between, those like the members of my own family, who were angry and bewildered by the civil rights movement but who were also moved—perhaps at a level that they wanted to deny—by the fundamental righteousness of the cause.

All of that left a writer, who was beginning his work in the 1960s, with instinctive understandings about the craft and the nature of the story that was there to be told. There were rich and inexplicable ambiguities that seemed to be the essence of the human condition. If most of us were doing the best we could, struggling with the values on which we were raised, it was a writer's opportunity to celebrate his place, with all its heroism and its flaws.

Then, as now, the Heart of Dixie held plenty of both.

PART I

"A Change Is Gonna Come"

On a February day in 1960, four black freshmen at North Carolina A&T University walked from their campus to the Woolworth's store in downtown Greensboro and took their seats at the segregated lunch counter. They were determined to draw their own line, to declare on a frigid winter afternoon that racial segregation is wrong. With their simple act of defiance, the Greensboro Four triggered a movement that quickly spread through the South.

In cities like Raleigh, Charlotte, Montgomery, and Nashville, other young people, acting with dignity, discipline, and courage, also decided to take up the cause. They sat in at lunch counters, rode interstate buses in integrated groups, and marched through the streets of the segregated South. They often paid a price for their resolve. Many were beaten; a few were killed, but they would not give in to the violence and terrorism of their day.

Where did it come from, this nonviolent crusade in which many of the foot soldiers were still in their teens? What was the source of their wisdom and bravery, their simple refusal to be turned around? This profile provides a partial answer to those questions. It begins with the memories of Franklin McCain, Joe McNeill, and Jibreel Khazan, the surviving members of the Greensboro Four.

Deliverance:
The Greensboro Four

The Big Lie

For Franklin McCain, there are moments when the memory of it comes rushing back—the feeling he had when he took his place at the counter, on the padded swivel stool beneath the laminated signs promoting lemon pie. He and his friends had given little thought to the history they were making. They were barely eighteen, and they didn't really care. All they knew was that the world was not what they thought it should be. Everywhere they turned there were White-Only signs and a way of life in the South and beyond that was rooted in the common affront of segregation.

As a young black man, McCain got the message—an insult that

was never very far from his mind. With his three closest friends on the dormitory hall, Joe McNeill, David Richmond, and Ezell Blair, he had made a decision so basic and clear that he couldn't believe he hadn't thought of it before. For the sake of his dignity and his pride, he simply was not going to take it anymore. As far as McCain and the others were concerned, the laws of segregation no longer applied.

And so it was that on February 1, 1960, they made their way to the Woolworth's lunch counter, a popular gathering place in Greensboro, and took their seats on the white people's stools. Forty years later, it was clear what it meant. It was the first sit-in of the 1960s, the day the civil rights movement finally came alive. Until then it had sputtered. There had been a victory or two here and there—the Montgomery bus boycott, for example, which had ended in 1956 and made a hero out of Martin Luther King Jr. But in the intervening years, Dr. King had struggled over what to do next. He had preached in pulpits all over the South, at times, in fact, all over the world, flashing his oratory and his passion, hoping somehow for a critical mass. But so far he had failed. The crowds most often would roar their approval, and the journalists came down from *Time* magazine and put him on the cover, but the movement itself—the great awakening that King had proclaimed—was nothing but a caricature of his dreams. White supremacy was the order of the day, and the battle against it, such as it was, seemed like the harmless buzzing of a fly.

Then came Greensboro. As the protests grew, one of King's colleagues, Fred Shuttlesworth, paid a visit to North Carolina to see what was happening. It didn't take him long to make his assessment. After seeing the demonstrators massing at the counters, he immediately telephoned King's headquarters. "Tell Martin," he said, "I think this is it."

In the days after that, the sit-ins spread to other cities in the South—Charlotte, Winston-Salem, Nashville—and that tactic soon gave way to others. The Freedom Rides, the March on Washington, Dr. King's "Letter from a Birmingham Jail"—each of those things built upon the last, but Greensboro was always first in the line. "It was the shot heard 'round the world," said King.

Whenever he thought about it that way, Franklin McCain had to smile. He never set out to be a pioneer. His motive instead was simply to find some sense of relief, some escape from the rage that was building inside him. He understood the irony of it very well. His anger was not yet focused on the whites. It was reserved instead for the members of his own generation and his parents'. They had lived with humiliation and oppression, and because so far they had failed to draw the line, he was afraid they were getting just what they deserved. It was a disturbing idea, and by the middle of his freshman year in college, he was beginning to think it would drive him insane.

He had come to Greensboro from a middle-class family in Washington, D.C., enrolling at North Carolina A&T. In many ways, he thought back fondly on the people who had raised him. His Grandmother Massey was always his favorite. She was a light-skinned woman from North Carolina, with a roundish face and soft, gentle eyes. For much of her life, she had spent her days in the white people's homes, helping raise their children, and as McCain remembers her, she had a kind of folk wisdom that set her apart.

There was the time, for example, when Franklin was maybe twelve or thirteen, bragging in the way that teenagers will about something he had done. Amanda Massey took him outside and pointed to the heavens. "Boy," she said, "there are stars up there that have not even been discovered—they are bigger than the Earth and the distances are such that you can't even imagine—and you are going to stand down here and tell me that you are so important."

For McCain, it was easily the most vivid memory of his childhood, a lesson in humility that he carried all his life. But there were other lessons that were more problematic. His energetic parents, Warner and Mattie, wanted their children to believe they could make it. For three generations, the McCains had gone to college, which was simply accepted as the thirteenth grade—an utterly unremarkable achievement—and the message for as long as Franklin could remember was that any young person who worked hard at his studies and did his best to stay out of trouble would find a way to make his mark on the world.

It sounded good at the time, but was it really true? In a world that was segregated and mean, did it really make sense to believe that a black man's virtue would find its reward? Franklin didn't think so, and by the beginning of his freshman year in college, he had quietly concluded with a mounting sense of rage that the teachings of his family—the articles of faith on which he was raised—had simply been a lie. He soon discovered that he was not alone. His roommate, David Richmond, for example, was a bright young man who had the same reflective turn of mind. Like Franklin he was planning to major in science (for McCain it was chemistry, for Richmond it was physics), and they both did well on advanced placement tests, both qualifying for upper-level classes. Soon, they met their neighbors down the hall, Joe McNeill and Ezell Blair, who lived in room 2123. The room became a place where all of them would gather, these four young scholars who would talk about their courses, but who would talk also about the world outside.

All of them hated the curse of segregation, and night after night, it became their obsession. Many of the other students thought they were strange, "the oddballs," as McCain now remembers it. They showed too little interest in football or girls or what they would do on a Saturday night. Instead, they were always poring over books, writings about Gandhi, or the works of W.E.B. Dubois as they tried to come to terms with the issue of race.

One night near the start of the second semester, it was too cold, they decided, to go anywhere, so they gathered after supper, as they had many times, in the cluttered dorm room of Joe and Ezell. It had always been a place of refuge, with *Atlantic Monthly*s scattered on the floor amid the philosophy texts and the most recent issues of *Physics Today*. On this particular night, January 31, 1960, there was another little book lying there with the rest, a paperback by the labor leader Eric Hoffer, extolling the virtue of the "true believers," the people who refused to take no for an answer.

In many ways, it would have been nice to see themselves that way. But the more they talked about it that night, the more apparent it became that they didn't really believe in very much at all. Or if they did, they had never taken it to heart. They were fond of criticizing their parents' generation for doing too little, and believing too much in the American Dream. The Big Lie, they called it. But what had they done, the four of them right there in the room? Had they ever taken their stand against the Lie? Had they ever confronted the white people's laws? Had they ever done anything except talk? They didn't care much for the answers to the questions, and as the evening wore on, their mood sank lower and lower by the hour. "I felt dirty," says McCain. "I felt ashamed."

But finally McNeill made a simple suggestion. "Let's do something," he said, and they realized suddenly that a corner had been turned. McNeill was serious. He began to talk about public accommodations—how the nearby stores like Walgreen's and Woolworth's would accept their money but refused to allow them to sit at their lunch counters.

Sometime around dawn on February 1, they decided that the time had come to take a stand. They would go that day, no need to put it off, to the lunch counter down at the Woolworth's store and demand to be served. A shiver of fear quickly went through the group. One of them asked, Are we really sure this is what we want to do?

Ezell Blair was the most uncertain. He remembered the day as a nine-year-old when he had boasted to friends that he would one day drink from the white people's fountains and eat at their lunch counters. He had always admired the racial pioneers—the Little Rock Nine, for example, who had braved the mobs in 1957, seeking to integrate their city's public schools. But now that his own moment had arrived, he was not really sure he was ready for the challenge.

Forty years later, he remembered tossing and turning that night, then calling his parents to ask their advice. His father, Ezell Sr., was a leader in the NAACP and a man who was willing to stand up for his family. His mother, Corene, was a member of the organization also, and when Ezell Jr. asked her opinion, she told him simply to do what he must and to carry himself with dignity and grace. After that, there was nothing more to say.

As Joe McNeill pointed out, they were all afraid. Under the circumstances, it was normal. The question was how they managed that fear—whether they let it cripple their resolve, or whether they were able to push it aside.

For McCain, the answer to that one was easy. They might go to jail. They might even be killed. But in a segregated world, they had to be prepared to pay such a price. "We had nothing to lose," he says, looking back. His anger, quite simply, was stronger than his fear, and before it was over the others felt the same. They knew that the following afternoon they would do it. The moment of their personal liberation was at hand.

The Movement

It was a twelve-minute walk from the A&T campus. They met at the library after spending most of the day in their classes. Mc-Cain says he made it through geometry and chemistry and a discussion of James Thurber in English Composition. But he picked up demerits in ROTC, his last class of the day, for speaking out of turn. Finally, at three thirty, he headed for the library, where the others soon arrived, and they began a quiet walk from the campus to the store. "We weren't talking very much," says McCain. When they got to the door, they split into pairs—McCain and McNeill, Richmond and Blair. They bought school supplies and kept the receipts, then McCain and McNeill, who happened to be the closest, decided it was time to move toward the counter. As McCain remembers it, they hesitated for maybe a minute, maybe even five, then took their seats, to the general astonishment of the people all around.

For McCain, it was a moment unique in his life, providing a sense of exhilaration and relief. "I can't even describe it," he says today. "Never have I experienced such an incredible emotion, such an uplift. . . . As a journalist friend of mine once put it, 'My soul was rested.'"

But soon the moment became more tense. McNeill says a policeman arrived on the scene and began to pace back and forth at the counter, tapping his nightstick firmly in his hand.

"Joe," said Franklin, "I think this is it."

"Yeah," said McNeill. "I think so."

The gesture, however, was merely a threat, and when the two young men at the counter didn't flinch, the policeman suddenly seemed to be confused. So did everybody else in authority, as Richmond and Blair made their way toward the stools, and the waitress tried to explain once again that they would have to leave. "We don't serve Negroes here," she said.

But McCain replied with manicured politeness, referring to the school supplies they had bought: "I beg to disagree. You do serve us and you have."

And McNeill added stubbornly, "We have the receipts to prove it."

C. L. Harris, the manager, soon arrived at the counter and told them again, "I just can't serve you."

The standoff continued until just before five, the tension building as the word began to spread. McNeill remembers an elderly white woman who patted their shoulders and told them that she was disappointed in a way—not by the fact that they had decided to protest but because, she said, "It should have been done twenty years ago."

That was the high point. The low point came when a black kitchen worker began to berate them, saying no good would come of what they were doing. "At that moment," says McCain, "we literally hated her."

It was a feeling that slowly changed as they began to understand the interplay of emotions, the threat that they had come to represent—even for many black people in the South. What kind of retaliation would there be, and who, in the end, would feel its effects? The answers, of course, were still unclear, and there were reasons for a kitchen worker to be afraid. But on February 1, 1960, McCain and the others did not want to hear it. They were there on a mission, and at the moment at least it was hard to muster any sympathy for an African American woman who opposed them.

And so it was that they rode their roller coaster of emotions until nearly five o'clock, when C. L. Harris decided to close down the counter. As stiffly polite as they had been from the start, the four of them left and headed back to campus, reveling together in their moment of deliverance but knowing already that this was a cause much bigger than themselves.

They called a meeting that night of the campus leadership—the student body president, the student newspaper editor, and anybody else who held an official position of authority. They talked about their adventure that day and the shimmering possibilities that lay just ahead, and they were startled at first by the response of the others. Nobody believed them. Nobody believed that four college freshmen, acting on their own, had taken on the system of white supremacy and lived to tell about it.

The exception to the skepticism that night was an upperclassman named Albert Rozier, the student newspaper editor. On the following morning, he put out an extra edition of his paper—the first in its history—and suddenly it seemed as though the whole world knew. McCain and the others tried to make it clear that this was not a fad, not a one-day adventure or a way of raising hell. This was serious business, they said. The important thing now was to keep pushing on.

On Tuesday morning, February 2, McCain, McNeill, and two other students, Billy Smith and Clarence Henderson, returned to the Woolworth's as soon as it opened. Blair and Richmond decided to go to class. A photographer arrived from the *Greensboro Record* and snapped a picture of four students sitting at the Woolworth's counter. For the next forty years, the picture was consistently misidentified as the first sit-in, and Smith and Henderson became Richmond and Blair in newspaper cut-lines all across the country. At the moment, however, they were simply caught up in the excitement of the day—a momentum that was clearly getting stronger by the hour. By Tuesday afternoon, there were two dozen students sitting in at the counter, and by the following Saturday there were nearly three thousand.

Bettye Davis was one of the newcomers. She was a freshman at Bennett College, not far from A&T—a Georgia girl whose parents had urged her to keep out of trouble. They were terrified at what might happen if their daughter became a part of the public demonstrations. They understood clearly that this was a frontal assault on the laws of segregation, and it seemed to be spreading to every city in the South. They knew there had to be trouble down the line.

On Saturday, February 7, as the demonstrators assembled by the thousands downtown, the streets were teeming with white people, too. There were bomb scares, and a lot of young toughs parading through the streets, screaming epithets and throwing water balloons from the fifteenth floor of a Greensboro hotel.

After a while it became a defining character of the movement—the dignity of the black students massing at the counters and the ugly obscenity of the mobs who opposed them. Even the segregationists had to notice. As one southern columnist put it at the time, "Here were the colored students, in coats, white shirts, ties, and one of them was reading Goethe and one was taking notes from a biology text. And here, on the sidewalk outside, was a gang of white boys come to heckle, a ragtag rabble, slack-jawed, black-jacketed, grinning fit to kill. . . . It gives one pause."

As the melodrama spread to fifty-four cities in nine southern states, the question that people kept asking was *Why*? Why now, and why had Greensboro been such a spark? There had been other sit-ins. The tactic, in fact, went back all the way to the 1870s, when a group of blacks in the city of Charlotte took their places in the white-only section of a downtown theater. In more recent times, there had been at least a dozen demonstrations before Greensboro, all of which were isolated events, unnoticed outside the places where they happened.

Greensboro was different, and Bettye Davis, among others, thought that maybe she understood the reason. She had to admit to a little bit of prejudice. She was falling in love with Franklin McCain and would soon become his wife. But there was something about his character, she said, and that of his friends. As far as she could tell they were fearless, full of anger and passion that was tempered somehow by a sense of perspective. They didn't really seem to have any egos. Not only were they exceptionally close to one another, but they were willing to share leadership with any student at any Greensboro college who seemed to have what it took.

They set up a committee called the Student Executive Committee for Justice, and Bettye was one of the members of the group—a lonely little core that continued to march when the weather turned rainy and the national reporters had moved on to other things. By the spring, she remembers, they were down to a handful, but Franklin and the others didn't seem to mind. They were rooted by now in their own sense of history, a connection they felt between their own modest efforts and the people they had read about in books—from Frederick Douglass to Mohandas Gandhi to Cinque the African, who had led a slave-ship rebellion in the middle of the Atlantic. They were sustained in the end by all of these things—the anger, the passion, the feeling of connection—and by spring it was clear that they simply wouldn't quit.

One person who took his measure of their resolve was Spencer Love, the CEO of Burlington Industries and the most powerful business leader in Greensboro. Love, quite clearly, was getting tired of the noise, and he dispatched an executive from Burlington Industries, a talented man named E. R. Zane, to sit down immediately with the leaders of the movement. Zane was different from the other white leaders. He was willing to listen. His motivation at its core may have been economic—the sit-in movement was not good for business—but Zane seemed to care about doing what was right. McCain and the others could see that at once, and by July they had managed to work out a solution. The restaurant owners in the city of

Greensboro, with only a couple of holdouts, would serve blacks on an equal basis with whites.

There would be other battles in the city down the line; theaters, for example, were unaffected by the truce. But for Franklin McCain and his dormitory friends, there was satisfaction in what they accomplished. Not only had they won their skirmish in Greensboro; they had triggered a movement that was spreading through the South.

As the momentum grew, the Greensboro Four understood their role, but then as now, they were always careful not to overstate it.

"Like many others," said Joe McNeill, "we are proud to have been able to contribute." But in the coming years, they also discovered, along with the other survivors of the movement, that it would not be easy to move on with their lives.

What, exactly, could they do for an encore?

The Long Morning After

In Greensboro, all of them worried about David Richmond. Some people said he was the best of the bunch—gentle, intelligent, generous to a fault, able to summon the courage to take a stand. Franklin thought he was a little bit shy, uncomfortable perhaps with that curious celebrity that went with the movement.

But there were other burdens that he carried also. He got married while he was still at A&T, and he was immediately faced with the prospect of juggling. There were the demands of his classes and the needs of his family, as well as the never-ending pressures of the movement. He began to fall behind on his schoolwork, cutting back on his class load, and as time went by he clearly came to envy the success of the others.

Ezell Blair, for example, was elected student body president, then moved on from there to Howard University Law School. McNeill graduated, accepted a commission in the Air Force, flew combat missions in Vietnam, and was eventually promoted all the way to general. McCain got his graduate degree in chemistry, then took a promising job with the Celanese Corporation in Charlotte.

Richmond, meanwhile, never got his degree, moving instead from one job to the next, none of which, in the opinion of his friends, was a match for his abilities. After a while, he began to drink. His marriage fell apart, and the drinking got worse, and his health seemed to be in a state of decline. There were times in the 1970s and 1980s when they would all get together and go back to Woolworth's, celebrating some of the round-numbered anniversaries. On many of those occasions, they worried about David. He seemed so gaunt, and sometimes when he talked to Franklin and the others, his conversation teetered on the edge of despair. In 1993, he died, perhaps from the effects of his alcohol problem, but Franklin thought it was really a broken heart. In a sense, David's life, like the others, had peaked at the fragile age of eighteen, when they decided together to do something grand. But the pressures of that decision were immense.

To Ezell Blair, the survivors of the movement were like veterans of combat, battered by the trauma, and health and alcohol problems were common. Blair himself had battled a variety of maladies, he said, serious enough to force him out of law school, and the first symptoms started at the height of the sit-ins. But looking back on it, there was nothing he would change. If the sit-ins were part of a political journey, they were also, for Blair, a journey of the heart. In his years after college, as he pondered the American legacy of racism, he decided to make his break with the South, the place of his birth. He made his way to New Bedford, Massachusetts, where he began to meet people from all over the world. His closest friend was a Holocaust survivor, and there were neighbors from Africa and the Middle East who looked at the world in a whole different way.

It was about that time that he converted to Islam. In 1970, he changed his name to Jibreel Khazan, and his family in North Carolina was shocked, particularly his father, Ezell Sr., who had been happy to have a son to carry on his name. Now it was gone, this tangible tie between the generations, and for the Blairs, temporarily, it was a moment of pain. But Jibreel Khazan never strayed very far from the example of his father or the lessons of the people he had known as a child. There were teachers in the segregated schools of the South who believed in the promise of the Constitution and the radical possibilities of the Bill of Rights, and Khazan himself had come to believe that the mission of the civil rights movement was to "take those things and try to make them live." It was therefore a movement that was rooted in the past, in the wisdom of the generation of his parents, which was a realization he shared with Franklin McCain.

There was a time when all of them had been impatient, when Franklin especially had been skeptical of the faith of the people who raised him, their affirmation that virtue would find its reward. He now understood that they were trying to give him hope, which was a heroic notion for people who lived in a segregated world, and without that hope there would have been no movement—no anger in the face of a frustrated promise, no passion to help them overcome their fears.

These were the things he came to understand. There were ways in which he was still disillusioned, for the world hadn't changed as much as he had hoped. There was the growing chasm between rich and poor, the final frontier on which the movement had stalled, and as the twentieth century came to an end he could feel the return of old attitudes—in Charlotte a push to resegregate the schools, in South Carolina a racist crusade for the Confederate flag. But there were bits and pieces of news that gave him hope. In Tallahassee, Florida, just before the fortieth anniversary of the Greensboro sit-in, a group of students and civil rights activists staged a modern sit-in of their own—a protest against Governor Jeb Bush's plans to dismantle affirmative action in his state.

McCain believes those things are important. Each generation has to keep on pushing, sustained in part by its knowledge of the past. So as the anniversary celebrations roll around, McCain is happy to reflect on the history, telling the people in Greensboro and beyond that he and his friends were not heroes. Whatever their motivations at the start, they were a part of something much bigger than themselves—a generation that was ready, that immediately knew at the first whisper of the news that the time had finally come to take a stand.

*As the sit-in movement quickly spread, one of the people who picked up
the torch was Charles Jones, a seminary student from down the road in
Charlotte. The demonstrations there, like those in other cities nearby, were
less publicized than the ground-breaking protests in Greensboro. But they
revealed as much or more about the character of the movement, and I was
happy to have a chance to interview the leaders as they came together some
forty years later to celebrate the anniversary of their achievement.*

The Power and the Glory
of a Tuna Fish Sandwich

He heard the news on a February night in 1960, in the desolate hours just before dawn. He was driving south through
Virginia on his way home to Charlotte, the radio crackling through
the cold morning air. The newscast offered only sketchy details, but
the report was exhilarating even so. Four young freshmen at North
Carolina A&T, an all-black university in Greensboro, had gone down
to the segregated lunch counter at Woolworth's and taken their seats
on the white people's stools.

Charles Jones listened to the story in amazement. For some time
now, he had been obsessed by the cruelty of southern segregation,
that maddening combination of customs and laws that had been in
place since the end of Reconstruction. Jones, the grandson of a slave,
came from a line of ambitious people, preachers mostly, including his
father, J. T. Jones, who wanted the best for the members of his family. But for every African American in the South, segregation was a
crippling, insulting reality, a daily reminder of inferiority from which
there seemed to be no escape.

Charles didn't want to believe that was true. He was a seminary
student at Johnson C. Smith, a young man of twenty-two, regarded
by many of his friends as a dreamer. He had begun to study the
philosophy of nonviolence—the writings of Gandhi and some of the
speeches of Martin Luther King Jr.—and a few years earlier, in 1956,
he was stirred by the photographs from Montgomery, the newspaper

images of Negro citizens trudging to work on the gray winter mornings, refusing to ride on the segregated buses.

Eventually, that particular protest had worked. The U.S. Supreme Court struck down segregation on the Alabama buses, and the Montgomery leaders such as King and Rosa Parks became national heroes for many black Americans. But in the rest of the South segregation survived, and four years after the Montgomery demonstrations, people like Jones and his friends at the college were still at a loss about how to combat it.

Then came the news reports out of Greensboro. More than forty years later, Jones remembered the adrenalin rush of that moment—how he heard that the students had taken their seats and refused to obey when the Woolworth's manager ordered them to leave. The straightforward dignity of it took his breath. These four students, whoever they were, had simply declared that the laws of segregation no longer applied. As he thought about the powerful thing they had done, Jones found himself shouting to the great, empty sky: "Thank you, God! This is how we can do it."

It was, he told a reporter years later, "like some kind of cosmic lightning bolt."

When he got back to campus, he met with a group of student council leaders and declared with a flourish, "I don't know about ya'll, but tomorrow morning I'm going downtown, and I'm gon' do what the students in Greensboro did." He had no way of knowing when he said it that his counterparts in more than fifty other southern towns were beginning to make the same kind of plans. Only later did he learn that all of them were part of the same great awakening.

The Charlotte protests came together quickly, and though Jones was the visionary, the spokesman quoted most often in the press, there were others who emerged from the ranks of the students. Heyward Davenport was a gifted strategist, and behind the scenes there was B. B. DeLaine, a quiet young man from South Carolina with soft, steady eyes and a gentle demeanor, a man who didn't think of himself as an activist. Some of the others thought that was strange, for DeLaine, as much as anybody on campus, had come of age with the civil rights movement.

His father was the Reverend J. A. DeLaine, a fiery leader from Clarendon County, South Carolina, who organized the farmers in that part of the state to file the country's first desegregation lawsuit. Eventually, the case of _Briggs vs. Elliott_ became one of five the Supreme Court considered in its landmark ruling of 1954, outlawing segregation in the schools.

As a child of twelve, B.B. DeLaine began attending mass meetings leading up to the lawsuit, and on a trip home from college a few years later, he witnessed firsthand the violent retributions that were now being regularly aimed at his father. One morning he was talking to his mother in the kitchen when he heard a crash near the front of the house. He rushed toward the sound and saw glass on the floor from the living room window and some white men driving away in a car. He grabbed immediately for the family shotgun, but his mother slowed him down, warning him frantically what would happen if he fired.

This was South Carolina, she said. The police would come and take him away, and nobody knew what would happen to him then.

A few years later at Johnson C. Smith, he was grateful for Mattie DeLaine's intervention, especially as he studied the theory of nonviolence, the new cornerstone of the civil rights movement. Charles Jones talked about it all the time, telling the students who volunteered for the sit-ins, "We are going to sit at the lunch counter, and we are not going to move. We are not going to cooperate with segregation, but we _are_ going to be on our best behavior. We are not going to talk back. We are not going to return any white people's blows. If you are uncomfortable with that, just remember we are outnumbered, outgunned, so we have to be disciplined and we have to be smart."

Early on the first morning of the protests, Jones put on "Sunday-go-to-meetin'" clothes and went down to the administration building on the campus, a handsome, nineteenth-century edifice constructed carefully out of handmade bricks. It was a symbol, he knew, of all the ancestors' hopes in the days just after emancipation, when the former slaves set out to build institutions—churches, schools, even a few universities where they could aspire to the highest educational opportunities.

On that cold winter morning in 1960, Jones could feel a connection between the hopes and dreams of the ancestors' time and the new possibilities of the civil rights movement. He wondered whether the other students felt it as well, but in a way he knew that it didn't really matter. The important thing was they were there in force— maybe two hundred strong, waiting to make the trek downtown. Some of them drove their personal cars, a few others walked, and most of them rode on the campus school bus, driven that day by B. B. DeLaine.

They sat in at the counters of a half dozen stores, and day after day they kept coming back. There were racial insults and scattered acts of violence, as young white toughs gathered periodically to spit or heckle or threaten further harm. DeLaine also remembered one policeman who elbowed a young woman squarely in the face, knocking her to the ground. But the police most often seemed to be restrained, and so did many of the city's white leaders. And perhaps most important in the eyes of Charles Jones, there were committed reporters from the *Charlotte Observer* and some of the radio and television stations who seemed to be serious about telling the story.

Their dispatches were usually even-handed and fair, and they reported not only what the demonstrators did but their explanations about why. Jones himself quoted the Constitution and the Old Testament prophets, talking about equality and Christian brotherhood, and "the great schism in the South between what this region says it believes and how it behaves." The stories went out on the national wires, and looking back on it later, Jones was convinced that the Charlotte demonstrations, as much as those in any other city, delivered an important message to the country.

By the summer of 1960, the combination of moral and economic pressure, intensified by the national publicity, took its toll on Charlotte's white leadership. Many of the businessmen downtown decided finally that enough was enough, and the word went out that it was time for a truce.

"There was an understanding," said Jones, "that if we would just quietly come down and eat, the restaurants and counters downtown would be open."

In early July, to test that promise, Jones went with his father to the Rexall Drugs and Trade and Tryon in the heart of downtown. As the two of them sat down together to order, Jones thought about all those people in the past who had persevered through the years of slavery and segregation. He glanced at his father and saw the glimmer of satisfaction in his eyes, and as he picked up his tuna fish sandwich, it seemed for a moment as if anything was possible.

But he also knew that the movement in Charlotte, however successful, was only one part of a much larger struggle. A few weeks earlier, he had met with activists from nine southern states—more than 150 sit-in veterans gathering in Raleigh at Shaw University. They met with national civil rights leaders, including the conference organizer, Ella Baker, Dr. Martin Luther King Jr., and the man they found most eloquent of all, a Methodist minister by the name of James Lawson.

Lawson framed the philosophy of the movement this way: "Love is the force by which God binds man to Himself and man to man. Such love goes to the extreme; it remains loving and forgiving even in the midst of hostility. It matches the capacity of evil to inflict suffering with an even more enduring capacity to absorb evil, all the while persisting in love."

What Lawson was saying was that the students were engaged in an odd kind of war, more heroic and courageous than a violent fit of rage at the massive injustice of the southern way of life. They would absorb the hatred at the heart of segregation, and through their example they would bring the institution of white supremacy to its knees.

Charles Jones was mesmerized by the notion, and throughout the three-day meeting, he met other students whose enthusiasm was equal to his own. One of those was Diane Nash from Fisk University, who seemed to embody, as much as anybody at the conference, some of the finest ideals of the movement. Many of her peers were struck by her beauty, her large, dark eyes that were gentle and sure, and her manner that at first seemed so unassuming.

In the early days, when she and her friends started meeting in Nashville, planning their first lunch-counter sit-ins, she says she was frightened by what they were doing. Growing up in the North, she had seen the horrible photos of Emmett Till, a teenager murdered on a trip to Mississippi when he allegedly said something fresh to a white woman. "I had heard stories of the brutality of the South," she said. "I was duly impressed."

Nevertheless, she became a leader in the Nashville movement, and one day in the spring she confronted the mayor on the steps of city hall. She demanded to know, as the reporters hovered around taking notes, whether he would use the power and prestige of his office to end segregation.

Ben West, one of the most powerful men in Nashville, drew himself up sharply and declared: "I appeal to all citizens to end discrimination, to have no bigotry, no bias, no hatred."

Nash continued to push. "Then, Mayor, do you recommend that lunch counters be desegregated?"

"Yes," said West, and among people in the movement, it became a legendary moment of triumph.

Following the meeting at Shaw University, Nash, like Jones, signed on with the Student Nonviolent Coordinating Committee (SNCC), a new organization formed at the conference to coordinate protests throughout the South. Early in 1961, they decided they needed to lend their support to sit-ins taking place in Rock Hill, South Carolina. There, a group of students from Friendship College, led by Thomas Gaither, a field organizer for the Congress of Racial Equality, were arrested and sentenced to thirty days' hard labor or fines of one hundred dollars apiece.

Nine of the students opted for the chain gang.

Their decision came at a time when the civil rights movement all over the South was running low on cash. Thousands of people had been arrested by now, and money for bail was getting harder to raise. In addition to that, the story was slowly growing stale, as the media and the country began to lose interest. But the specter of students on a Carolina chain gang was something that the nation had not yet seen.

It caught the attention of the national press corps, and even more than that, it caught the attention of the leaders in SNCC. At a conference in Atlanta, Charles Jones and the others were deeply moved by the Gandhian example of the Rock Hill students and immediately set out to join them in jail. The expedition included Jones and Diane Nash and two of the other young sit-in veterans, Charles Sherrod and Ruby Doris Smith.

They were arrested together on February 6, 1961, and Nash's mother in Chicago saw it that night on the television news. It was part of the generational agony that was one of the undercurrents of the civil rights movement—parents who were frightened by the risks and vulnerability of their children but who also knew that the children were right. Nash did her best to sooth those fears, writing letters home from her cell in the jail. She also wrote a letter to the *Rock Hill Herald*, the local newspaper, trying to explain the philosophy of the movement.

"Segregation is immoral," she told the white community of Rock Hill. "Seek a world where all men may be as free as you yourself want to be."

For the next thirty days, she did a lot of reading—the autobiography of Mohandas Gandhi, the patron saint of the nonviolent movement—and along with her cellmate, Ruby Doris Smith, she told one reporter who came to the jail, "The days pass quickly."

For Charles Jones and his comrade Charles Sherrod, the days also went by in a blur. Life on the chain gang was brutally hard. They dug ditches and shoveled wet sand from the bed of a creek, using it later to build concrete pipes. They cleaned up trash from the sides of the highways and helped sweep the streets—doing whatever, as Jones later put it, "the gatekeepers felt would be humiliating."

But Jones, Sherrod, and the other demonstrators in the Rock Hill jail seemed to be immune to humiliation. To the astonishment of the South Carolina authorities, the young people worked harder than anybody else. They sang the old spirituals every day on the road crew, inspired, said Jones, by the example of the slaves from a hundred years before. The music gave a rhythm and a purpose to the work, a feeling of unity.

"We called it the chain gang shuffle," said Jones.

And every night, no matter how tired, when they returned to the large holding cell at the jail, herded in like cattle, Jones and Sherrod led the others in devotions. Both young men were seminary students, Jones in Charlotte, Sherrod in Virginia, and they would read from the scriptures, and one or the other would give a brief sermon.

To the jailers' horror, all the black prisoners and even the whites in the cells across the hall began to participate in the services. "Shut up that fuss!" the authorities commanded, and when it continued, the civil rights prisoners were taken away to solitary confinement—a concrete cell with a toilet and no bed. But even there, they would not relent.

Word of their example quickly spread through the movement, and as the historian Taylor Branch later put it, the Rock Hill students and those who came to go to jail with them "set a new standard of psychological commitment." They helped to underscore a new understanding in the ranks of the civil rights demonstrators that "the entire South was a common battlefield."

When his jail term was over, Charles Jones knew he would never be the same. Many years later, he remembered how one of the chain gang guards, a grizzled white man who had presided over this curious young crew with a wad of tobacco and a double-barreled shotgun, called him aside and declared with a kind of bewildered admiration, "I don't agree with what you boys are doing, but you're good boys."

Jones thought then that they were starting to see a little bit of progress, taking their first few steps toward a color-blind society where "all God's children could live together with respect." He had no illusions that the battle was won, or that it would ever be in his own lifetime.

But at least, he said, they had finally made a start.

For some of the young people in the civil rights movement, despite the dangers of their undertaking, there was sustenance and hope in the journey that they were sharing with their peers. But there were others, as we would learn later on, who could not possibly have felt more alone.

Perry Wallace:
The Long Road Home

He stood at the center of the hardwood floor and did his best to take it all in. There had been other times, other moments when the cheering had swept through the building, but he had never imagined it could feel like this. On a February day in 2004, playing once again to an overflow crowd, Perry Wallace had come back home to the Vanderbilt University gym, the place where he'd made his own piece of history.

Starting in the summer of 1966, this young man from the north side of Nashville entered the student body at Vanderbilt. He was a basketball star at Pearl High School and the valedictorian of his all-black class, and there were a hundred colleges scattered across the country who wanted him to come play basketball for them. But he had chosen instead to stay close to home, becoming the first black player in the Southeastern Conference (SEC), and there were people who said from the very beginning that he carried himself like a young Jackie Robinson. There was a dignity about him, an air of self-possession and restraint, and a gentle courage that you could see in his eyes. But out on the court, he showed a certain ferocity also—his game played mostly above the rim, blocking shots, snatching rebounds with a snap of his hands. And even in the dingy little gyms of Mississippi, where the crowds would threaten and greet him with a slur, there were the occasional gasps of astonishment and awe at the things they had never seen anybody else do.

In many ways, it was an experience as rich as he could have imagined. But there was a bitterness about it that was slow to recede, and it wasn't just the ugly racism of the road—the choreographed hatred in Deep South arenas where the cheerleaders jeered and epithets flew from every corner of the room. Back at Vanderbilt also, there were nights he would lie by himself in the dorm and wonder at the icy silence of his classmates. Not all of them, of course. There were people who were kind, and people he admired for their honest confrontation with the issue of race. And yet too often, there were students who looked right past him in the halls, as if somehow he were not even there.

He found it a lonely way to spend his years, and when graduation came in 1970 he told one reporter who was working in Nashville: "I have been there by myself. There were many people who knew my name, but they were not interested in knowing me. It was not so much that I was treated badly. It was just that I wasn't treated at all."

The official relationship cooled after that. People began to talk about "Perry's blast," his public criticism of the subtle racism he encountered at his school. Vanderbilt's vice chancellor, Rob Roy Purdy, spoke for many others when he told the same reporter: "Perry has become quite bitter, you know. He seems to remember the trauma and not the good side of it. He has made a lot of people unhappy."

For a time at least, the hurt ran deep, as Vanderbilt and Wallace went their own separate ways, neither one talking very much about the other. But now here he was in 2004, standing once again at center court. He was a gray-haired man of fifty-six, a law professor at American University, and he thought the emotions might sweep him away as he glanced at his jersey now hanging in the rafters: number 25 in black and gold, just the third time in the history of the school that an athlete had had his jersey retired.

Wallace was honored, he told one reporter, and he was happy for Vanderbilt also—proud of the decision the university had made to lay claim to its own little corner of history. There was a symmetry now, as Wallace understood it. A story once overflowing with pain had finally come full circle—fulfilling, more than thirty years later, the delicate promise it had held from the start.

It began in the final days of segregation.

Perry Wallace was the youngest of six children, coming of age in an all-black world. His father, Perry Sr., had moved the family to Nashville in the 1930s, joining the massive urban migration in search of greater economic opportunity. They had all been farmers until that time, and Perry Sr. applied the hardheaded ethic he had learned in the fields to the task of earning a living for his family. In the early years he got a job laying brick, and after a while he was doing well enough to start his own company.

Sometime late in the 1950s, the family moved again to a sturdy new home, nestled near the boundary of a white neighborhood. For Perry Jr., the effect was like living in a no-man's land, especially in the winter of 1960, when the sit-ins began in the heart of downtown. There were white toughs roaming the streets every day, inflamed by the students from the black universities—young men and women who dressed as if they were on their way to church. The demonstrators carried themselves with resolve, silent in the face of the insults and violence, as they took their seats in the segregated restaurants.

At the age of twelve, Perry was fascinated by the drama. Sometimes on a dare, he and his friends would venture downtown, lured by the danger but drawn also by a new and intoxicating kind of hope.

"People were talking," he remembers, "about the possibility of change. We were scared, but curious, especially as kids. We wanted to help, wanted to get involved, but there was also a lot of conflict and hostility—white guys throwing rocks, calling you names, pointing guns at you. You would think to yourself, 'This doesn't make any sense.'"

Many times he thought about getting away. He knew already that he might have special gifts as an athlete, and while he suffered periodically from attacks of asthma, he also knew from the example of his parents that there were obstacles in the world that could be overcome. He thought about how it might be to go north. It was what you did, after all, if you were ambitious and black and wanted to go to college. You could go to an all-black school in the South, or you could go to an integrated school in the North.

He was drawn especially to the latter possibility, and with that in mind, he worked hard at his game, even harder at his studies, at one of those segregated schools in the South where the faculty was strong and the standards were demanding. By his senior year, Perry had emerged as valedictorian and a high school all-American on a championship team that had gone undefeated. He knew his parents were proud of what he'd done, and not just the accolades or acclaim, or the scholarship offers that poured by the dozens. They seemed to be proudest of all about his effort—his energy and drive and dedication to a goal.

Perry Wallace Sr. was that kind of man. He was always a stoic, work-toughened father who understood clearly that the world didn't surrender its rewards without a fight. But Perry's mother also exerted a major influence on his life. She, too, was a worker, a gentle woman with an eighth grade education who had a job cleaning office buildings downtown. She often brought home the old magazines discarded from the waiting rooms where she worked—*Time, Life*, it didn't really matter. All of it was part of her love of learning, and she worked hard to impart the same values to her son.

"I remember," says Perry, "taking those magazines as a boy, and looking at all those people on the pages. These were people living better, and I wanted a part of what they had. Because of that dream, I said to myself at a very early age, 'I am going to be a student-athlete, probably at a big university up north.'"

That was always the expectation and the hope, a given almost in his high school years, encouraged by his family and the teachers at his school. But then he met the person who turned things around. Roy Skinner was the basketball coach at Vanderbilt, a plain-spoken man born and raised in the South, who was having great success in the 1960s. His teams most often were nationally ranked, and his players in general were a credit to the school—student-athletes who knew they were expected to show up for class.

Skinner thought Wallace might fit in well and told him so at a meeting at his home. Wallace, by then, was a senior and a star, deluged already with scholarship offers, and Skinner knew he had some catching up to do. But he had an advantage the other coaches didn't have. He was a smallish man with a manner that was quiet, unassuming and direct, and to the Wallace family, he seemed to be southern all the way to the bone. Curiously enough that put them at ease. They might well have assumed before the conversation started that a southern white man in the 1960s was more likely than not to be a segregationist. But Skinner gave off none of that aura. Instead, he seemed to be "just folks," a phrase that both of Perry's parents would use, and theirs was not a superficial assessment.

"My parents knew people, and they knew life," Perry remembered years later. "And they had a feeling about Coach Skinner. When he came over that day and sat down in our house, he had a certain manner about him, a certain honesty and decency, a rhythm and a style that seemed easy-going. My parents, of course, were looking at him hard. They were asking themselves, 'Who is this man who wants to take our son into dangerous territory?' And they liked what they saw."

Perry, meanwhile, in that same conversation, was struck by something quite simple and direct. The coach called his parents "Mr. and Mrs. Wallace," and it was not a common practice at the time for a white man to use such courtesy titles. For Skinner, however, they seemed to come easily, and for Perry and his family, the whole experience tapped in subtly, and then with great force, to the hopes and dreams of the civil rights era.

It had been a preoccupation for years, this powerful movement in pursuit of simple justice that was pulling more and more at the heart of the country. They had watched it on television in the fifties—the riots in Little Rock and the startling heroism of nine black children at Central High School—and they had seen it firsthand in the Nashville sit-ins. Now in the mind of young Perry Wallace the hopes and opportunities created by the movement suddenly seemed to be more personal and real.

"I had a sense of possibility," he says. "I had a sense that I could play some role."

So he decided to cast his lot with Vanderbilt, and to take his place as a racial pioneer. It gave him at least some measure of comfort to know from the start that he was not alone. Coach Skinner, as it happened, had also recruited another black player that year, an outspoken young man by the name of Godfrey Dillard.

Perry was happy about that piece of news. He figured he would need all the company he could find.

He enrolled in the summer of 1966, taking some introductory courses, and the problems came at him almost from the start. He began attending services at a church near the campus, the only African American to do so, and after a while a couple of the elders called him aside. They seemed a little uncomfortable about it, and they worked hard to be pleasant as they delivered the news. But the bottom line, they said, was that some of the older members of the church were threatening to write it out of their wills if the racial purity of the congregation were breached. The elders said it would probably be best if Perry could find another place to worship.

"I didn't hang my head," he remembers. "I wasn't really hurt. The old instincts of segregation kicked in. I simply understood that this was one of those places in the South where colored people weren't welcome."

The larger melodramas took shape on the road, when the freshman basketball season began. Those were the days when first-year recruits were not yet eligible to play for the varsity. Ole Miss cancelled the freshman game that year, rather than host black players on its campus, and the story at Kentucky was even more strange. As Wallace remembers it, early in the game or maybe even in the warmups, he decided to dunk—a stylish habit he had developed in high school. As soon as he did it, he happened to glance at the Kentucky sideline and saw the scowl on the face of Coach Adolph Rupp. Later, he learned that his own little dunk had triggered a case of déjà vu. The season before, Kentucky had lost the national championship game to Texas Western, an unlikely collection of thunder-dunking blacks, led by a guard named David Lattin. Rupp was appalled, and now here was Wallace, threatening to bring the same style of play to a conference as traditional as the SEC. In defense of the "purity" of the game as he had known it, Rupp set out to change the rules. He persuaded the National Collegiate Athletic Association to ban the dunk for the next several years—a move that robbed Perry Wallace of his offense.

Wallace, however, took it in stride. He simply worked a little harder on his jump shot. But there were other events in that freshman season that were not as easy to put out of his mind. The most disturbing of those was the game they played at Mississippi State. The arena itself was a sweltering place with the look and feel of an airplane hangar, the dressing rooms tiny with concrete floors, the bleachers like something from a high school gym. They were filled this night with a howling group of fans, shouting curses and slurs, and Wallace thought it seemed like a preview of hell.

He remembered years later how his hands, improbably, were as cold as ice, despite the stifling heat in the place, and he remembered also that when both teams left the floor for the half, he and Godfrey Dillard sat together on a bench, clasping tightly to each other's hands.

"We were trying to be in denial," he said. "We didn't want it to be this bad. But it was such an outrageous display of racism, like the blaring of trombones. The crowd was starting to shatter our denial."

They made it through the game and played well enough in the second half, and Perry took some comfort from the fact that they won. But back at Vanderbilt, a fundamental question started playing with his mind. Like many of the other black students at the school, he began to ask more skeptically what he could really expect from America. He had been raised with the expectation and the hope—the quite remarkable leap of faith, given the realities of racial segregation—that a person of talent and commitment and drive could somehow manage to make his own way. The country in the end would yield its rewards.

Now, however, he and the others were starting to doubt it. Less than a year into this noble experiment, he was starting to wonder whether his assumption of fairness was nothing but a cruel, self-inflicted illusion. Not that there weren't a few reasons for hope. Among other things, Wallace and his friends were impressed by the serious discussion of race that was quietly taking shape in certain quarters of the campus. It was driven in part by the Impact Symposium, a student-run group bringing in speakers like Martin Luther King Jr. and the black power advocate Stokely Carmichael.

Most impressively to Wallace, the students who were running the program were white, and almost all of them came from the South. They seemed to understand that the region had to change, that segregation was an anchor that was pulling them down, and Vanderbilt was not immune to the problem. But even these students were somehow remote, somehow out of touch with that undertow of loneliness that was pulling at the blacks.

In the end, of course, the white students were different, no matter how decent they intended to be. And there were others still tied to the bigotry of the past. More than once, walking into his dorm, Wallace heard cries of "Nigger on the hall," and there was another experience that stayed with him even more. He was invited one evening to have dinner with some friends, and they decided to go to the women's quadrangle. About halfway through the cafeteria line, he was suddenly aware that the women were staring—dozens of them with a look that was equal parts fear and disdain. That at least was the way it felt to Wallace, and his mind flashed back to the story of Emmett Till, the black teenager lynched and mutilated in Mississippi for the simple crime of speaking to a white woman.

His parents had warned him about such things, and his mother especially had told him many times, "Stay away from white girls." Now at the women's cafeteria and Vanderbilt, he felt a powerful urge to get away.

"It occurred to me," he said years later, "maybe I could just get up and run."

Instead, he rode it out, and it was not the final time as the months went by that he encountered the residues of old blindness, or at the very least, a feeling of being walled away from his peers. All of it was intensified by the feelings of hatred he encountered on the road. During his sophomore year in 1968, there was a trip to Ole Miss that seemed to say it all. Godfrey Dillard, his black teammate, was gone by then. He had injured his knee and left the team, and though many of the white players tried to be supportive, there were ways in which Wallace was out there alone.

Against Ole Miss he injured his eye. He was fighting for a rebound when one of his opponents hit him in the face, and even today Wallace says he isn't sure whether the blow was deliberate. But his eye was bloodied, and the fans in the bleachers responded with delight. They taunted and jeered as he walked off the court and dared him to return, and as the trainers worked on his eye at half-time, he had to fight through a feeling of dread.

By the time the medical personnel had finished, his teammates were already back on the court. Perry knew what was waiting on the other side of the wall, and he paused for a minute at the locker room door, gathering his resolve. It was then that he noticed a remarkable thing. There was a small group of fans, all of them white, who had made the trip from Vanderbilt to Ole Miss. They stood and cheered as he stepped through the door, and if their voices were quickly overwhelmed by the boos, Wallace was nevertheless grateful they were there.

Even so, there was a distance somehow that couldn't be bridged. He may have had his supporters in the crowd, people, in fact, who were there at some risk. But in the final analysis, the strength he needed had to come from himself.

"I realized," he explained to one friend, "how much I had to carry this thing by myself."

By nearly any measure, he carried it well. That night at Ole Miss, he played the second half like a man possessed, snatching a dozen or more rebounds, and by his senior year he led the team in scoring, averaging more than seventeen points a game. In addition to that, as he approached his graduation in 1970, he was deeply admired on the Vanderbilt campus—chosen, in fact, by a vote of the students as the most respected leader at the school. He graduated with a degree in engineering, a demanding regimen by anybody's standards, and however hard the whole thing may have been, there were many people impressed by his triumph.

"Whenever we would talk," says Vereen Bell, a professor of English who knew Wallace well, "I would think about how I was when I was in college, and then I would look at Perry. He was so much wiser, so much more reflective. It was the difference between a teenager and a grown man."

Because that perception was widespread, when Wallace spoke out near the time of graduation, referring to the subtle racism he had encountered at the university, even a few of his hard-earned admirers reacted with mixture of astonishment and shock. What was he talking about anyway? Didn't he hear the cheering in the stands? Didn't he appreciate the accolades and awards? Didn't he value his Vanderbilt degree?

For many years, in many different corners of the Vanderbilt community, there were whispered accusations of ingratitude—and some people, in fact, didn't bother to whisper. But there were a few who sprang to Wallace's defense. His coach, Roy Skinner, the plain-spoken southerner who had lured him to the school, told one reporter, "I think Perry was trying to help us."

Vereen Bell certainly thought that was true. On many different evenings in the 1960s, he would listen with a mounting sense of heartbreak as Wallace and some of the other black students would talk about the bewildering reality of the times. All of them seemed to understand well enough that they had not been marooned in a nest of naked bigots. There were many white students, probably even a majority, who wanted very much to be decent and fair. But the footing sometimes was difficult to find, for many of the old habits of racial segregation were still institutionalized at the school.

All-white fraternities, for example, still dominated the campus social life, and the idea of desegregation was still new. The first black undergraduates had arrived on campus in 1964, and even as the sixties drew to a close their numbers were small. But they shared in the mounting impatience nationwide that was sweeping through the African American community—that intermingling of expectation and anger that followed inevitably from the civil rights movement. They were tired of the procrastinations of America and at Vanderbilt, the intimate microcosm where they lived, they were a little bit hurt beneath all the rage to find people still resistant to the notion of equality.

To a person with the sensitivity of Perry Wallace, the time finally came when it was more than he could stand.

It took him a decade to work it all out, to sort through the contradictions and fatigue. He left Vanderbilt and made a brief run at pro basketball (playing only on a minor league team), before taking a job with the Urban League and then entering law school at Columbia University. All the while, he was sifting through the memories of his Vanderbilt experience—the wounds and scars from the Deep South arenas, and the quieter racism he encountered on the campus. He remembered the time in his junior year when a group of white men paid a visit to his room. They invited him to come and worship at their church, and they were members, as it happened, of the same denomination where the elders had told him in his freshman year that it might be better if he didn't come back. Wallace felt tired just listening to their pitch, and told them bluntly it was too much to ask.

"I said 'Thanks, but no thanks,'" he remembered, "'because I am tired and weary of this race thing. I am tired of the pioneering. I don't want to take on any more.'"

And for a while at least, that was how it was. He simply wanted to put the whole thing behind him. But then the exhaustion began to recede, and in its place was a different set of memories. He knew, in a sense, they had always been there, but now with time they seemed to be rising more easily to the surface. He thought often, of course, about the other black students—what a brave and intelligent group they were—and there were white students too that he had to admire, for they seemed to be embarked on the same kind of journey. They were living on the crest of a monumental change, and they seemed to believe in it as deeply as he did.

There were also the pillars of the institution itself. His coach, Roy Skinner, had lived up to his billing, a demanding presence on the basketball court but patient and steady, and there were professors like his friend Dr. Bell who went out of their way to make him feel at home. He was also impressed with Chancellor Alexander Heard, a man who exuded great dignity and strength, as he led the university down the path to integration, and when he thought about all of those things together, there was a richness about his Vanderbilt days that left him inevitably with a new sense of pride.

By the time he had started a family of his own and taken his place on the faculty of American University, he was proud of what he had accomplished in college and proud of Vanderbilt for giving him the chance. But the final moment of reconciliation didn't come until 2004, when the university decided to retire his jersey.

It was not an idea handed down from the top. Rather it started with the work of three students—Zach Thomas, Justin Wood, and Sara Ruby, who chose for their political science project to do a documentary on Wallace. Their professor, Richard Pride, had come to Vanderbilt about the time Wallace was emerging as a star, and he encouraged the students to dive into the story.

"The diversity issue had been percolating on campus," says Pride, "and the students could see that back in the sixties, Vanderbilt had done something extraordinary."

When the film was completed, Pride gave it an A but encouraged the students not to leave it at that. Zach Thomas, a leader in the Student Government Association, proposed a resolution calling for the retirement of the Perry Wallace jersey, and Vanderbilt Chancellor Gordon Gee was receptive.

And so it was that on February 21, Wallace stood once again at center court, and the cheering filled the room as it had so often in the days when he played. But there was no ambivalence about it this time—as far as anybody knew, no racist whispers out there in the crowd—and Wallace himself was deeply moved by the moment. Already, he had spoken to the student body, and then to the members of the basketball team.

He says the current coach, Kevin Stallings, had urged him simply to speak from his heart. "He wanted me to talk about race as well as basketball," says Wallace. "He wanted it to be a learning experience for his team."

There was no recording of what Wallace said, but a few weeks later he offered this account:

> I told them that I was older than they were, and I have gray hair, but we are part of a family with a magnificent heritage. We are students and athletes with one feeding the other. You can get all perfectionist about it if you want to, but perfection can become the enemy of understanding. The simple truth is, Vanderbilt took a chance and let all the horses run, and when you look at that history against the current backdrop of athletic problems—the way some coaches and players are acting—this university can say with great pride, "We got that right more than thirty years ago."

Kevin Stallings said later he was "mesmerized" by the talk, and it seemed clear enough that his players were too. On television that afternoon, they beat LSU 74–54.

The Sheriff Without a Gun

It was February 1965 when Thomas Gilmore came back home. He had gotten tired of Alabama for a while, the meanness of it, the rigid segregation, and in 1963 he had moved his family out to California. But he discovered early on that he couldn't run away, and in any case, the city of Los Angeles was not a happy destination for his flight. "The bigness of it and the wildness of it" were a little too much for a country boy from Greene County, and he decided he missed those swampy bottomlands, where he had fished and hunted and learned to be a man.

The civil rights movement was gaining momentum at the time of his return, even making its way to those Black Belt counties where it sometimes seemed as though nothing ever changed. Gilmore hadn't really thought much about it, not in terms of his own participation, for it was a distant reality from his life in California—and certainly it had never even crossed his mind that he would one day become a symbol of liberation. He was simply homesick, lonesome for the sight of Forkland, Alabama, where he had grown up poor on a patch of land that had been in his family for five generations.

He began his life in a rough wooden cabin, which was later replaced by a white frame house, down in the southern end of the county. The Warrior River was just a stone's throw away, and he and the others who lived in the area were known as "swamp people." They were an independent lot, especially the Gilmores, who traced their ancestry back to Joe Winn, a slave who managed to buy enough land, in the days just after emancipation, to give his six children eighty acres each. Clara Gilmore, Thomas's grandmother, was still a farmer on one of those plots, raising a little bit of everything—pigs, chickens, milk cows, and vegetables.

Overlaid against the strength of his family and the legacy of independence going back a hundred years was the specter of racism. Like virtually every other black southerner his age, Gilmore carried a picture in his mind of the horrible, misshapen face of Emmett Till, and there were lesser cruelties in Alabama as well. As a child on shopping trips to Demopolis, the nearest town with a store, he was troubled by the segregated drinking fountains, for what difference did it make where a child got his water? Later, as a teenager, he could see the purpose of the segregated order, how it was not a simple matter of separation, polite and benign, as many whites insisted, but a tool for keeping black people in their place.

Once in a field not far from his house, two young men, one black and one white, got into a good-natured wrestling match that abruptly turned dark and almost deadly when the black youth threw the white boy to the ground. Sometime later, this young black man was paddling across the Warrior River in his skiff, when the same white boy and several of his friends rowed out to meet him. Somewhere out near the middle of the river, they flipped his boat and threw him in the water, and the black youth had to swim for his life.

Gilmore absorbed these lessons of the times, and as a young man early in the 1960s, he was torn between the pull of being a minister in Forkland, or getting as far away from it as possible. In 1963, he left for Los Angeles, where he never felt at home, and when he returned to Alabama after only two years, his life took a sudden and unexpected turn. On a gray and dreary February day, he had driven to Demopolis to pick up some baby formula for his child, and he saw an old friend at a service station. He pulled in to greet him, and as he did so, he hit a mud puddle and splashed dirty water on a state trooper's car. He immediately got out and told the trooper, "I'm sorry about that." The officer, however, took one look at this tall and gangly black man in his twenties, with his big-city beard and his California plates, and immediately assumed that this was an agitator looking for some trouble. He and his partner made Gilmore stand with his palms on the gas pumps, while they frisked him for weapons.

"You are going to wash this car yourself," the trooper informed him, with a look of Alabama meanness in his eye. Gilmore was startled but kept his composure. "Officer," he said, "I will pay to have your car washed."

The policeman was not impressed by the courtesy. "I'll get your ass," he said. "I know where you're headed."

Gilmore assumed that the trooper meant Selma, where, in 1965, the voting rights protests were in full swing, and although it had not been a part of his plans, it occurred to him then that he ought to go to work for the civil rights movement. He decided to look up an old mentor and friend, the Reverend William McKinley Branch, who was the founder of the fledgling Greene County movement. Reverend Branch, as it happened, had long been one of Thomas Gilmore's heroes. He was a smallish man in his forties, dark-skinned, with a merry disposition and an air of authority, and not even the trace of a wrinkle in his face. He had been a child in Greene County in the 1930s, when the times were as hard as anybody could remember. His father was a sharecropper trying to pay off a five-hundred-dollar loan from a white man. Every fall he put up a share of his cotton, but no matter how many acres he plowed, or how many cotton bales he produced, he always seemed to fall a little short. "Boy," the white man said every year, "if you had just made one more bale . . ."

They subsisted many days on parched corn and water, and "were glad to get it," William Branch said later. But one day when there wasn't any meat in the house, William prayed to the heavens for some kind of relief. "Lord," he said, "let a turtle come up in the yard." He was maybe eleven years old at the time and could imagine the savory tang of turtle soup; and thirty minutes later, when a turtle, in fact, came crawling toward the house, it was easy to see it as the answer to a prayer. Having already heard the call to be a preacher, he decided he was ready to give his life to the Lord.

He knew he needed some more education, and before he had

graduated from high school he set out one day for Selma University. He caught a milk truck to the town of Demopolis, paid a driver a quarter to take him to Uniontown, then walked the rest of the way to Selma. It was another thirty miles or so, he guessed, and he made it to the outskirts of town around dusk. With no place to sleep, he sat up all night in a Selma juke joint, and the following morning, he appeared on the doorstep of William Dinkins, the president of the college. Dinkins was impressed with this tenacious young man, polite and disheveled, who was standing at his door, but he said he needed some more education.

"Finish high school," Dinkins told him, "and then come back."

In 1941, Branch did, and after earning his two-year degree, he went back to Greene County and accepted the pastorate at Ebenezer Baptist, working for the salary of twelve dollars a Sunday. He was never at ease with the racial order in the South, and as the civil rights movement gained momentum, he dreamed of the day when it would come to Greene County. He knew the resistance was sure to be fierce, for this had been, as Branch often put it, "a slave county" before the Civil War—a place where blacks outnumbered whites, and a hundred years later, the ratio was the same. If Negroes ever registered to vote, they would hold a majority of nearly two to one.

Sometime early in the 1960s, Branch set out to try to make it happen. He set up a chapter of the NAACP, and many years later, he remembered the tension when the word got around. Before one of the organizational meetings, "my people heard a whisper," he said—a rumor that the Klan was planning an attack. That night at the church, ten or twelve of Branch's supporters came with their guns and slipped out to the graveyard just behind the building. They crouched in the bushes and hid in the trees, and after a while the Kluxers did come—a group of armed men crawling toward the church on their stomachs. They were inching toward a window at the back of the building, which looked in on the pulpit where Branch was already starting to speak, when the Negro sentries took them by surprise.

"Stick 'em up!" they commanded from the darkness, using a phrase that was popular in the cowboy movies, and the startled Klansmen ran howling for the trees.

"The Lord took care of me," said Branch.

By 1965, when Thomas Gilmore returned from California, Branch had amassed a solid group of followers, but he was happy for the new addition to the ranks. He thought of Thomas as one of the brightest young men in the county, recently married, devoted to his family, a quiet and reflective person overall but tough enough to confront the status quo. Together, they worked to get people registered to vote and addressed other issues that came up as well.

Once in Greene County, during a voting rights march in 1965, a young woman was struck by a deputy sheriff, and Gilmore tried to have the deputy arrested. When the authorities treated the suggestion as a joke, he brought thirty people to the district attorney's office, and they refused to leave until their grievances were heard. The police came quickly, and as Gilmore remembered it, "They beat us up pretty badly." He talked about the beatings with William Branch and James Orange, an organizer with the Southern Christian Leadership Conference, and Orange came up with a radical suggestion.

"You be the sheriff," he said.

For the next several months, Reverend Branch refused to let it go. He talked about the aura of repression and fear that hung over the lives of black people in the county, and although it was true that the incumbent sheriff, a former football player by the name of Bill Lee, was a kinder, more complicated man than some of his other southern counterparts, he was also a segregationist at heart. Lee had played in the Rose Bowl for the University of Alabama, and his father and brother had both been sheriff. The office, in fact, had been in the family since 1922, and when Gilmore finally decided to run, Lee was heard to vow that "a cotton patch nigger" would never take it away.

Undeterred, in the spring of 1966 Gilmore hit the campaign trail—the churches, the farms, the juke joints on the weekend. Some of the people seemed to be excited, nursing the hope that things would really change. But Gilmore discovered a frustrating thing. There was still a vast residue of fatalism, old feelings of resignation and defeat, that took many forms. He went one morning to speak at a church, and a black deacon told him, "I'm not gonna vote for you. If I vote for you and you win, they'll kill you. It's a nail in your coffin. I'm not gonna help kill you."

Another time at a little juke joint on the road to Greensboro,

Gilmore went in on a Saturday night and asked to put a poster behind the jukebox. "There was this brother standing there," he remembered, "wearing bib overalls. I said, 'I sure need your vote, man. We got to bring down Mr. Bill Lee.' He said, 'Man, why don't you cut out that bullshit?' This was such a new idea for black folks. There was such cynicism built up over time that people just couldn't conceive of the difference."

Still, he knew that the overall numbers were strongly in his favor. By election day, May 3, there were thirty-four hundred black people registered in the county and only two thousand whites, and if the blacks turned out and there wasn't any fraud, the results were virtually a foregone conclusion. But then the stories began to trickle in—white people voting who were not on the rolls, people who had moved from the county years ago either coming back to cast their ballots themselves or designating somebody else to do it for them. One black woman told Gilmore later that when she went to the polls, the white election worker asked her, "Do you want to vote for Sheriff Lee or Bill Lee?"

The reports were disturbing, but on that warm Tuesday evening as he waited for the count, Gilmore refused to give up hope, refused to listen anymore to those cynical voices he could hear somewhere in the back of his mind. "I just can't believe," he told a reporter from *Newsweek*, "they'd actually take this thing away from me now. . . . Not even them."

The whites, meanwhile, gathered at the courthouse, as they might at a high school football game. It was a Greene County tradition—the people coming together at dusk, assembling at the square in the county seat of Eutaw and waiting for the returns. The actual count took place in a second-floor office, hidden away in a stucco building at the back of the square. There was a wrought-iron staircase leading to the door, and on the night of May 3, the people glanced anxiously in that direction. Ordinarily, there were running tabulations posted through the evening, scribbled on a blackboard in the hall of the courthouse, and it was part of the suspense and anticipation that could make election night one of the most festive occasions of the year. But not this time. There was no blackboard, no attempt at entertainment, for in the first week of May 1966, most of the people who gathered at the square thought the stakes were too high—nothing less than their whole way of life. They could hardly imagine a black man as sheriff, as the ultimate symbol of small-town authority, and rumors early in the evening were grim. Gilmore was said to be in the lead.

But then came the total from the absentee ballots—only one black vote among the two hundred cast—and Sheriff Bill Lee back in front, back where his followers thought he should be. When the evening was over, and the tension finally died, Lee won by a total of three hundred votes, and as he made his way through the slaphappy throng, shaking their hands, thanking them graciously for all their support, he seemed to know even then that it was only temporary. The white minority, he admitted, could not hold off the majority forever.

For Thomas Gilmore, it was only after he knew he had lost, when the cold reality of it set in, that he knew how badly he wanted to be sheriff. All along, he thought it was important, and he would talk philosophically about giving his children and the others in the black community of Greene County "somebody they can look up to without being afraid." But those, he discovered, were the reasons in his head, the intellectual understanding of the need for a change. Now in defeat, he was coming to terms with a level of yearning that he hadn't really grasped. His ambitions for himself and the people of the county were abruptly and exponentially magnified.

He filed a lawsuit against the Democratic Party, citing irregularities in the primary, and as the case made its torturous way through the courts he prepared for the election of 1970. There was, however, one event that intervened, a deeply moving interlude in his life that made him reexamine his commitment to the office; made him wonder, in fact, if he could really be a sheriff.

The event was a visit from Martin Luther King Jr., early in the spring of 1968.

King, by then, was in a difficult place—a moment in his life and public career that was probably more exhausting and more ambitious than anything else that had happened through the years. On April 4, 1967, he had appeared at the Riverside Church in New York and denounced the war in Vietnam. It was not the first time. He had also spoken at his own church in Atlanta, but the media was listening at the Riverside service, and the word went out across America that the greatest civil rights leader in the land had now waded in on the issue of foreign policy. The denunciations were swift and unrelenting. From Senator Barry Goldwater on the right to Senator Edward Brooke of Massachusetts—the first black senator since Reconstruction—there were suggestions that King had stepped out of line, putting the civil rights movement at risk by breaking with a president who had been its friend. But King held fast to his antiwar position.

"The bombs of Vietnam explode at home," he said. "They destroy the dreams and possibility of a decent America."

More specifically, they were sapping the resources of the War on Poverty at a time when the country was exploding in rage. In the summer of 1967, there were riots in a hundred American cities, and eighty people died. King was convinced that poverty in a land of plenty was to blame—the grinding, soul-numbing daily existence of people in the cities and people in the rural backwaters of the South who didn't have jobs or food for their families. In August 1967, a young black activist named Marian Wright, who had worked in Mississippi and seen the terrible poverty of the Delta, came to King and suggested a poor people's pilgrimage to Washington. King immediately agreed, and with his staff in Atlanta he began to make plans.

On March 20, 1968, he came to Alabama, following stops in Mississippi and Memphis, stumping for support for the poor people's march. Gilmore was his driver, and happy to serve, for he and King had been friends for several years. In 1966, King had come to Greene County to campaign for him, and two years later he asked Gilmore to help coordinate the march. On March 20, as the evening shadows settled on the highway, King and his inner circle of advisers were driving from the little town of Eutaw to Marion, and as usual they were late. As luck would have it, they were caught on a curving road behind a truck, six of them crowded into Gilmore's car, a '63 Chevy, two-tone green. In the front seat with Gilmore were Ralph Abernathy and Dr. King, Abernathy in the middle, and in the back seat were three of King's other advisers—Barnard Lee, Dorothy Cotton, and Hosea Williams. They were talking about the Poor People's March and their plans for a mule train out of Mississippi, picking up people as it made its deliberate journey through the South.

As the conversation bounced from seriousness to banter, Gilmore thought that King looked tired. It was clear he was worried again about the movement—about the future of nonviolence in an era of riots, about the specter of poverty and the fading commitment of the U.S. government, and about his own ability to set a new agenda. King had battled for integration and the ballot, but there was still so much that needed to be done, and he was not a man to rest on his laurels.

On the road to Marion, as Gilmore was listening to the stream of conversation, he was grumbling to himself about the eighteen-wheeler, grinding its gears as it slowed for the curves, making King later than he already was. Finally, he thought he saw an opening, and whipped out to pass—a dangerous maneuver, he thought when it was over. But everybody laughed, and there was a sudden burst of hard-edged teasing about Gilmore trying to kill Dr. King. About that time, the road straightened out, and the eighteen-wheeler pulled back alongside and turned deliberately into their lane. At the moment they were passing a tiny gas station, and Gilmore swerved from the path of the truck and pulled to a stop not far from the pumps.

The driver of the truck, a white man in his twenties, pulled over also and jumped from his cab. He stalked to the driver's window of the car and demanded, "Nigger, get those lights out of my rear view mirror."

"Can you believe this?" mumbled Ralph Abernathy, and in the back seat Hosea Williams was telling Gilmore to roll his window up on the truck driver's throat. Only King seemed calm. "Young man," he said, in that baritone voice that was always serene, "get in your rig and go ahead now. You're starting trouble, and you don't need to do that."

The driver stood frozen as he recognized King, then slowly backed away.

As Gilmore started again down the highway, King began to talk about the state of the nation, how troubled it was, and how the sickness now was even closer to the surface. Two weeks later, Gilmore remembered that curious episode when he heard the news out of Memphis—the terrible, unbelievable report that King had been murdered on his hotel balcony. Only a few minutes earlier the most gifted civil rights leader in the nation had been in a pillow fight with his friends, but then the rifle bullet tore through his neck, leaving the country and the movement with a new kind of martyr—a man who was always larger than life, even to those who saw his humanity.

All over America, as the news quickly spread, the inner cities erupted into riots, and for thousands of African American people, nonviolence died on the balcony in Memphis. For Thomas Gilmore the effect was just the opposite. He found himself haunted by the greatness of King, a man with his frailties like anybody else, but a leader with a powerful vision for his country. His stubborn, unflinching proclamations of nonviolence were clearly no contrivance, as Gilmore had seen on the highway to Marion. Over the next several weeks, as he struggled with his grief, Gilmore decided to pay honor to the memory by adopting nonviolence as his own way of life. Before, he had always seen it as a tactic, a sensible approach to the goal of liberation, but now it needed to be something more.

The decision, however, raised a fundamental question. Was it possible to be a nonviolent sheriff? In a rural community as tough as Greene County, could you enforce the law without carrying a gun? With the approach of the 1970 elections, Gilmore decided he would give it a try. The ambition still burned, along with the steady realization that in a county like his own there was no other office more important than that of the sheriff.

In the breakthrough campaign of 1970, Gilmore was part of a slate of black candidates who won every governmental seat in Greene County. William Branch, the respected elder statesman of the movement, was elected probate judge, the first black since Reconstruction to hold that position, and Thomas Gilmore became the new sheriff.

As Gilmore saw it, the challenge now was to govern with integrity. He allowed his deputies to carry handguns, a concession, he said, to the reality of the job, but Gilmore himself remained committed to his oath of nonviolence. There were some dicey moments in the course of his thirteen years in the office. There was an armed black man on an Alabama back road, threatening violence, and Gilmore, who never carried a gun, trying to talk him out of it. "Man," he said, in a soft, easy voice, "it would do me good if you would put that gun down."

There were white people, too, who drifted near the edge, and Gilmore would spend a lot of time in conversation—in kitchens and living rooms sipping cups of coffee—telling a man who was having trouble with his wife: "Man, I'm trying to work this out so you don't go to jail. That'll just end up costing you money. I don't know about you, but I'm a country boy from down in the swamp. I don't have money to waste."

The key, he said, was to respect the humanity of the people in trouble, and it was one of the things he had wanted all along, to soothe the irrationality and the fears that had become so inflamed by the issue of race. He wanted the people of Greene County to see that there wasn't any reason anymore to be afraid.

By the end of his term, having slowly but surely won the respect of whites as well as blacks, he thought they were making a little bit of progress. He said it was the least he could do for Dr. King.

This is a story as bittersweet as any that I have ever written. It is the memoir of a night, so exuberant and filled with promise, and the terrible loss and emptiness that followed.

RFK: A Night at Vanderbilt

I t's approaching forty years as I write about it now, and the thing I remember is the crush of the crowd—how they jammed together and filled up the airport and screamed and waved signs and surged forward at the sight of him, trying to shake his hand or just touch him.

He made it halfway from the plane to his car, a step-at-a-time journey of maybe fifteen minutes. But finally he was surrounded, and there was nowhere to move; so they hoisted him unsteadily to an escalator railing, and as he balanced there precariously looking frail and very tired, he made a brief speech about the problems of the country.

These were urgent times, he said, full of war and injustice and pointless human pain. But they were not impossible times, not an occasion for cynicism or despair.

There was nothing revolutionary about the words that he spoke; platitudes were as abundant as startling insights. But somewhere imbedded in his Massachusetts twang, somewhere in the strange and enigmatic intensity of his icy blue stare, in the jab of his forefinger and the tousle of his hair, in all the little components that made up his presence, there was an urgency and a passion that were soon to disappear. For this was March 21, 1968, and the man was Robert Kennedy, newly announced candidate for president of the United States.

He had come to Nashville on this particular occasion, where he was to deliver a speech at Vanderbilt University. More than ten thousand people waited for him there, but the people at the airport wanted a glimpse of him too, and when he climbed down from the railing and resumed his slow journey in the direction of the car, the force of the crowd was nearly overwhelming.

I was in the middle of it, wide-eyed and trying to stay upright, shoving to keep up with Kennedy, whom I was supposed to introduce. When we finally squeezed through the doors of the airport terminal, it was raining outside—a cold and windy drizzle that would soon turn to ice.

I had an umbrella clutched tightly in my hand, but it was still closed, and in the delirious surge of bodies there was no way to open it, or even to lift my arm. It struck me then that the crowd, though friendly, was edging toward a mob, caught up in a kind of Pied Piper blindness for which I feel no nostalgia. But for the slouched and slender man at the center of it, there are those—and I suppose I am one—who still feel a nostalgia that borders on an ache.

When he died seventy-seven days later, you knew with a certainty beyond shock and grief that American politics would never be the same. And it isn't. Kennedy came to Vanderbilt to serve as keynoter for the Impact symposium, a student-run speakers program that had brought a number of celebrities to the campus—William Buckley, Martin Luther King Jr., Stokely Carmichael, and Barry Goldwater, to name just a few. Kennedy's speech was at least as memorable as any of the others. He spoke during a time of war and division, of urban riots and racial injustice, and against that backdrop he talked about the patriotism of dissent. It was, he thought, the duty of the people who loved their country to speak out strongly against its imperfections.

"There are millions of Americans," he declared, "living in hidden places, whose faces and names we will never know. But I have seen children starving in Mississippi, idling their lives away in the ghetto, living without hope or future amid the despair on Indian reservations, with no jobs and little hope. I have seen proud men in the hills of Appalachia, who wish only to work in dignity—but the mines are closed, and the jobs are gone and no one, neither industry or labor or government, has cared enough to help. Those conditions will change, those children will live, only if we dissent. So I dissent, and I know you do too."

For some of us at least, those words are still haunting in the twenty-first century as we enter a new era of national division—a profound and agonizing disagreement about what kind of country we want to become in a time of terrorism and war. The killing fields of Iraq and the divisions at home have become, already, a kind of tortured replay, a terrible echo, of the 1960s. And what some of us fear is that there are no Robert Kennedy's among us today—no political leaders who have yet stepped forward with the wisdom and the vision to lead us through the pain.

I don't mean to idealize Kennedy. For some time now, there have been scholars who have picked their way through his record, revealing his contradictions and his flaws. Even in the sixties, there were those who were unconvinced by his urgency, who saw him and a cynical and ruthless politician. And even his admirers had to acknowledge that he could be ruthless, or at least so driven that you couldn't tell the difference. But he was not cynical.

I remember the car ride from the airport to Vanderbilt—three Tennessee politicians crowded into the front seat, while Kennedy shared the back with John Glenn and one slightly awed student who was astonished by the frankness of it all as the politicians tried to tell Kennedy what to say and not to say. It's a campus audience, they told him, so talk about the Vietnam War if you want. But this is still the South, so go a little easy on the issue of race.

Kennedy listened for a while, then turned to me and asked without warning, "What do you think I ought to say tonight?"

I hesitated briefly, then told him it was fine to talk about the war, but I also thought he should talk about poverty and injustice at home. I told him it was true those subjects were still sensitive in the South, but that was all the more reason to address them there—and that he might be surprised by the sympathy of the crowd.

"Thank you," he said. "That's what I'll do."

Then he sank into himself and rode along in silence, brooding enigmatically as the politicians in the front seat laughed and joked and exchanged old stories. I had no idea what Kennedy was thinking, but there was certainly a great deal for him to brood about. He could have reflected, as he did sometimes, about the shabbier contradictions of his earlier career—his time as attorney general in his brother's administration when he permitted wiretaps on civil rights leaders and angered groups of blacks who came to him regularly with horror stories from the South, telling them abruptly and with no apparent sense of irony, "Well, you know we've all suffered."

But in the end, of course, Kennedy did suffer, and for a brief time—less than five years, in fact, for that was all there was between his brother's death and his—Kennedy embodied an identification with pain. He spoke at every campaign stop, including the one at the Vanderbilt gymnasium, about the troubling things he had seen in the country—"the slow destruction of a child by hunger, and schools without books, and homes without any heat in the winter."

Despite his pleadings, the wounds of the country only seemed to grow worse, culminating on April 4, 1968, when Martin Luther King was murdered in Memphis. Kennedy heard the news on a plane to Indianapolis, where he was scheduled to appear that night at a campaign rally in a black neighborhood. All across the country the ghettos were burning, with looting and bombs and sniper fire from the high-rise apartments. But Kennedy insisted on keeping his appointment.

Standing alone on a flatbed truck, hunched against the cold in his black overcoat, he told the crowd what had had happened to King, and as the people cried out in disbelief, he told them he understood how they felt.

"In this difficult day," he said, "in this difficult time for the United States, it is perhaps well to ask what kind of nation we are and what direction we want to move in. For those of you who are black, you can be filled with bitterness, with hatred and a desire for revenge. We can move in that direction as a country, in great polarization—black people amongst black, white people amongst white, filled with hatred toward one another.

"Or we can make an effort, as Martin Luther King did, to understand and to comprehend, and to replace that violence, that stain of bloodshed that has spread across our land, with an effort to understand.

"My favorite poet was Aeschylus. He wrote: 'In our sleep, pain which cannot forget falls drop by drop upon the heart until, in our own despair, against our will, comes wisdom through the awful grace of God.'"

There were no riots in Indianapolis that night. "I guess the thing that kept us going," said one of King's aides, "was that maybe Bobby Kennedy would come up with some answers."

For the next two months, a lot of people held grimly to that hope, especially as Kennedy did well in the primaries, and the thought began slowly to form in our minds that despite all the tragedy and despair of the decade—the war and the riots and the murder of good men—Robert Kennedy might be the next president.

He might find the policies to implement his vision, and the

country might find a way through its pain. But then in the first week of June he was gone, following unbelievably in the martyred path of Dr. King. In a way, it was the culmination of the sixties, the death of a promise that had been so strong.

Four decades later, it seems clear enough that the wound to the country has never really healed. There is only the scar—the cynicism born on a California night when the most decent politician of our time lay in a spreading pool of his blood and whispered to the people who were rushing to his side, "Is everybody all right?"

The answer, of course, was that none of us was. In the political life of our troubled young country, there was simply no cure for that kind of loss.

One of the great tragedies of the 1960s, in addition to the assassinations of the Kennedys, was the murder of Martin Luther King Jr. in Memphis. In this profile, Lewis Baldwin, once a teenaged follower of Dr. King, talks about a life of scholarship—and his hard-headed hope that writing and teaching can help keep the civil rights legacy alive.

Free at Last, Free at Last

History is a part of becoming truly free.
—John Hope Franklin

Lewis Baldwin remembers the day in 1965—February 15, a Monday afternoon, chilly perhaps and just a bit cloudy, though some of those specifics are beginning to fade. But there is still the mental picture of the crowd, right there in the heart of the Alabama black belt, where the civil rights movement was then in its infancy. Several hundred African Americans, including himself, had gathered on the lawn of Antioch Baptist, coming together at the little wooden church to listen to the words of Martin Luther King Jr. King was speaking that day in the village of Camden, telling the people who had turned out to hear him that they were living on the threshold of history.

For many, it was a curious message even then, for they were residents of Wilcox County, just a few miles south of Selma, and this was a part of rural Alabama where the white minority had grown frightened and hard. The movement that was gaining momentum in Selma was spilling over now to the counties around it, and almost everybody understood the stakes. The issue in 1965 was the right of African Americans to vote—a revolutionary demand in a part of the South where that privilege had long been denied.

Dr. King promised there would soon be a change. They were on the move, he said, and would not be defeated, for the arc of justice was on their side. Looking back on the moment after more than forty years, Baldwin understood that King and his followers were

61

only a few months away from winning their fight. He came to see that clearly as a King biographer and professor of religion, a twenty-year member of the Vanderbilt faculty, who studied the history and theology of the movement. But at the time it was happening he was only fifteen, standing with his brother at the back of the crowd, and seeing everything through a teenager's eyes.

He noticed, oddly, that Dr. King was short, not even as tall as Baldwin's own father, a Baptist preacher who traveled back then from one country church in Alabama to another. The elder Baldwin, also named Lewis, was a passionate believer in civil rights, willing to let his own children march, particularly the boys, and the younger Lewis was often in the ranks. Like many others, he was emboldened on the day that King came to town, seeing this man, so small and unimposing in stature, confronting the sheriff of Wilcox County.

Sheriff P. L. "Lummie" Jenkins had a fearsome reputation—a small-town lawman with an overbearing style. But now here he was shaking hands with Dr. King, responding politely to King's overtures on behalf of black citizens who were seeking to vote. From Baldwin's position near the back of the crowd, he couldn't hear much of what was being said, but he remembered King's poise and attitude of calm, and many years later he knew this was a part of the triumph. The movement was confronting the old culture of fear, all those years of domination by whites, when the slightest misstep could cost a black man his life. The fear was crumbling as the people came together, and with the passage of the Voting Rights Act in the summer, 1965 became a watershed year. It was the moment when the balance of power would change, and African Americans in the segregated South would take on a greater control of their lives.

As a high school sophomore, Baldwin was too young to really understand it—not reflective enough at this point in his life to look for the larger meaning of the moment. Instead, he simply scrawled in his yearbook, "I saw Dr. King."

But two years later, when he finished high school and went away to Talladega College, he began to grow serious about the history he had witnessed. Talladega itself was an inspiration to him. It was the first black college in Alabama, founded in 1867 by a pair of former slaves, William Savary and Thomas Tarrant. On the walls of the library were murals depicting the Amistad rebellion—a slave-ship uprising in 1839 led by Cinque the African, a Mende tribesman from Sierra Leone. Baldwin learned the story during orientation, and it blended easily with the civil rights dramas that he had lived through.

He developed, he says, a "growing sense of black history, and before he finished his time at Talladega, he began to consider his own contribution. He was fascinated by Martin Luther King, and he came to believe that understanding King's movement could become, in a sense, a final piece of liberation.

"I began to ask myself," he says, "how can I contribute to the ongoing struggle? More and more the answer seemed to be that I would devote myself to scholarship and teaching. My first semester at Talladega, I took black history under Dr. Harold Franklin, and he was a major source of inspiration. He was tall and impressive, a dark-skinned man about six-feet-one, and a very serious teacher in class. On the first day, he scared the devil out of all of us. But I began to think about what I was learning, and to put it into the context of my own life—my father, for example, this man who had a fifth-grade education, driving people to the polls to register to vote.

"He used to pastor four little churches, getting paid ten dollars and a sack of corn, and sometimes he would preach about the social gospel, about the need for justice in the here and now. I remember he would show us the lynching trees, where terrible things had happened in the past. He wanted to see a change. He had a deep interest in civil rights."

Even now, says Baldwin, his scholarship is driven by a combination of memory and academic study, which continued to grow as he finished his history degree at Talladega and set out for Crozer Theological Seminary—the place where Martin Luther King had studied. In 1973, Baldwin earned a master's degree in black church studies and in 1975, his master of divinity. In 1980, he finished his Ph.D. at Northwestern and four years later joined the Vanderbilt faculty.

In the years that followed, he became more convinced that despite the growing body of work on King, there was a place where he could make his own mark. In many ways, he admired the work of other King scholars—David Garrow, for example, who won the Pulitzer Prize for his King biography *Bearing the Cross*, or Taylor Branch, who followed soon after with *Parting the Waters*. But these were white authors, and in Baldwin's mind there was a certain myopia at the heart of their work.

They tended, he thought, to underplay the importance of King's black southern roots—to emphasize, for example, the simmering tensions between King and his father, rather than seeing King's family as a "bulwark." In studying such things, Baldwin discovered that he often confirmed his own intuitions, for he, like King, was a preacher's kid from the South—a black southern Baptist who saw the church as an extension of the family. It came as no surprise, therefore, that King drew heavily on the strength of his raising, and was moved by the lessons of his childhood faith.

> *There is a balm in Gilead*
> *To make the wounded whole;*
> *There is a balm in Gilead*
> *To heal the sin-sick soul.*

That old southern hymn, which traced its roots to slavery, embodied Dr. King's understanding of the church. It was a place of optimism and hope, where people came together in the midst of their despair, knowing that better times were ahead. It was true that his thinking evolved and he chafed, for example, at the fierce fundamentalism of his father. But in the end, all the new notions he absorbed in his life only deepened the identity of his youth. "It was part of the air," said Baldwin, "part of the ground on which he stood."

As a result, Baldwin wrote, "Black southerners recognized King as one of their own—one who shared their cultural roots and experiences, spoke their language, reflected their profound spirituality and rhythmic consciousness, possessed their gift for story-telling and deep laughter, embraced their festive and celebrative approach to life. . . . The black experience and black Christian tradition were the most important sources in the shaping of King's life."

Each week in his classes at Vanderbilt, Baldwin talks to his students about such things, pacing behind a broad wooden desk, his lecture notes scattered across the top of it. His classes are nearly always full—forty-one students in 2007 registered for his course

"Martin Luther King Jr. and the Social Roles of Religion." They are divided equally between black and white, listening intently to the lecture, which, for most of the hour, echoes the cadence of a black Baptist preacher.

Baldwin tries not to deify King, tries to keep him "real," as one student puts it, but he also talks about King's vision. In thirteen years on the public stage, from 1955 to 1968, King crusaded successively against segregation and in favor of the vote and then turned his attention to poverty and peace. There was danger at every step, as Baldwin himself had seen in Alabama—policemen swinging their clubs with such force that the skin was torn off a protester's skull. But in the final years of his life, when King shifted focus to the American economy, the stakes and the dangers increased exponentially.

"When you start talking about people giving up wealth and power," Baldwin told his students, "they are going to kill you."

After one class session in late January, a few of the young people waited behind, debating the lessons among themselves. "In my formal education," said Dante Bryant, a master's candidate in theological studies, "King was presented almost like a messiah. He becomes untouchable. But in this class, we are learning about him in a much different way—his faults, his honesty. I come away thinking, 'I'd follow him.'"

Baldwin smiles when he hears such things. It carries him back to his own college days, and the doors of the mind that were opened for him then. It was a time when King and the movement grew real, and that is a quality he wants to preserve. Too often in the popular culture, he says, King's legacy is sanitized into irrelevance. But King was killed precisely when his message for the country was at its most radical. He had shifted his focus to economic justice and the people still trapped in a culture of poverty. And though he was, in Baldwin's view, still sorting through the implications of his thinking, his prophetic anchor remained with his faith.

"One day," said King, in one of the final speeches of his life, "we must stand before the God of history and account for what we've done. And I believe I can hear the God of history saying, 'You didn't do enough. For I was hungry, and you fed me not.'"

For Lewis Baldwin, there was a heartbreaking sadness at the

heart of that speech, and a reminder of the relevance of the message even now. Certainly, he says, it adds an urgency to his own scholarship. Baldwin's article of faith, the deeper conviction at the heart of his work, is that an honest understanding of Martin Luther King can still change the world—or at least prompt a few young people to try.

PART II

"Amazing Grace"

After writing for some years about the civil rights movement, I found myself introduced to the renegade Baptist preacher Will Campbell—partly because he had supported the cause, and partly because he understood its Christian roots. The more I talked to Campbell, the more intrigued I became with the role of Christianity in America, and the more I wanted to write about the faith. The chapters that follow, beginning with an extended profile of Campbell, tell the stories of disparate people for whom the Judeo-Christian tradition has been central to their lives. Some are famous, some are not; some were effective in accomplishing what they set out to do, some were less so. But they all have in common a commitment to the faith as they understood it—while for the rest of us there is mystery and perhaps a bit of inspiration in the remarkable variety of those understandings.

The Gospel According to Will

I stopped off in Nashville a little while back for a few days of R&R with my friend Will Campbell—a Baptist-bred drinking buddy and spiritual adviser who has emerged over the years as a kind of Socratic southern gadfly, a thorn in the flesh of the conventional wisdom. I arrived a little late for the christening—the spiritual dedication of the newborn son of Waylon Jennings (an event attended by, among others, Muhammad Ali). But I did catch a glimpse of the burial of Bill Jenkins, which was in itself a remarkable occasion. Jenkins had been a neighbor of Campbell's—an eighty-five-year-old black man who lived alone and who would peer from his farmhouse porch across the rolling Tennessee countryside, recalling the days when it all belonged to him, before the depression came and the banks foreclosed and his children grew up and moved away. "The younger generation," he would say, "they so crazy. Always causin' trouble 'bout this or that. Me," he would say, "I ain't ever been in no trouble . . ." then adding for the sake of clinical accuracy after gazing discreetly at the curling, light-skinned scar that ran across his wrist and left thumb, "'cept when I killed my wife.'"

But all that was a long time ago, and Jenkins had long since done his time and paid his debts and lived hard and clean for more than fifty years. Then he died, and as the mourners poured into the sandstone church, making their way across a rubble-strewn field of briars and Johnson grass and Queen Anne's lace, Campbell stood before them, grimly buoyed by the swelling amens and the grief-stricken moans, and he declared in sonorous tones: "He was my neighbor. We used to lean against the fence and swap stories in the evenin' time, but that wasn't enough. No it wasn't enough because he was also my friend. It didn't matter that he was old, and I was not so old, or that his skin was black and mine was white, or that he owned a lot of land and I owned a little. He was my friend. But that wasn't enough either 'cause he was also my brother."

And later, when a friend with no connection to the event beyond curiosity offered lame compliments on the quality of the sermon, Campbell simply grunted and cleared his throat. "Hell," he affirmed, his boot kicking idly at the Tennessee sod, "if you can't preach to a bunch of broken-hearted people, there ain't much use in you trying to preach."

Campbell can preach, of course. He's been at it now for more than forty years, ever since the steamy June Sunday in south Mississippi, when he preached his first sermon at East Fork Baptist, a tiny wooden church near the town of Liberty—hidden away in the murky Amite County bottom lands, amid the stands of pine and the shadowy streams of gray Spanish moss. He gazed out nervously across the upturned faces—a skinny, soft-eyed kid of seventeen, with oversized ears and a runaway shock of dark brown hair. He peered through a pair of black-rimmed glasses, and after checking the hand-me-down pocket watch on the lectern beside him, he launched into a short, fiery sermon on the first verse of Genesis.

Later, after thinking it over and praying about it some, the elders of the church—preacher J. Price Brock and a half dozen others—took him aside and declared him ordained to go and preach the gospel. He made a few detours along the way, through Yale Divinity School, among other places, but he has emerged in the end as one of the South's leading preachers—an earthy, erudite theologian and author who takes satisfaction in giving offense, in proclaiming a kind of scandalous, radicalized vision of the faith, producing shock and astonishment nearly anywhere he goes.

He is not a William Sloane Coffin. Nor is he Billy Graham. He is instead an odd and unsettling combination of the two—a radical, slow-moving Bible-belt preacher with a hand-carved cane and a floppy hat, meandering his way through the crises of life. He's developed a kind of cult-figure fame in American theology, partly through his books, and partly through his unpretentious, one-man ministry to the nation's dispossessed. He's an ardent proponent of black civil rights, a friend to the bigots in the Ku Klux Klan, and most recently, an unlikely champion for the men and women of death row.

He began in the fifties with the issue of race. First as chaplain at the University of Mississippi, and later as a Deep South staffer for the National Council of Churches, he allied himself with the civil rights movement—traveling the bumpy southern back roads from one upheaval to the next, from Montgomery to Nashville to St. Augustine, Florida.

It's hard to say exactly what he did. He was simply there, moving among the people and offering what he could. In 1957, for example, he was one of three white ministers with Elizabeth Eckford, walking by her side as she and eight other black teenagers made their way through the Little Rock mobs, braving taunts and rocks and bayoneted rifles, seeking to enroll in an all-white school.

Gradually, he became a friend to the leaders of the movement—Andrew Young, John Lewis, and Martin Luther King Jr.—but also to the bright young radicals of lesser charisma, many of them filled with foolhardy courage, as they drifted into Selma or Marks, Mississippi, defying the wrath of the most brutal South. Campbell was awed by the bravery of it all, and yet he couldn't shake a feeling in the back of his mind—a troublesome sense that however right and righteous it was, however important that the South be confronted with the sins of its past, there was something incomplete about the whole crusade, some failure to understand, as he would put it later, "that Mr. Jesus died for the bigots as well."

So he began to work the other side of the street, mingling with the racists and Klansmen, as well as the blacks, setting out from home in the early morning hours, rumbling through the Delta in his cherry-red pick-up. Armed with a guitar and a Bible and an occasional bottle of Tennessee whiskey, he would point himself toward the flat and muddy fields of Sunflower County, toward the straight and endless rows of picked-over cotton and the barbed-wire fences of Parchman Penitentiary.

At Parchman, he would visit a young friend of his—a terrorist, as it happened, whose name was Tommy Tarrants. He was a Klansman, a tough and lanky young man then in his twenties, with scruffy brown hair and a head full of hate. He had moved to Mississippi from Mobile, Alabama, becoming, while he was still in his teens, a leading strategist in a campaign of violence. But he was shot and nearly killed in 1968, ambushed by the FBI, as he sought to bomb the home of a liberal Jewish merchant. For his trouble, he was sentenced to thirty years in prison, and at the time that Campbell came along, he was still in a struggle with the passions of his youth.

They spent a lot of time behind the barbed wire of Parchman, settling occasionally under the shade of an oak and letting the conversation ramble where it would. Eventually, after visits from Campbell and a handful of others who took an interest in his case, Tarrants began to change. He renounced his racism, proclaimed a newfound belief in the Christian faith, and got himself paroled. He enrolled in Ole Miss, got a degree, and became an evangelical minister.

Campbell is pleased by that but takes no credit for it. Conversions, he says, are not his calling. He is embarked instead on an unconditional ministry, a simple reaching out to angry young blacks, Ku Kluxers, and the alienated rich—leaving it to them what they do with the message. That's a little unsettling to many fundamentalists, and also to his liberal friends, to the people who are involved in a push for social change. But for Campbell, it's all very clear, and he will rummage through the clutter on his roll-top desk, producing a well-worn copy of the King James Bible, fumbling through the parchment to the writings of Paul.

"Here," he will say, "it's all right here in Second Corinthians, right down here at the end of chapter five: 'God was in Christ, reconciling the world unto himself, not imputing their trespasses against them. . . .

"There," he continues, with a fierce, sudden swipe at his gray fringe of hair, "that's what it's all about. You can read it there, or in Mark or Matthew, or over in Luke. But what it all means is so damn simple: We are bastards, but God loves us anyway. We're forgiven, and if we can somehow manage to get hold of that fact, we can find the power to go and do likewise. Go and hate no more, go and kill no more. Old Tommy Tarrants got his mind around that one, and if the rest of us could do the same . . . but of course we don't want to do the same 'cause it would change the way we all do our business.

So we keep foolin' around with all the false messiahs," and he shrugs philosophically, folds up the Bible, and returns it roughly to the clutter on his desk.

But despite his fatalism and occasional despair, Campbell has set out to proclaim the message—giving little thought to measurable results, for if he did much of that, he would give up the ghost. He is a peculiar sort of gospel existentialist, like some strange character from the mind of Camus, behaving as though the odds were not insurmountable—as though the world were not full of murder, mendacity, executions and prejudice. It is, he admits, a mission so pure and pitiful that it's almost a joke. But it isn't a joke, for not everyone is amused when he pays a visit to a rich liberal church, surveying the stained glass windows and the prosperous people in the hand-carved pews, and suggesting, when they ask how their faith should be applied, that they leave the door to the sanctuary open, so the downtown winos will have a place to sleep.

"I agree," he says, "that they'll use bad language, and maybe piss on your rug. But it's scriptural."

And if that sounds outrageous to the point of buffoonery, there are other moments when he can't be dismissed, when the scandal of his message is so inescapable that the people in the audience will wince, or even cry, as the words tumble out. He is strangely unimposing as he stands before them, looking thoroughly uncomfortable, tugging at his earlobe or the end of his sideburn, ignoring, or trying to, the knot of fear and insecurity that is there in his gut. There is the trace of a tremor around the edges of his voice, and yet through it all a kind of resonant, stentorian certainty as he begins to tell the story.

It is a brutal story and the telling is as wrenching as Campbell can make it.

"Thirty-four years ago," he says, speaking this time to more than twelve thousand teenagers, Lutherans as it happens, who are gathered in Kansas City for their annual convention, "I stood with my buddies on the island of Saipan, overlooking the crystal blue waters of the Pacific Ocean. Not far from where we stood was a little island, looking to us almost like an aircraft carrier—a little island called Tinian. We used to stand in the early morning and watch the big airplanes take off and gather in the afternoon to watch them return. That day, August 6, 1945, . . . was no ordinary day. It was the day two hundred thousand human beings would die. It was the day the first atom bomb was dropped. . . .

"We knew as we gathered that afternoon that the bomb had fallen, two hundred thousand people left dead in its wake . . . and I cheered! My young brothers and sisters, I yelled and cheered and slapped my buddies on the back and threw my army helmet into the sea at the news that two hundred thousand people, those for whom Christ died, no longer lived. Because I wanted to go home. Fry the bastards. Kill the slant-eyed, slope-head sons-of-bitches. I want to go home."

He pauses now to let the words sink in, his expression a mixture of outrage and grief, eyes glistening, his hand trembling slightly at the side of the lectern. But his words are soft and sure as he resumes the narrative, shifting the scene to another cheering crowd of more recent vintage—to the people who gathered on May 25, 1979, to applaud the excruciating end to the life of John Spenkelink. Shortly after ten o'clock on that sunny spring morning, amid the taunting of guards and the jubilant chanting of the people outside, Spenkelink was strapped to a white wooden chair at the Florida state prison. And on the final orders of Gov. Bob Graham, seventy-five hundred volts of electricity were sent through his body, causing his flesh to burn, and six minutes later, his heart to stop beating.

In the aftermath of that execution, one of the first after the nation's restoration of the death penalty, Campbell emerged as a vocal opponent—denouncing capital punishment, testifying against it wherever he could. For he knew Spenkelink's ambiguous history, knew that he was guilty of killing another man but knew also that in his nearly six years of facing death himself, he had become caught up in a quiet Christian search, not showy or pious but a final private grappling with what it all means. He was the acknowledged leader among the men of death row—aggressive in defense of other prisoners' rights but with an emerging sensitivity that was sometimes startling. Two hours before his death, for example, he turned to his minister and friend, Tom Feamster, and said, "Let's pray for the governor," adding when the prayer was over, "Don't tell the press. That's not why I did it."

Campbell told all that to his young Lutheran audience, then compared it starkly to the things that happened next.

"When all was in readiness," he said, his voice low and husky but strangely calm, "when Brother John, bound and gagged, was strapped in the electric chair, the curtain was opened for the witnesses. The first surge, twenty-five hundred volts of electricity, singed the skin off his right calf, sending smoke into the death chamber. He clenched his left fist, then his hands began to curl and blacken. Listen to me now. The doctor stepped forth, unbuttoned his white shirt and placed a stethoscope on his chest. He was not yet dead. The doctor stepped back. Another surge of twenty-five hundred volts of electricity, then another, and the deed was done. And outside the walls, a group of teenage hecklers about your age, fifteen, sixteen, nineteen years, were chanting in unison, again and again: 'Spark Spenk, Spark Spenk, Bring on the barbecue sauce.' I wanted to cry, to run, to vomit. And I did cry, for I was hearing myself, thirty-four years ago, cheering on the cliffs of a faraway island . . . 'Fry the bastards, kill the sons-of-bitches. I want to go home.'"

And there in the auditorium filled with silence and shock, just before the outburst of a standing ovation, Campbell added six words—sounding at first like an afterthought, but making, he says, the only real point that he knows how to make: "May Christ have mercy upon us."

That is his hope, his pitch, his final affirmation when it all gets crazy. Though his thinking is systematic in its own peculiar way, it is more than an abstraction from Saint Augustine or Saint Paul, more than an echo of his professors back at Yale. There's a kind of brutal intuition about reality and religion, a sure wrathful instinct that keeps him on course. But where does it come from? What is it, finally, that saves him from despair, yet removes him as well from the pristine and pious?

To get a sense of that, it helps to tag along on a swing through the South—when he strikes out from Nashville in a small rented car, heading southwest toward the state of Mississippi, humming through the Delta on the long flat roads, toward the town of Yazoo where the hills begin, past the cotton and the rice and the dingy green pastures where the cattle are grazing. There'll be a few stops along the way—a dinnertime visit with a lawyer-friend, a strategy session with a young black activist—but his real destination lies deeper in the state.

He is headed toward the home place down in Amite, singing country songs or telling bawdy tales, backseat driving while a friend takes the wheel.

"Dammit," he says with peevish good humor, "will you please slow down. How you gonna see when the countryside's a blur? There're some historic sites along in here. Right over there, on up around the curve, that's where ole man Tweet McKelvin used to live. He was the only Republican I'd ever seen 'til I was grown. I remember the first time an automobile ever came by his place, he said, 'My God, son, the automobiles are gonna be the ruination of this country.' God, that ole guy had it all figured out, right down to what we are talking about today. He didn't call it an energy shortage, but he knew . . . and then he'd want a ride into town."

He laughs and spits tobacco toward the chilly night air and then begins to talk about his family. "Right down there," he says, "down at the turn at the bottom of the hill, that's where my daddy let me drive the old '34 Ford right into the ditch. I was going too fast but he didn't say a word, just sat there, and when we landed he said, 'Well I guess there's nothin' to do but go on up to the house; eat a little supper and come back tomorrow with the chain.' He never even raised his voice. How you gon' rebel against that? I tell you, he's one of the gentlest, most generous human beings I've ever known. He got it from his daddy, and he did what he could to pass it down the line."

He is rolling now, and as the stories tumble out, we pause for a while at an ancient-looking farmhouse, tidy and green, set back from the road on Highway 24. It has a TV antenna and a fresh coat of paint, but other than that it has changed very little since Campbell's grandfather, known in the family as Grandpa Bunt, raised ten children in its four small rooms. He was a stoic Baptist deacon of determined good cheer—a small-time cotton farmer, gaunt and slightly stooped, with a sun-crinkled face and wispy gray hair that grew thinner with age. In his later years, when the children grew up and the grandchildren came, he would lean against a stump in his barren front yard smiling to himself at the games that they played. They were a hearty consolation against the tragedies of his past—against the unrelenting memories from his early years of marriage, when his first three children, Myrtis, Claudie, and little Sophia, all died within weeks of the same disease. But he came through it all with no trace of bitterness—with a kind of dogged, undismayed understanding that the world is full of suffering and caprice, and that the mission of a man is not to add to the total.

"I remember one time," says his grandson Will, "we were playing in the yard over there by the fence. It looked a little different back in those days, which was right during the heart of the Great Depression. The road was made out of gravel and clay, and it was farther from the house than it is today—kinda curling past us toward a thick stand of pines. We were playing tag or some such game, me and about a dozen cousins and friends, when we noticed a black man coming up the road. His name was John Walker, and we thought he was a character. He had recently been beaten for stealing a sack of corn, and some of us laughed at the way he told the story: 'Lawd, they got me nekked as a jaybird. Took a gin belt to me. Whipped me till I almost shat.' So when he came shuffling by us on this particular day, we began to taunt him: 'Hey nigger, hey nigger.' But he didn't even look up, kept his eyes pointed straight at the road, as if he hadn't noticed. But Grandpa noticed, and he called us over and said very quietly: 'Now hon'—that's what he called everybody in that way that he had—'now hon, there's no more niggers. Those days are dead. All that's left now is the colored people.'"

And suddenly as you listen, it begins to make sense. You begin to understand what Campbell is about—to see why his diploma from Yale is no longer on display, and why, pasted over it on the wall above his mantel, is a certificate of ordination from East Fork Baptist—lying slightly crooked in its simple black frame but affirming that in the eyes of his fellow believers, of people like his grandfather, he is now ordained to go and preach the gospel.

He has tried to do simply that, armed with gritty understandings of the Sermon on the Mount, of the first being last and the meek and humble emerging triumphant. And the radical causes into which it all thrust him—his strategy sessions with Martin Luther King, his prison visits to death row killers—never seriously estranged him from most members of his family. He could always return from his travels through the South, his free-lance pastorate to the centers of turmoil, and he would know that on some level—often more instinctive than openly expressed—his father and his brothers would approve of his calling.

He usually spared them the harrowing specifics, the nerve-racking scenes in the midst of demonstrations, when he was threatened occasionally by mobs of whites or trailed by deputies in the middle of the night. But there was one particular story that he related in detail, for it was, he said, a kind of conversion—a sudden, agonizing moment of truth when his faith took on a heightened sense of clarity. It was the moment when he learned that Jonathan Daniels, a gentle-spirited Episcopal priest who had spoken out for civil rights in the dusty reaches of rural Alabama, had been murdered, torn apart by a shotgun blast in the slumbering, sun-baked village of Hayneville. Campbell was devastated. But in the midst of his grief, he found himself forced by his own theology to affirm that the sins of the murderer were already forgiven—that the undeserved shower of divine forgiveness rains upon us all, and that the astonishing, common-thread human opportunity is simply to accept it.

"It was a revelation," he says. But it was also something more personal than that; it was a rediscovery of the things that his grand-father knew—that in a world full of tragedy, you don't choose sides; that you can stand for what's right and yet reject condemnation for those who are wrong. So when an all-white jury freed Daniels's killer, Campbell made a point of endorsing the verdict. It was shocking news back in 1966, when he wrote in a liberal Christian quarterly: "Jonathan can never have died in vain, because he loved his killer—by his own last written words. And since he loved his murderer, his death is its own meaning. And what it means is that Tom Coleman, this man who pulled the trigger, is forgiven. If Jonathan forgives him, then it is not for me to cry for his blood, his execution. Any act on my part which is even akin to avenging Jonathan's death is sacrilege. . . . For when Thomas killed Jonathan, he committed a crime against the State. When Thomas killed Jonathan, he commit-ted a crime against God. The strange, the near maddening thing about this case is that both the offended parties have rendered the same verdict—not for the same reasons, not in the same way, but the verdict is the same—acquittal."

Later, he admits with a sort of rueful self-bemusement, "A whole bunch of my civil rights friends came to me and said, with considerable embellishment, 'Good God, Campbell, you stupid idiot, you can't go saying things like that to a bunch of rednecks. Man, that just gives 'em license.' But of course, I told 'em, that's not true. What the jury told Tom Coleman was, 'You are forgiven. Go thou and kill again, if you want.' But what the gospel says, and what we are obliged to say is, 'Your sins are already forgiven you, brother. Go thou and kill no more.' That's the difference, and it's all the differ-ence in the world."

And for those who regard such words as the ravings of a madman or the babblings of a fool (and there are many who fall into each of these categories), Campbell has a different answer. Instead of arguing the efficacy of conversions through divine compassion, he shifts his ground and attacks the alternative. "The law," he says. "We are forever arguing that people must be restrained, so we pass a law and set about enforcing it. But if the law is for the purpose of preventing crime, of securing a just and civilized society, then every wail of a siren calls out its failure. Every civil rights demonstration attests to the inability of the courts to provide racial justice. Every police chief who asks for a larger appropriation because of rising crime rates is admitting his own failure. Every time a law has to be enforced, then it has failed to do what we hoped it would. So what I am saying is, for God's sake, let's try something else."

In the 1970s and 1980s, he built an organization on precisely that premise—a haphazard collection of like-minded people, ranging from John Spenkelink to the novelist Walker Percy. It was an otherwise ill-defined group called the Committee of Southern Churchmen, subsisting year-to-year on patched-together budgets of thirty thousand dollars—most of it coming from small foundations. The committee published a quarterly Christian journal, with contributors ranging from Percy to Robert Coles. But its primary function was to provide a base of operations for Campbell—a subsistence salary, a generous travel budget and a log cabin office in the hills near Nashville.

Then as later, people often asked him exactly what he did, and the answer wasn't easy. He listened to the problems of bewildered individuals, and wrote magazine articles and occasional books. The first major seller, *Brother to a Dragonfly*, was a finalist for the National Book Award, and the accolades have continued through the years.

But one of the clearest demonstrations of Campbell's calling occurred early on in the 1980s when Billy Graham came to Nashville, arriving on a warm summer Saturday and sending word to Campbell that he'd like to get together. Graham was preparing for a crusade at Vanderbilt, and through an intermediary, he invited Campbell to meet him backstage—"just to get acquainted," the intermediary said.

Campbell considered it a strange invitation. He had never met Graham, though he'd tried on occasion, and he knew that their differences had been well publicized. Some eight years earlier, at the height of the killing in Vietnam, he had written an open letter in a Christian magazine, chastising Graham for his support of Richard Nixon. And more recently than that, speaking to a convention of ministers in Graham's hometown, he had scoffed at the blandness of mass market evangelism. But despite such differences, and despite his theology, Campbell was inclined to like Billy Graham—to respect him grudgingly for his personal decency and for his stubborn refusal in the 1950s to allow his crusades to be segregated racially. So he looked forward to their meeting for many of the same reasons that Graham proposed it—he wanted an opportunity to discuss their disagreements but also to affirm that they were brothers in the faith.

It looked for a while, however, as though it would all fall through. For as Graham preached to the multitudes at Vanderbilt, inveighing against divorce and premarital sex, Campbell was absorbed in his own Christian witness. He had a wedding and a baptism to perform and a visit to make to death row. Then, after a counseling session with a troubled seminarian, came the funeral of Bill Jenkins, where he preached a sermon and cried with the family—cursing his lapse of pastoral detachment, while one of Jenkins's daughters, a big, friendly woman with a robust grin, patted him on the arm and consoled him gently: "Now, now, preacher, we all know how you loved Papa. You just go ahead and cry."

But the most wrenching moments came later in the week, just a few hours before he was supposed to meet Graham. He traveled to the town of Lebanon, Tennessee, a medium-sized hamlet some thirty miles from Nashville, with flat-roofed stores along its downtown streets and a Confederate monument in the center of its square. And there in the shadows of early afternoon, amid the tension and humidity of a crowded courtroom, he pleaded for the life of Tyrone Bowers.

Bowers was a black man, twenty-two years old and stocky, with close-cropped hair and hard, steady eyes that stared straight ahead. Though he insisted he was innocent, five separate witnesses linked him to a murder—to the death of an amiable white man whose name was Glenn Taylor, a forty-one-year-old father of two and a popular figure among the people of Lebanon. According to the witnesses, Bowers admitted robbing Taylor on a cold winter midnight, leading him through a field of waist-high sage and putting six bullets in the back of his head. They said he pulled the trigger until the gun failed to fire, after his victim had moaned and begged for his life.

Campbell knew Taylor and was shocked by his death. But as an opponent of capital punishment, he made no exceptions, and when an all-white jury found Bowers guilty, Campbell agreed to testify at the sentencing hearing. He was asked to appear as an expert witness—a Christian ethicist who had studied at Yale and written extensively on the subject of justice. And the testimony began that way, with Campbell offering theological arguments and recounting his history of opposing executions—his occasional appearances at legislative hearings, his televised debates, and his private pleadings with assorted public officials.

But when he acknowledged participation in public demonstrations, the character of the testimony began to change—to become less cerebral and considerably more emotional, as the attorney general Tommy Thompson, tall and sandy-haired, with a penetrating mind and an overbearing style, sought to paint Campbell as an out-of-step radical. But in the jousting that followed, Campbell simply sidestepped and presented himself as something very different—a God-fearing, Jesus-loving preacher who takes it all seriously.

> Thompson: So you were one of the masses in the streets that we see on television? Would that be fair to say?
> Campbell: It would not be fair to say.
> Thompson: Well, would it surprise you to know that eighty-five percent of the general population is in favor of capital punishment?
> Campbell: Of the general population? No sir, it would not surprise me. It may well be, sir, that we say one thing in church and another thing outside of church.
> Thompson: All right, well let me ask you this. Would the fact that 85 percent of these people are for capital punishment make them any less of a Christian than you, sir?
> Campbell: It would not make them any less the people for whom our Lord died.
> Thompson: Yes sir. Well you are so concerned about capital punishment, I want you to look at that picture right there

(showing him a photo of the dead man, his right arm folded beneath his head, mud on his clothes, and six bullet holes in the base of his skull).

Campbell: I have already looked at it, sir.

Thompson: And if I told you that the evidence in this case indicated that this was a hard-working man, fifteen hours a day . . .

Campbell: I know, I know. I was in his business many times.

Thompson: Well, what do you think would be an answer to a person who would not only rob him but have him walk through a sage field, make him lay down, put his head in his hands, and sit there and shoot him once with a pistol, and when he started moaning shoot him five more times? What is the answer to that, Reverend?

Campbell paused before he offered a response, and for a moment it seemed as though he had nothing to say. But he did, of course, and the reaction was stunning in the small country courtroom, with the people jammed into the rough wooden pews, fanning themselves against the Tennessee heat and gazing steadily in the direction of the bench.

"Mr. Thompson," said Campbell, with his thoughts now collected, "apparently we do not know the answer to your question. I believe the answer is to evangelize the country in the name of Jesus Christ, so that it will simply not occur to anyone to commit the kind of violence that is shown in that picture, or the kind we are contemplating in this courtroom today. Until we do come to that kind of commitment and understanding of the Christian faith, I believe the spiral of violence will continue in this country. We have tried everything else we know to try. So I'm citing the only answer I know. I'm a Christian minister."

And in the astonishment that followed, Campbell knew that the point was made. The jury seemed absorbed in his simple proclamation, and several hours later he received word of the verdict—life imprisonment, rather than death in the chair. "The Spirit," he said. "Maybe it got loose in the Court of Mr. Caesar."

He considered telling the story to his brother, Billy Graham, for he thought it was possible that they could find a common ground, some mutual, substantial affirmation about the gospel—that it is effective and powerful amid the tawdriness of life, and that it's a sacrilegious shame to bury it in sweetness. But when he arrived at the stadium at seven o'clock that evening, with the choir and the crowds and the floodlight falling on the artificial turf, he immediately understood that it would not work. He found himself amused at his own presumption—at the notion that he, Will Campbell, could evangelize the best-known evangelist in the Christian world. So he simply smiled and joked and said gracious things, and chuckled to himself at his own private foolishness. And after basking backstage in the friendliness and charm, he moved to the stands for the public performance—staring in dismay at the slickness of it all. Then he shook his head sadly at what religion had become and laughed a little wanly when a friend turned and said, "Let's get out of here and go get drunk."

Well, how was it?" Brenda Campbell demanded. She was a formidable woman who had spent her whole adult life with Will Campbell and had become accustomed to the odd array of people who streamed through her kitchen—an unsuccessful songwriter with no place to stay, a frightened young marine who had run away from boot camp. But on this particular night, it was just a pair of journalists, and she seemed more relaxed as she gave her husband a drink and informed him again in her booming southern voice: "I want to hear all about it."

"Well," he said, burping discreetly and settling in beside her on a lumpy brown couch, "there ain't much to tell. He's a nice guy, but it's easy to be nice when you're in that position. And the problem with it is that people see how nice you are, and how pure you are, and they get to focusing their attention on you. I even have that problem from time to time; somebody'll read what I write or hear some sermon, and before long they'll be callin' me up, or some seminarian will be comin' along to write a Ph.D. on Will Campbellism. And I try to tell 'em, 'Don't do that. There's nothin' here. You don't look to me, and you don't look to Billy, because that ain't where the Christian faith is.' It ain't in niceness or eloquence or even social commitment, and we seem to have some trouble gettin' hold of that point."

Then a writer friend who was, as Campbell put it, "well into the hops," cut into the soliloquy to demand a clarification: "You keep saying what the Christian faith isn't. Well, what the hell is it, if it isn't those things?"

So Campbell smiled and picked up his guitar, and he began to answer with his own graphic parable. He told a story from a decade earlier, about a journey he made over to North Carolina—to the town of Granite Quarry in the lush, wooded flatlands just east of Charlotte. His purpose in going was to be with Bob Jones, then the Grand Dragon of the Ku Klux Klan, on the night before Jones was shipped off to prison. It was a strangely festive occasion with all the kinfolk and Klanfolk gathered in the Dragon's cinder block home telling funny stories and trying to be jolly and unconcerned. The whiskey flowed and the laughter continued until about two in the morning, when Campbell proposed communion. "Hell yes," said Jones "let's have communion." So the people gathered in a circle, and Campbell unpacked his guitar and said: "I'm gonna sing a song that to me is the essence of the Christian faith. It's called 'Anna I'm Takin' You Home' and it's about a whore and a lover who forgives her and takes her home. That's what Christianity is all about—being forgiven and taken home to where you're loved." Then, strumming softly on his guitar, he began to pray, "Lord, ole brother Bob is going off to jail for a while. We gonna ask you to kind of keep an eye on him. Lord, you know he's not a saint. And you also know that we sho ain't. But the Book tells us that's why you died. So that God and sinners could be reconciled. And we gon' drink to that and if it's all the same, we gon' sing our song in Jesus' name: Anna, I'm takin' you home."

Over the span of more than twenty years, I had the good fortune to write about Billy Graham for a variety of regional and national publications, including the Washington Post, *the* Charlotte Observer, *the* Progressive *magazine,* Creative Loafing, *and the* (NC) Independent. *The profile that follows is a synthesis from all of those stories, my take on a man I respected—and wanted to admire even more than I did.*

The Double-Edged Legacy of Billy Graham

He looked so frail as he entered the stadium, hunched forward slightly on the seat of the golf cart, then rising unsteadily at the edge of the podium. Two men had to help him up the steps, each at an elbow providing support.

That was not the way I remembered Billy Graham. Early in the 1980s, when I first began writing about him a lot, he seemed to be the picture of health, as the stadiums would fill with the sound of his voice, rich and honey-toned and gently pleading, the words familiar after so many years. His thoughts and phrases were mostly unremarkable, streams of certainty about the power of the faith, and the disaster that loomed at the end of other paths.

"You come forward now, men and women, black or white; you come, hundreds of you. It'll only take a moment to come. Mothers, fathers, young people too. The ushers will show you. You may be an elder or a deacon in the church, but you come."

And of course they came, moving forward silently in numbers that were startling—some weeping softly, others holding hands and popping Juicy Fruit gum, but coming, streaming down the aisles from throughout the arena, the choir as always singing, "Just as I Am." And above it all the same hypnotic voice: "You come now. . . . It's important that you come. There's something about coming forward and standing here that helps settle it in your mind."

When you saw Billy Graham in that kind of setting—when he

stood before the crowd with his sun-tanned face and his pale blue stare, with the odd, lingering innocence of some aging surfer—it was a little hard to fathom what it all really meant. There was an air about him of absolute sincerity. But what about the substance? What were the crowds left with when the service was over? What vision, what understanding of the depths of Christianity?

His critics have answered such questions harshly, contending over the years that there's a clunking banality at the heart of Graham's message, a sanitized, Americanized understanding of Jesus that rendered him irrelevant to the world and its pain. Reinhold Niebuhr was one of the first to make the charge. In the tumultuous summer of 1956—a time when Martin Luther King Jr. and his followers were boycotting buses in pursuit of integration—Niebuhr wrote an article for the *Christian Century* magazine. He quoted the epistle of First John ("If a man sayeth he loves God and hateth his brother, he is a liar") and urged Graham to speak out about racial upheavals.

Other critics emerged in the sixties and seventies, culminating in 1979, when the journalist Marshall Frady produced a biography of Graham—an eloquent critique that drew wide acclaim. Frady concluded that Graham, the farm boy evangelist from the outskirts of Charlotte, was so affected by the wooings of the powerful that he could no longer distinguish between Richard Nixon's America and the Kingdom of God.

"It is no accident," wrote Frady, "that Graham has wound up now with his image translated into a stained-glass window in Washington's National Presbyterian Cathedral. He constitutes finally the apotheosis of the American Innocence itself—that plain, cheerful, rigorous, ferociously wholesome earnestness which, to some, as one Egyptian editor put it during the days of Vietnam, 'has made you nice Americans the most dangerous people on the face of the earth.'"

It was not that Graham's critics doubted his character or the fundamental honesty of his intent. They knew he had sought to be a good steward, that at a time when evangelism was being disgraced—rendered hypocritical by the Bakkers and the Swaggerts, and the vicious hate-mongers screaming from the right—Graham had held to his own steady course. That was no small achievement, and it seemed to be rooted not only in his faith but in the simple decency at the heart of who he was. In an interview in the 1980s, even Frady was moved to declare, "From the very first moment I met him, I thought this was as good a man, basically, as I had been in the presence of."

But it was also possible, as Graham was moving toward the end of his life, to detect in some of the things he said a sense of uncertainty about what he'd accomplished. Among other things, the world as a whole was a rebuke to his faith, for it was still a violent and sinful place, where people could hate and even kill in the name of God. Not that he blamed himself altogether. But in the looming shadow of his eightieth birthday, he worried in an interview with ABC's Peter Jennings about the "mistakes" he had made in the course of his ministry—and there were, in fact, some reasons for regret. Certainly, it was true that except for one brief period in the 1980s, he seldom swam against the currents of his country.

He had started as a patriot in the 1940s, a young evangelist who lived in a world of black and white, where communists were waging a war against God and America was the last great hope of resistance. In 1949, that message attracted the attention of the newspaper magnate William Randolph Hearst, who ordered his army of obedient reporters to "puff Graham."

The reporters did, and Graham soon emerged as a national celebrity—a friend of presidents from Eisenhower to Nixon, who saw the benefits of his visits to the White House. Graham, for his part, relished the attention. Then as later, he was a man of deep and genuine humility, astonished by the warm regard of great men, and he did his best to return their affection—in part by voicing support for their policies.

In the 1960s, amid all the agony over Vietnam, he would pound the pulpit of his TV crusades and castigate those who were critics of the country. "There is too much negativism," he would say, "too many people who are knocking our institutions." And he would call to the podium earnest young Marines who explained how God had helped them kill communists. On domestic issues, he sounded much the same. In 1971, in his hometown of Charlotte, the city's powerful gathered in his honor—at a private reception featuring cross-shaped sandwiches and a thirty-pound cake in the shape of a Bible. There was a public ceremony with twelve thousand people, and in a country grappling with inner-city poverty, Graham offered this recollection from his boyhood: "We also wrestled with poverty, if you go by today's standards, except we did not know we were poor. . . . We also had the problem of rats. The only difference between then and now is that we didn't call on the federal government to kill them."

Soon, however, this world that had always been so pleasant came crashing down around him. The Watergate scandal brought Graham up short, for he had felt deep affection for Richard Nixon—more than for any of his other White House suitors. When he began to listen to the Watergate tapes, with all their vulgarities and sinister plottings, he was bewildered by the cynicism they contained. "I just couldn't understand it," he told Marshall Frady. "I thought he was a man of integrity . . . and all those people around him, they seemed so clean."

In the wake of that scandal, and Graham's own measure of disillusionment and pain, he emerged in the 1980s as a more reflective person. He had always been a man of answers. Now suddenly there were questions, and they only became more troubling over the next several years as he made several trips to Iron Curtain countries and began to reexamine the Cold War rhetoric that had shaped his career. During his trips to Poland and Hungary, and a few years later, the Soviet Union, he came to see the humanity of America's adversaries. In any final showdown between East and West, he now understood, the casualties might include these people in his audience.

During the same period, he visited India, Bangladesh, and other third world countries, where the gravity of world hunger hit him with a force that hadn't been there before. Starving people, like the communists, were no longer an abstraction. Thus, in 1982, he stood before seven hundred people at Harvard University, speaking softly, informally, freely admitting the limits of his vision.

"As a Christian," he said, "I believe that God has a special concern for the poor of the world. . . . I believe God has a special concern for things like peace, racism, the responsible use of the Earth's resources, economic and social justice, the use of power and the sacredness of human life. I confess that I have not always seen all the complexities. . . . I am still learning. But I have come to see in deeper ways the implications of my faith and the message I have been proclaiming.

"I often spoke on the wonderful little story in the tenth chapter of Luke where Jesus told the story of the Good Samaritan, teaching us our social responsibilities. From the very beginning, I felt that if I came upon a person who had been beaten and robbed and left for dead that I'd do my best to help him. I also felt that this applied to my relatives and friends and immediate neighbors.

"But I never thought in terms of corporate responsibility. I had no real idea that millions of people throughout the world lived on the knife-edge of starvation and that the teachings of my reference point demanded that I have a responsibility toward them. Later, as I traveled and studied the Bible more, I changed."

He continued from there, admitting his mistakes and affirming that his "pilgrimage" was not yet complete. He talked especially about the arms race, calling for the negotiated destruction of all nuclear weapons. "I think it's possible," he said, "maybe not probable, but possible."

In many circles, the speech drew acclaim. Reporters and editorial writers began dashing off essays about Graham's growth as a Christian—the enlargements of his vision and definition of sin. No longer, they noted, did he define evil in the world solely as the debaucheries of individual people. He had come to see that pervasive social ills—poverty and war and nuclear weapons—were collective symptoms of the sinful human heart. Harvard theologian Harvey Cox summed up the sentiments of many of his colleagues when he said with a smile: "I'm very cheered at ol' Billy. He's doing good."

Three months later, during this time of approval from unaccustomed quarters, Graham set out on a trip to Moscow. He planned to deliver a speech at an international religious conference on nuclear disarmament, hoping, he said, "to make whatever small contribution I can to the cause of world peace." But even as he was leaving, an old reluctance began to show itself. He fretted with reporters about changes in his image—the publicity about his pleas for disarmament, his passionate denunciations of oppression and hunger. "I don't want to get sidetracked," he said, "and have the press always building me up as the leader of some peace movement."

From the beginning of his trip, he seemed to be unsure and off stride, stumbling as he dealt with difficult issues. He praised the Soviet Union for its increasing levels of religious freedom, precisely at a time when Soviet dissidents were denouncing their oppression. At one of his speeches, a Baptist protester unfurled a banner demanding greater freedom and was quickly led away by police. Falling back on his earlier instincts, Graham immediately defended the police.

"Some people can be detained for all kinds of reasons," he said.

"We detain people in the United States if we catch people doing things that are wrong. I've had people come to my services in the U.S. causing disturbances, and they have been taken away by police."

Because of such statements, Graham took a battering. *Newsweek* columnist George Will called him "America's most embarrassing export." Other critics were equally harsh, and in the midst of it all the original purpose of his trip became lost. Much of the media had moved on to other things by the time he spoke at the conference on disarmament, gathering himself and delivering one of the most powerful speeches of his career. At the heart of his message was a quotation from Albert Einstein: "The unleashed power of the atom has changed everything except our way of thinking. Thus we are drifting toward a catastrophe beyond comparison. We shall require a substantially new manner of thinking if mankind is to survive."

Graham echoed the sentiment. "We need a new breakthrough," he declared, "in how the terrifying problem of nuclear war is approached. The vicious cycle of propaganda and counterpropaganda, charge and countercharge must somehow be broken. The unending and escalating cycle of relying on deterrents should also be defused." Graham called once again for negotiated arms control, with the ultimate aim of total disarmament. He acknowledged that the process was difficult and far beyond the realms of his own expertise—and so he offered no plan, no concrete proposals for how the negotiations should go. What he did offer was a ringing conviction that arms negotiations would not succeed, could *never* succeed, without a change in the diplomatic climate.

"Our purpose is to rise above narrow national interests," he said, "and give humanity a spiritual vision of the way to peace. . . . Let us call the nations and leaders of our world to repentance. We need to repent as nations over our past failures—the failure to accept each other, the failure to be concerned about the needs of the poor and the starving of the world, the failure to place top priority on peace instead of war. . . ."

"I would urge the leaders of the nations," he said, "especially the major powers, to declare a moratorium on hostile rhetoric. Peace does not grow in a climate of mistrust, in which each side to a greater and greater degree is constantly accusing the other of false motives and hidden actions."

Throughout the speech and the interviews that followed, Graham insisted that our nationalistic ways of thinking had failed—and even worse, were attached to a technology where one miscalculation or a single excess of cynicism could lead to Armageddon. And for millions of the world's people, he added, Armageddon had arrived—for they existed day to day on the edge of starvation, while the world's powerful nations, those with the resources to make a dent in the suffering, squandered billions instead on weapons of mass destruction.

"Have we gone mad?" he demanded. "Are we seeking the genocide of the whole human race?"

For many of us who had watched him through the years, that speech was the high point of Graham's career, the bravest moment in his long Christian witness. But stung by the controversy that it brought him, he seemed to become more cautious after that, retreating to the safety of his own crusades. I remember a conversation at his mountaintop home in North Carolina. It was a misty spring Sunday with a chill in the air, and Graham was just returning from church. He entered the living room of his spacious log house, moving with a slouching, good-natured gait, his arms dangling loosely at his side. On this particular day, when he was still in his sixties, he seemed tanned, relaxed, but even in the cloister of this mountain retreat, with its flock of friendly dogs and expansive hearth of old-fashioned brick, he was inescapably aware that he was an institution. His identity was tied to his sense of mission, and he made it clear that he would let nothing—absolutely nothing—interfere with his calling.

"My main focus is the Gospel," he explained, deflecting a compliment about his statements on peace. "I'm concerned about what it can do for you, for a person's life. There may be issues that are distantly related to the Gospel, or perhaps they are deeply related. But the gift of an evangelist is a very narrow gift."

For the rest of his life, as his vigor slowly left him, he still spoke gently on behalf of the poor and for reconciliation among the world's different races. But the prophetic force of his speeches in Moscow and his lecture at Harvard seldom showed itself anymore. Instead, he retreated to the safety of his gift, preaching his sermons on the power of the faith, and then calling people forward: "You come now. It's important that you come. There's something about coming forward that helps to settle it in your mind."

For those of us who admired him, and wished him the best, it was clear that his life was a pilgrimage of faith, and that he managed on occasion to make people think. But did he do it enough? In the course of his ministry, did he demand enough of the people coming forward? Did he insist that they love their neighbors as themselves, black or white, rich or poor, gay or straight? Did he encourage the millions who answered his call to live on the hardest edge of their faith?

Or did the world too often absorb his words and simply move on about its business, fundamentally unchanged by the things he said?

It seemed clear enough the last time I saw him, speaking at a crusade in his hometown of Charlotte, that his sincerity and goodness were beyond all dispute. And yet the troubling questions remained. A few of us in the audience that night could not help wishing, despite our respect, that over the long and honorable course of his life, he had offered a tougher definition of his faith.

Starting late in the 1970s, when I became religion writer at the Charlotte
Observer, *my editors and I agreed from the start that we would cover
not only the religious personalities—Charlotte native Billy Graham, for
example—and the more extreme voices shouting from the fringe but the
ordinary people and churches who were the religious backbone of the community. After leaving the* Observer *some years later, I was still intrigued by
the currents of religious life in the South, and the city of Charlotte, where
I was living, seemed to be a revealing laboratory. In this story, written in
2005, I set out to examine the religious debate in a New South city, some of it
healthy, some of it disturbing, but all of it important in trying to understand
how a modern community struggles with its values.*

Charlotte's Holy Wars:
Religion in a New South City

It was the middle of spring in 2005, a time when the Mecklenburg
County Commission was considering an insurance plan for un-
married couples, gay or straight, who worked for local government.
Dan Burrell, the senior minister at Northside Baptist Church—a
man who had emerged in recent years as one of Charlotte's leading
fundamentalists—issued a mass e-mail denouncing the plan and
calling on his fellow conservatives to join him.

By his own account, Burrell was not a throwback, not a twenty-
first-century embodiment of the stereotype of southern fundamentalists. Beneath the warm wooden dome of Northside Baptist,
he preaches a sunnier gospel on Sundays than Jack Hudson, his
fire-and-brimstone predecessor, did. He rejects, for example, the old
hang-ups of race that once tainted the message from many southern
pulpits. He proclaims instead that "the Scriptures scream racial
unity" and says it's dangerous when the Christian faith is used to
justify a moral wrong.

Burrell sees his ministry as part of a rich and noble tradition
going back to the abolitionists of the nineteenth century, but he also
believes that the stakes in the moral battle are high. Whether the
issue is race, right to life, or the sanctity of marriage between a man

and a woman, Burrell says the time has come to take a stand—to defend with no hesitation or shame the "eternal and absolute authority" of the Bible.

In recent months, Burrell has begun meeting regularly with other conservative ministers in the city, trying to put together a coalition that will speak out strongly on a whole host of issues. He has found an ally in County Commissioner Bill James, arguably the most conservative politician in the city, and a man whose career on the public stage has been driven by his strong fundamentalist faith. James believes the fundamentalists are winning. He believes, in fact, that at this moment in the moral history of the city, there are no voices of consequence to oppose them.

James understands that for the last half century, churches have played a major role in the politics of Charlotte, at least in the broadest sense of that term. Led and prodded by several generations of outspoken ministers, they have tried to put a stamp on the public debate. Some of those ministers have been regarded as liberal, others conservative; some have been black, others white, but they have battled with a kind of genteel ferocity in an effort to assume the moral high ground.

Today, says James, he is satisfied about the state of that struggle. "I don't know any liberal preachers of note anymore," he declared in the spring of 2004. "The left doesn't seem to have any activist ministers. . . . Liberals in Charlotte have given up on busing, effectively given up on affirmative action, and won't even bring up gay rights. I don't know if there are any true liberals in Charlotte."

But James conceded that if that is true, it represents a seismic shift in the city. There once was a time when liberal voices thundered from some of the most prominent pulpits in town. Beginning at Myers Park Baptist Church back in the 1950s and 1960s, a pipe-smoking intellectual named Carlyle Marney spoke out strongly on the issue of civil rights. Those were the days when the city of Charlotte was searching for its conscience, when blacks were sitting in at local restaurants or demanding the total integration of the schools. The eloquent liberals like Marney and Warner Hall of Covenant Presbyterian sought to give aide and comfort to the cause, calling on the prominent members of their flocks to be better Christians. At its heart, their argument was simple: All men and women are children of God, and therefore brothers and sisters of one another. But these were men of powerful intellect, who could preach and teach and inspire admiration, even among people who didn't quite agree.

Their opposite number back in those days was the fiery Jack Hudson of Northside Baptist. He was a plain-spoken man with slicked down hair and a hunch to his shoulders, and he had a substantial following of his own. He built one of the first of Charlotte's mega churches, but in the battle for the conscience of the people of the city, Hudson was simply no match for the liberals. He spoke out against assorted sins of the flesh and the dangers he saw in racial integration, and slowly but surely respectable opinion began to tune him out.

And so it was that the day of the liberals lasted well into the 1970s, and perhaps even longer, as a second generation began to emerge. These were men like Carlyle Marney's successor, Gene Owens, and Doug Oldenburg, who followed Warner Hall to Covenant Presbyterian. There was Charlie Milford at Park Road Baptist and Randy Taylor at Myers Park Presbyterian and Father Jim Devereaux at St. Peter's Catholic.

The most flamboyant of the group was Owens, a silver-haired theologian, born in eastern North Carolina, a man who gradually developed a poetic affinity for the well-spoken word. He seemed to revel in shaking up the flock. He marched for busing to integrate the schools and called for peace in Vietnam and invited Carter Heyward, an Episcopal priest who had recently acknowledged to the world that she was gay, to preach from the pulpit at Myers Park Baptist.

A few miles away at Covenant Presbyterian, Doug Oldenburg was a quieter presence but no less firm. He was a handsome man with soft, gentle eyes, and he was caught, he said, "in a lover's quarrel" with the capitalist system. On many a Sunday during his time at Covenant, he proclaimed to the influential people in the pews that the church had a special mission for the poor. Part of it was simply a matter of compassion, like giving to the Crisis Assistance Ministry or helping build houses for Habitat for Humanity. But at least as important in Oldenburg's view was the church's obligation to roll up its sleeves and represent the poor in the halls of government.

The Bible, he thought, was full of those commands, inconvenient reminders for people who wanted to enjoy their own wealth. But if you took them seriously, the sermons of Jesus and the lessons of the prophets were a powerful force to make the world more just. That at least was Oldenburg's view, and like the others in the Myers Park pulpits, he was not afraid to lay it on the line.

Dale Mullennix remembers those days. He came to Charlotte in 1979 as an assistant minister at Myers Park Baptist. He was fresh out of seminary in Louisville and was embarked on a personal mission at the time "to save the world for the left." He was astonished by the message from the Myers Park ministers, these graceful, intelligent voices of compassion, and he was surprised also by the gradual discovery that the more he got to know these men, the more impressive they seemed.

"They used to get together for breakfast once a month," he remembers, "and I'd finagle a reason to be invited, just for the quality and depth of conversation. There was not a word of competitiveness among them. They were asking instead, what is good for the community? What is right? What will work? There was seldom any talk about parking problems, and the old idea that the church should lower its voice to raise its income just never came up."

But what about now? Is Bill James correct? Have the powerful liberal voices disappeared? The simplest answer to that question is no. At Myers Park Baptist, the current minister, Steve Shoemaker, is not as colorful, certainly, as Owens. But there are few, if any, who fault his courage, or the depth and intelligence of his Sunday morning sermons.

Shoemaker grew up in Charlotte, a preacher's son who went away to seminary and then to other pulpits in other parts of the country. He came back home after serving at an inner-city church in Houston. He enjoyed it there, enjoyed the location in the heart of downtown, where he could urge the homeless people in the streets not only to come in for handouts of food but to join the church and participate fully in everything it did—the Sunday morning worship, the family dinners, even the missions to people in need.

He knew that Myers Park was a different kind of place. It was nestled away in one of Charlotte's oldest suburbs, an area of handsome, two-story houses, where the wind rustled gently through the magnolia leaves. The church had always struggled against the elegant isolation of its setting, but Shoemaker knew that his predecessors, Marney and Owens, had encouraged the congregation to be involved in the community and to wrestle with the ethical issues of the day.

Shoemaker was happy for the chance to do the same. Late in the fall of 2002, with the country in the looming shadow of a war, he decided to preach a sermon about Iraq. He talked about the teachings of Jesus, that troubling pronouncement about loving your enemies, and he talked about the practical tendency of the world to ignore a command so completely inconvenient.

"We kneel," he said, "before the mystery of God and the terrors of life, in bafflement and moral anguish. We pray for our President and our nation's leaders, and we pray for the leaders of all nations and peoples. And we pray for our enemies, though our hearts recoil—how could they not recoil? For Saddam Hussein and all who would do us harm. We pray for our soldiers and for the people of Iraq and Afghanistan, and for a world which seems never to know the things that make for peace. Amen."

On other Sundays since his arrival at Myers Park nearly four years ago, Shoemaker has spoken out against the resegregation of the public schools and in favor of tolerance for people who are gay. He understands that he is not alone. Just a few blocks away at Myers Park United Methodist, James Howell is settling in as the new senior minister, and so far it seems to be going well. The pews are packed on most Sunday mornings, the balconies full, with folding chairs on the ends of many rows, as Howell gazes out across the faces in the crowd and urges people "out into a pained and broken world—and thanks be to God for the high and holy privilege."

Howell came to Myers Park from the college town of Davidson, North Carolina, where the people were struck by the haunting beauty of his sermons. "He's maybe the best preacher I've ever heard," says Caroline Hicks, a member at Davidson. But Howell says it gets harder all the time.

"Twenty-five years ago," he contends, "the highest compliment for a minister at the end of a sermon was, 'You stepped on my toes. You really made me think.' Today, the highest compliment is, 'I agree with you.' Some axis has shifted."

Howell says he still tries to talk about difficult things—peace in the aftermath of 9/11, public schools in a time of resegregation, greed in a land of material wealth. But he tries to do it gently, with sensitivity and style, and even so, he understands clearly he is taking a chance. "I think we're living in an era," he says, "when we no longer understand the virtue of disagreement. We have these litmus tests. We don't really talk to each other anymore."

William Wood shares that troubling assessment. The veteran minister at First Presbyterian Church in the heart of downtown has studied the statistics of the mainline churches. "If you project out the membership losses since 1965," he says, "by the year 2038 at noon on Sunday, there will be no more Presbyterians."

Wood says there are many different reasons for that. But he believes primarily that polarization has taken its toll, and divisive issues such as homosexuality and abortion have torn at the unity of churches like his own, costing them members. So he finds himself becoming more cautious, pulling his punches sometimes in his Sunday morning sermons in what often seems like a delicate time. There are certain subjects that he will not avoid, especially the rights and needs of the poor, and his church has been known through the years for its outreach.

Its members build houses for Habitat for Humanity, and two nights a week the church building serves as a shelter for the homeless. There are, in fact, more than thirty-five programs for people in need, and Wood says that "is a permanent part of the identity of this church." But he also says at a time when the issues are becoming more complicated, when people of good will can disagree about the foreign policy of the country or the pros and cons of homosexual marriage, he tries to balance the desire to speak out with the need to preserve the unity of the church. "Sometimes you just can't help it," he says. "But in this climate, I don't go picking fights."

Though he tends to resist it, Clifford Jones understands the current inclination to be more cautious. He says it's not just the white community that has changed but also his own. Jones is the pastor at Friendship Missionary Baptist Church, one of the most prominent black churches in town, and under his leadership, one of the most involved in the total community. But Jones has moments of deep frustration, moments when it seems as though his own institution, which, for generations now, has stood like a beacon on Beatties Ford Road, is becoming "sinfully incestuous" in its definition of the faith.

"I don't sense the same kind of urgency in the African American community," he says, "not the same kind of involvement in political and social issues that I saw twenty years ago. The rising middle class of African Americans doesn't seem to have the same commitment. I sense that the emerging church of the twenty-first century places more emphasis on what goes on within its walls than it does on the hungry, the homeless, the AIDS patient."

Jones, for his part, continues to beat the old drums of compassion. "I'm a leftover from the sixties," he explains. But he also believes that Charlotte has now become a different place. There once was a time when there were many more voices like his own, and though there are still a few of them today, it is not as clear who is paying attention. To Jones, that is the most fundamental of ironies. Charlotte, he says, is no longer the same southern city that it was, no longer as cohesive, and as it has changed, it has become less compassionate—less sensitive, he believes, to people in need, including, of course, its racial minorities.

"On the heels of the civil rights movement," he contends, "there seemed to be a sense and a desire to do what was right—if not for right's sake, then at least for image sake." It was a civic morality undergirded by faith, but Jones doesn't see it as much anymore. As Charlotte has grown, and people have begun to move in from other places, he thinks that something important has been lost.

Andy Baxter agrees. Baxter, an ordained Methodist minister, is executive director of Mecklenburg Ministries, a loose alliance of church people in Charlotte who are seeking to raise issues of justice and reconciliation. Baxter says it keeps getting harder when the city is growing at a breakneck pace, and in the new and far-flung sprawl of suburbia, the feeling of community has all but disappeared. In addition, says Baxter, Charlotte, like the rest of the country, is caught in the aftershock of 9/11, a time when people are seeking reassurance and really don't want to be prodded to think. They are looking instead for a message of certainty, and to the extent that they find it coming from the pulpit, it is coming most often from conservative churches.

"I think 9/11 changed the ballgame a lot," agrees David Chadwick, minister at Forest Hill Church in southeast Charlotte. "There are now a lot more people looking for answers, and conservative churches are giving answers that liberal churches don't."

Certainly, it's true that for more than twenty years in Charlotte, conservatives have played a major role in the public debate, dispensing their own understanding of the truth with a fiery certitude that among other things has dominated the newspaper headlines. Some say it began with Joseph Chambers, minister at the Paw Creek Church of God, who began attracting attention in the 1980s with his public crusades against pornography. He picketed outside the *Charlotte Observer*, accusing the paper of being soft on the issue, and later he picketed a local theater that was showing *The Last Temptation of Christ*.

Later in the eighties, the conservatives were out in force again as part of the demonstrations by Operation Rescue, a militant anti-abortion group that tried to blockade the doors of the clinics. They were supported by ministers such as Harry Reeder from Christ Covenant Church in nearby Matthews, and as the controversy swirled, the conservatives continued to become more visible.

Then came the nineties, when maybe the most prominent conservative of all suddenly burst onto the scene. He was not a minister this time, but a passionate layman who emerged from the pews of Calvary Church, the great cathedral in southeast Charlotte, to assume his place as one of the most strident voices in the city. Bill James makes no apology for that. "I have often told folks," he says, "that God commands individuals and churches to be both 'salt and light.' While 'light' is informing folks about the love of Christ and his redemption of mankind, salt is about being a change agent. When salt gets in a wound it inflames and causes irritation. In short, I have been the proverbial 'salt in the wound' on occasion because I and others, in trying to rid society of behavior that is un-Christian and wrong, will inflame certain segments of the public."

James began to dish out the salt during what he calls "the great arts war of 1997." He was a county commissioner by then, and he and his fellow conservatives lashed out at the production of *Angels in America*, a play with a homosexual theme staged by the Charlotte Repertoire Theater. Because Charlotte Rep had gotten Arts and Science Council funding, some of which was public money, James and his allies attacked the morality of a play with such a message.

He believes they accomplished at least two things: They helped energize the Christian right, and they pressured the arts community in Charlotte—or at least part of it—to move in the direction of self-censorship. "That was, in my opinion, a win," he says. "The key is to keep vigilant and make sure the other side knows that you mean business."

James is clear about his public crusades. These are causes that go beyond politics; they are, instead, a defense of good in the war against evil, a defense of the truth against those who don't even think it exists.

"Most evangelical Christians," he declares, "don't even view liberals as being Christians. To be called a Christian means accepting that Christ is the only intercessor between God and man. Historically, this inability to accept that Christ is the only way to God is, I think, at the heart of why liberals espouse some of the views they do. Without the anchor of Christianity . . . they just make it up as they go along."

James says he's happy there are like-minded people in the pulpits of Charlotte, especially Dan Burrell at Northside Baptist, who shares his view of the fundamentalist mission. "It's a conflict of world views," says Burrell. "I believe I am fighting for eternal truths."

Early in 2005, Burrell attended a meeting at Myers Park Baptist, where he was asked to speak on the possibility of dialogue. "I was happy to do it," he recalled. "I enjoy talking about issues of faith, and I don't take it personally when people disagree. But I had to ask why? Dialogue isn't going to result in a change of mind on my part, and I doubt if it will on theirs. This is a fundamental difference in the way we view truth. Compromise is the life-blood of politics, but the death knell of theology. We are fighting over the absolute authority of the Scriptures."

If Burrell is right, if Charlotte's churches have drifted in the past generation into a kind of holy war of ideas, who is winning? Is it the conservatives, as Bill James believes? Do they have the liberals on the run? Or is the truth more subtle than that?

Dale Mullennix believes that it is. For one thing, he says, some of the most prominent churches in the area—Myers Park Baptist, Myers Park Methodist—have kept hiring ministers who pull them "in directions that did not make them feel comfortable." Mullennix, the former assistant minister at Myers Park Baptist, believes the habit of being challenged by liberal ministers has now become ingrained, at least in certain parts of the city.

In addition to that, when it comes to the interlocking issues of poverty and race, always a litmus test for the liberals, there are literally hundreds of churches in Charlotte reaching out to the poor, and some of those are theologically conservative. One of the most prominent is Forest Hill Presbyterian, where the charismatic minister David Chadwick preaches often about sexual sin. "If we reserved sex," he says, "for a man and a woman in the context of marriage, how many social ills would we cure in one generation?" But he also rejects the old dichotomy between the Bible's pronouncements about personal morality and its cry for justice and reconciliation.

"We have to speak out against racial injustice," he says. "Few of us in the white community know what it's like to be black—to fear racial profiling or wonder why you're not getting a job. And we have to talk also about the growing disparity between rich and poor, and the quagmire of poverty. I say to our congregation all the time, 'You can't love your brother if you don't know your brother.'"

Among other things, Forest Hill has tried to reach out to inner-city churches, supporting the work, for example, of Rev. Barbara Cameron, pastor of the Community Outreach Church in a neighborhood knows as Genesis Park. Nestled just north and west of downtown, it was once the most drug-infested part of the city. But in 1983, Pastor Cameron set up her church on a little hill overlooking the skyline. She began holding Sunday school classes for the children, and then started working with nonprofit agencies to build better housing, and with community police officers to make the neighborhood safer.

Within a decade, Genesis Park was a very different place, and Chadwick and other members of his church tried to help where they could. They offered volunteers, and before they built a new sanctuary for themselves, they raised five hundred thousand dollars for Cameron's church building in Genesis Park. "You have to be intentional," says Chadwick, "about breaking down barriers, about building relationships that really matter."

Rev. Kelvin Smith agrees, though his approach through the years has been slightly different. Smith is a native Charlottean, a Baptist in his raising, who, unlike some of his peers in the eighties, developed an interest in the issue of poverty. After graduating from Gardner-Webb College, he started a ministry in Jackson Park, an at-risk neighborhood near the Charlotte airport, where the red-brick apartments were scattered all around, and the people were poor, and the drug dealers came and went as they pleased.

When Smith moved in, he started a basketball league for the kids, which they could join only after being tutored to pull up their grades. He gave out emergency food and supplies, and in the abandoned apartments just behind his church, he set up a program of transitional housing for families trying to get back on their feet. There were classes in parenting and financial management—and in what Smith saw as some of the most basic tenets of the Bible: treating each other with civility and respect.

Today, that program is still going strong, and in the Steele Creek neighborhood not far away, Smith has started a new church to go along with it. With more than forty nationalities represented, his nondenominational congregation is one of the most integrated in the city. The Sunday morning services are evangelical, filled with exuberant anthems of praise, and an absolute faith in the authority of the Bible. It's a style and theology that many would identify as conservative, but Smith's motivations are different than some. "One of our core values," he concludes, "is to break down the old walls of racism, classism, denominationalism. We want to show people that the races can indeed live together."

B ack in Myers Park, Steve Shoemaker is impressed by the spirit of Smith's undertaking. In many ways, he says, he is happy enough with the current state of religion in Charlotte—happy with the diversity of strong pulpit voices and undismayed by the fact that his own church and a handful of others no longer enjoy the monopoly of influence they had in the past. "We are past the time," he says, "when the elite congregations on our side of town even *ought* to be speaking for the city."

But Shoemaker worries more and more that the city is divided, that in a community that is less cohesive than it was, there isn't the same old search for common ground. Certainly it's true that for many of the conservatives, that search is irrelevant or even worse. Bill James, among others, takes pride in the stridency of his positions and even the more mild-mannered Dan Burrell sees the debate in terms of black and white: "I believe I am fighting for eternal truths."

There is, in that fundamentalist view, not much common ground to be found, and those who pursue it are either insincere or simply not committed to the things that they believe. But the problem, in the eyes of the Christian moderates, is that there are times when fundamentalist certainty can shade into prejudice or personal attack. In the spring of 2005, for example, as Burrell lashed out at the county commissioners for considering equal benefits for homosexuals, he denounced Parks Helms, the commissioners' chairman, as an "arrogant and extremist liberal."

It is not a charge that has been heard very often in the course of Helms's long political career. Among most of his constituency through the years, he has been widely regarded as a moderate Democrat, willing to listen to other points of view. But these are different times in Charlotte, and that reality concerns Clifford Jones, the African American minister at Friendship Baptist.

To Jones, the conservatives' unbending certitude is chilling, and he decries "those Christians so blinded by faith that they become deaf to the realities of life." He thinks those voices are getting louder all the time, and sometimes ugly, and he worries about what it means for the city.

Jones is far from alone in that, and his concerns came sharply into focus late in the autumn of 2004. Shortly after the November elections, Commissioner Bill James sent out an e-mail, ostensibly about the problems of public education. At the age of forty-eight, James was riding high at the time. He had just been re-elected, without opposition, to his fifth straight term on the County Commission. Even his critics had developed a grudging respect for his tenacity. But they were startled by the tenor of his newest pronouncements, delivered in an e-mail to more than twelve hundred people.

"Most people know why CMS [the Charlotte-Mecklenburg Schools] can't teach kids in the urban black community," James declared. "They live in a moral sewer with parents who lack the desire to act properly."

Leaders in the black community were appalled, and so were their friends. Steve Shoemaker, for example, thought it was a "poisonous" moment for the people of Charlotte, a time when the community could be torn apart. So did William Wood, the firm but cautious minister at First Presbyterian, and the two of them appeared before the County Commission to tell Bill James he had gone too far.

Wood carried a petition signed by several hundred Presbyterians, expressing their anger at the "moral sewer" e-mail and the message of racism that lay at its core. Shoemaker shared their feeling of outrage, but he also saw it as a chance to make a point. The community, he wrote in a letter that was published in the *Charlotte Observer*, "must find ways of moral discourse which do not demonize the opponent." But the troubling unknown to the ministers on the left, including Shoemaker, was whether it was possible to find such a path when at least one side in the moral debate was sure of its total monopoly on the truth.

Was it true, as the fundamentalists were saying, that there was no possibility of consensus anymore? As the debates continued in 2005, that was one question hanging over Charlotte. And there was another one just as disturbing, at least in certain parts of the city: If the pulpit pronouncements were becoming more divisive, what about the people out there in the pews? Was anybody listening to what was being said?

One former minister at a Myers Park church had occasion in 2004 to visit several times at one of the new churches in southeast Charlotte. It was a mainline institution in a new neighborhood where the symbols of prosperity seemed to be all around—the two-story houses, the newly planted trees, the expensive foreign cars that were parked in the driveways. When he took his seat on that first Sunday morning, the minister was shocked. The people, he said, seemed "spiritually dead." They showed little interest in being challenged by their faith, and it didn't seem to matter if the minister was liberal, preaching a gospel of justice and reconciliation, or somebody more conservative, preaching about homosexuality or abortion.

The people didn't care. The preacher wondered what was going on. Was it the cynicism of the times, the low-grade fear that followed 9/11, now making people numb? Was it the blare of too many voices? Or was it simply the triumph of greed, people living their lives in a cocoon of affluence, indifferent to anything else in the world?

Whatever it was, for this particular minister, many of the signs of the times were not good. He was troubled by the arrogance of the new fundamentalists, and troubled even more by the new wave of apathy that seemed to be spreading through the suburbs of Charlotte. Because of those realities, he had to admit, it was hard to escape a subtle feeling of relief that he didn't have to be in a pulpit anymore.

One of the most intriguing people I've met through the years, even among those who were serious about their faith, was Karen Graham, an anti-abortion activist in North Carolina. Graham was one of the leaders in the movement—one of those, in fact, on the radical edge. She had joined a group called Operation Rescue, whose primary tactic at the time was blockading the doors of abortion clinics and forcing the police to drag them away. As I began to write about this movement, and thus began to interview Graham, it soon became clear that she was as out of step with the true believers around her as she was with the values of society at large. This is the story of one young woman and her leap of faith and the disillusionment that followed.

The Lonely Crusade
of Karen Graham

Karen Graham stood before the grave, running her hands through her wind-blown hair. It was her first time back since the day of the funeral. She folded her arms across her faded t-shirt, then squatted and stared at the grave some more. It was a warm spring day at Belmont Abbey, with the smell of honeysuckle on the breeze, and a cloud bank moving in from the west. Graham was nearly alone in the Catholic cemetery, and she said it was hard to know how to feel—hard even to remember the day of the funeral. Was it sunny? Cold? How big was the crowd?

The details were receding now in her mind, but even in her current state of depression, it was easy to remember what had happened just before. Starting in the summer of 1992, Graham was a member of a grisly expedition. She had clearly emerged in the previous four years as her city's most talked-about pro-life radical, and was regarded by some as an important national leader in Operation Rescue. Privately at least, she had always acknowledged the complications of abortion—how it was a reflection of the conflicting values of the culture and the private desperation of individual women. But she also thought it was simple at its core: These were babies being killed in the clinics, tiny human beings with fingers, toes, and a heart—and perhaps more terrible in a great many cases, the ability to feel pain as they were being ripped apart. She knew that many people didn't see it that way, but she was also convinced that if they did—if they could somehow see the evidence for themselves—then the pressure would build for abortion to stop. That was essentially her article of faith, and if it was wrong, what hope was there anyway?

So in the summer of 1992, she set out to prove it. She and several other people from the movement began sifting through the contents of plastic bags they had found in the dumpster of an abortion clinic in Charlotte, the city where she lived. She says they made seven expeditions in all, and on every one their discoveries were appalling. They found discarded medical waste—bloody sheets and suction bags, and inside the bags there were pieces of tissue, many of them recognizable as human.

One night in August, she took two reporters on the expedition with her. They found a human hand in one bag—a right hand, two and a half inches from elbow to fingertip. The thumb was distinct from the other four fingers. The fingernails were tiny. They also found a left foot and a hand with a broken forearm and a right foot torn and severed at the ankle. The reporters wrote the story in two different papers—the *Charlotte Observer* and *Creative Loafing*—and Graham was expectant, hoping that at last her message was clear. But the operators of the clinic fought back, suggesting that Graham and other pro-life zealots had planted the material in the dumpster themselves. She tried to argue that the charge was absurd. As the reporters who wrote the original stories could attest, these weren't body parts taken from a jar. The blood from the abortions was not yet dry. "We couldn't have planted this material," she said, "unless we performed the abortions ourselves."

But it seemed that almost nobody believed her, and the story quickly died with no apparent change in the public attitude. For Graham it was a startling moment of truth—evidence of the power of the backlash against her, created in part by her movement's own failures: its insensitivity and shrillness and the scattered acts of violence by people on the fringe. In the months after that, the backlash grew, with the Clinton administration coming to power and signing tougher laws against abortion protests. By the summer of 1994, Graham was slowly but surely becoming disillusioned, frustrated with the struggle and her own place in it.

"We have been stonewalled," she said. "We are at this turning point in the movement, whether we want to face it or not. I have to ask myself now, why am I in this? What is my role?"

In her search for answers she came in May 1993 to the wind-blown cemetery at Belmont Abbey, where they had buried the remains of the babies from the dumpster. Squatting there beside the granite headstone, which had no names, unlike the other markers around it, she sifted through the memories of her lonely crusade and hoped that maybe the answers might come. She knew it was an unlikely role in the first place. Private and shy, Karen Graham was never meant to be a public figure. She was a frail-looking woman of twenty-nine—five-feet-six and about a hundred pounds. She was born in Florida but raised in Charlotte by her mother, before entering the University of Florida. There, she took her bachelor's degree in journalism and often thought of herself as a liberal. She was opposed to capital punishment as well as abortion, called herself a pacifist, and chafed at the sexism she saw all around her.

But at the University of Florida she began to brood about the subject of abortion. She says it took on a reality one night when she saw a fetus that someone had thrown in a dumpster. "I got there about the same time as the police," she remembers, "and there it was, lying on a blanket on the ground. We couldn't tell for sure if it was a miscarriage or an abortion. But the baby was a girl."

When she graduated in 1988, with the issue of abortion now on her mind, she went to Atlanta to offer her support to Operation Rescue. The organization was making its first wave of headlines, blockading the doors to abortion clinics while the media was in town for the Democratic National Convention. During the week that Graham arrived, the frustration of Atlanta's police boiled over. They had already spent more than thirty-eight thousand man-hours and a half-million dollars hauling protesters away from clinic doors. The police decided to take off the gloves. As screams rang out through the streets of downtown, the officers did the work that they had been assigned, twisting arms, gouging pressure points on the demonstrators' necks.

"We know," explained one officer in charge, "how to get people from point A to point B."

Whether it was the drama of the moment or the theology that was preached in the Rescue rallies—a theology of sacrifice and a resistance to the lures of self-righteousness and pride—Graham was hooked. Later, she would see a widening gap between the preaching and the practice of many people in the movement, including its leaders. But in the autumn of 1988, she said she saw it as "a move of God."

She came home to Charlotte, and on October 29, 1988, she organized the first in a series of rescues. They were often tense and chaotic affairs, with protesters swarming toward the doors of the clinics, then lying inert as policemen hauled them away on stretchers. With the passage of time, and the rise of frustration and anger in the streets, Graham found herself becoming more shrill. "They like to kill babies!" she began to scream, and many of her opponents came to see her as extreme. More than that, they regarded her tactics as a final indignity against women whose lives were already full of pain.

Graham understood that there is truth in the charge. She remembered one scene from a clinic in Atlanta, when three young women arrived for abortions, looking pale and terrified, as they were led through a crowd of Rescue demonstrators. One of the women held her jacket to cover her face, the way criminals often do in the presence of a camera, while the protesters screamed, "Don't kill your baby!" Privately at least, Graham admitted that insensitivity to women was one of the great failings of the anti-abortion movement. Too many times, she said years later, she had seen disdain rather than compassion for women who were pregnant and didn't want to be. But she also turned the issue around. "A lot of feminists," she argued, "seem to be saying that women are strong and can handle anything—except a pregnancy that they didn't intend."

In the early days, Graham saw her movement as having deep roots, reaching back at least to the Underground Railroad—the attempt to free black slaves just before the Civil War. In Graham's mind, the analogy was this: The people who supported the Underground Railroad went beyond a simple advocacy of abolition. They broke the law, risking their lives or time in prison to help the runaways make it to freedom.

That, she said, was essentially the stance of Operation Rescue— an attempt to save the lives of unborn children, even if it meant defying civil law.

But there was another analogy from the days of abolition. The ultimate casualty of that crusade was the plantation economy of the antebellum South—a fact that produced powerful arguments of necessity. So it was also with the pro-choice side of the debate on abortion—which argued not that abortion was good but that terrible, real-life circumstances sometimes made it simply the least tragic option.

"That's the point they don't understand," said one young woman, standing on the fringes of one of Graham's demonstrations. She explained to a reporter that she had once been raped—impregnated by a man who had been her husband. But despite the horror of that ordeal, she said she decided in the end to keep the baby. "I couldn't do it," she explained. "I couldn't bring myself to get an abortion. But I'm also a clinical psychologist. I hear the stories all the time of women who are raped, or abandoned, or young girls overwhelmed by an older boyfriend. I have my own views. But I can't impose them on other people in a crisis. So I guess I believe in the morality of choice."

So do most Americans, and it was against that reality that the anti-abortion movement finally stalled, splintering into factions in the dispute over tactics. The most extreme of those factions favored an escalation into violence. According to abortion rights activists, there were at least thirty-six bombings at abortion clinics between 1977 and 1993—an average of more than two bombings a year. And then came the killings—a string of seven assassinations nationwide, including two on the morning of July 29, 1994.

When Karen Graham heard the news that day, she was not surprised. She had had her own encounter with the killer, a defrocked Presbyterian minister by the name of Paul Hill. She had known for months he intended to kill, and now he had finally made good on his threat. He had waited outside an abortion clinic in Pensacola, Florida, a 12-gauge shotgun cradled at his side, and at seven thirty in the morning, he had opened fire. He killed Dr. John Britton and a man who was with him and shouted defiantly as police arrived to carry him away: "One thing is for sure, no innocent babies will die in that clinic today!"

When Graham heard the reports, she thought back to a time a few months earlier when she was working in the city of Jackson, Mississippi, helping to coordinate a pro-life protest. Hill was there, and he had refused to sign the pledge of nonviolence that Graham and the other organizers were demanding. Graham understood that Hill was serious. There was something about his dark brown eyes, something in the chilling certainty of his stare that made it clear he was moving toward violence.

"This needs to be denounced and stopped," Graham told one reporter. "It makes no sense to shoot someone and claim to be pro-life. But the level of frustration is much higher today. You have people now talking themselves into believing that what we need to do is become violent." For Graham it was a line that couldn't be crossed, and that day in Jackson, she and two other pro-life leaders walked with the abortion doctor to the clinic. They put themselves deliberately between Paul Hill and the man they believed he was planning to kill. "It was terrifying," said Graham. And although violence was averted that day, her terror and revulsion came swirling back after Hill made good on his threats in Pensacola.

Soon after that, she began to back away. So much had changed since she joined the movement in 1988. Some of its moral clarity had been lost, blurred by deep frustrations in the ranks, and later by a theology she didn't fully share. By the middle of 1990s, there were many in the ranks of Operation Rescue who wanted to expand their focus of concern to include opposition to homosexuality. "My focus was much more narrow," said Graham. "There are all kinds of sin, and none of us are free. The reason I felt abortion was different—worth putting myself and others in danger—was because a life was at stake. The child was not making a choice to die.

"So I was still pro-life and still am today, but I began to think that maybe I wasn't the person to try to be a leader in the movement anymore. I really thought when I got into it that we would be able to change people's hearts and minds, and I would work myself out of a job. But then all sides began to try to use killing as the answer. Paul Hill did it, and so did the state of Florida when it sentenced him to die. If you are really pro-life, I think it has to be a seamless garment. 'The least of these' are also the criminals in prison, and who are we to play God and decide who should live and who should die? If God is really the giver of life and holds us all in his hands, that's a message of hope, not hate. But in our culture today, and the culture of the world, that's not an easy message to get across."

In the wake of her own political disillusionment, Graham continued to work around the edges of the movement, supporting organizations for unwed mothers and for children born into hard circumstances—poverty, disease, or the culture of drugs. Much more privately, there were also the days in her search for perspective when she returned to the cemetery at Belmont Abbey, standing there beside the gray granite marker with no names on it. "There are 128 babies buried here," she said. "They are together now in one grave. I still believe if we can make them human, the people out there will not want to kill them."

But Graham admitted that it might not happen, for even she, in her unintended way, denied the humanity she was seeking to proclaim. Back in 1992, after gathering the remains from the dumpster at the clinic, she had kept them floating for months in a jar, seeing them as possible evidence in a trial, not as human beings in need of a funeral.

But now that error had been corrected, and she said there were others she was working on as well. She recounted a trip she had taken to Norway for pro-life protests during the Winter Olympics. The Norwegian pastors that she met on that occasion had a different philosophy from those in this country—a longer view of history perhaps, as well as a different understanding of God. These were gentler people, less given to extremes, and as Graham put it, "They didn't seem to worship our American God, who's only into winning."

She also remembered the story of Will Campbell, the renegade Baptist preacher from Tennessee who had been asked by a group of civil rights activists—people frustrated by the slow pace of change—what he thought they ought to do next.

"Do?" said Campbell. "Nothing, just be."

Graham smiled as she recounted the story. She said there were days when she still felt guilty about the decision she had made out of self-preservation to try to live a more normal life. But in the end, there was simply no choice. She accepted a job in the corporate world and shared an apartment with her golden retriever, and if she was exhausted now from her years in the movement, and more sober about the ways of the world, she still had her faith in the mysteries of God.

That, she said, was a gift that was simply too important to lose.

Part salesman, part Christian activist, <u>Millard Fuller</u> was the founder of Habitat for Humanity, one of the most remarkable success stories in American philanthropy. After a sputtering start in the 1960s, Habitat soon became an international organization, mobilizing volunteers in every corner of the world to help build livable houses for the poor. The story that follows recounts the birth of the Habitat idea. It's a story full of irony and sadness but one that took a turn toward redemption at a Christian commune in southwest Georgia.

Koinonia: The Birth
of Habitat for Humanity

It began essentially with a broken heart. Linda Fuller sat on her bed with her husband beside her—a stricken look in his eyes as he listened in disbelief to her words. She said she was going away for a while. She needed time to think, to try to decide whether their marriage had a future.

Millard tried to argue with her at first. He talked about the house and the farm, the place at the lake, and the Lincoln Continental parked outside. What more could she want, he demanded to know. Linda merely sighed. She wanted to shake him, to run out the door—anything to escape this terrible blindness, his maddening inability to see or understand. Millard was a man with a one-track mind, a workaholic husband who, at the start, intended to be a good provider but became caught up in the demands of his work. Now it seemed that they were drowning in things—the symbols of wealth— and she felt as though she hardly knew him anymore. He was never at home, never there to listen or take her in his arms or chase away the lonely feelings in her heart.

It hadn't been that way at first. When she met him that day in 1958, at her house in Tuscaloosa, Alabama, he was courtly and kind, a gangly law student full of energy and charm, a man who could stir the fires in a girl of seventeen. Not that she was looking to fall in love. Mostly, she wanted somebody to be with. Her father, like Millard, was a hardworking man, a stranger sometimes in his own household. Linda was lonesome and Millard was tall, which was one of the things she liked in a boy, and they walked and talked, and he listened in a way that nobody ever had.

But there were warning signs even from the start. Their very introduction was a reflection of one of his manic obsessions, for he had called her looking for somebody else—a girl named Joan that he had met at a theater. He thought her last name might be Caldwell, which happened to be Linda's last name as well, and he was calling every Caldwell number in the book. When he came to Linda, they began to chat, and Millard abruptly called off his search, deciding instead that Linda was his girl.

It was a strange beginning, but after a while it didn't seem out of character. Millard's attention span was short. His mind could drift in the middle of a sentence; yet sometimes he could be so focused, so intense and energetic, capable of getting so absorbed in his work that he seemed to lose track of everything else. In the 1950s, Millard was a hustler. He and his law-school partner, Morris Dees, began a direct-mail company that sold holly wreaths, tractor cushions, doormats, and books—anything at all that might turn a profit. They stayed most often within the letter of the law, but they made their share of moral compromises.

These were tumultuous times in Alabama, when the civil rights movement was gaining momentum, and in deference to the prevailing opinion of the day, Millard was careful to speak out against it. During a political campaign in 1958, he made a speech to the Ku Klux Klan, telling these ominous men in their robes exactly what he thought they wanted to hear. He knew better, of course. In 1961, when the Freedom Riders made their way to Montgomery, Millard was sickened by the scene at the station—the mob that was waiting when the bus pulled in. It was May 20, a Saturday, when the twenty-one riders, black and white, began to disembark from the bus. There was an eerie silence for the first few seconds, and then the mob descended, screaming and beating anybody they could find. There were reports of families at the edge of the crowd lifting their children to "see the niggers run."

Millard Fuller was in the crowd that day, a bystander shocked at what he saw. The next morning, he made an entry in his diary recording his horror and noting that even as the violence grew worse, there were no policemen anywhere to stop it. Montgomery officials had made a deal with the Klan, simply deciding to let the whole thing happen. Fuller was disgusted, but, at least in 1961, he was not yet prepared to speak out against it. It pained him some to put it this way, but he knew that it wouldn't be good for his business.

There was nothing, of course, in that set of calculations to suggest the future directions of his life, and certainly Linda Fuller never gave it any thought—never pictured her husband as the leader of a great and quixotic crusade to eradicate the blight of substandard housing. All she saw in the 1960s was a self-centered man doing his best to make money, ignoring his wife and children in the process, and the time finally came when she could no longer stand it. On a November Saturday in 1965, she told him she was leaving, going away to New York to sort through her confusion. There was a minister there that she knew and trusted, and though she didn't tell Millard the whole story at the time, she carried some guilty feelings of her own.

For nearly two years, she had been seeing another man. At least for a while, the stolen moments had given her relief, and they were always easy enough to arrange. Millard was much too busy to notice. But she also knew it was no way to live, for a woman either loved her husband or she didn't, and an affair, she decided as she left for New York, was not a good substitute for a marriage.

She went away on a Sunday, and Millard was left to deal with his pain. He was an extrovert, not given to introspection, but suddenly the thought of losing his wife was almost more than his system could bear. "I was in agony," he remembered years later. "Never before or since have I suffered like that." Prowling through the empty rooms of his house, he cringed at the image staring back in the mirrors— the image of failure dressed up as success—and after a week he could no longer stand it. He pleaded with Linda to let him come to New York, and with a little hesitation, she finally agreed.

Many years later, she remembered the frightened look on his face—the fear in his eyes as he walked through the door of the Wellington Hotel. It was not a look she had seen very often—not in her husband's eyes at least—but as he stood before her in his black overcoat, he seemed to be moving in a slow-motion fog, and the thought flashed quickly across her mind that it looked like death had walked through the door. Their conversation was awkward at first, and that night in an effort to lighten things up, they decided to go out together for a movie. It was a comedy, as Millard remembered it later, but as soon as it was over, Linda burst into tears—deep and uncontrollable sobs that only grew worse as Millard led her outside and they began to walk the streets of New York. Now it was Linda's turn to be afraid. She knew she was about to offer her confession, and she gathered her nerve as they settled on the steps of Saint Patrick's Cathedral. "I thought he would walk away," she remembers, but instead he reached out and took her in his arms, and as the people hurried by on the Manhattan sidewalk, the two of them sat there together and wept.

She saw a different side of Millard Fuller that night. He was stronger than she ever knew he could be, and loved her more, and as part of his commitment to a different kind of life, he told her he was willing to give away his business. Actually, he said, he was planning to sell it and give away the money to people in need, and he vowed that never again in his life would he allow himself to be a prisoner of greed. He had always thought of himself as a Christian, and he told her that night in their hotel room that the time had come to live like he meant it.

Linda was a little bit skeptical at first. Despite her gratitude and relief, and a flood of affection that took her by surprise, she knew such conversions don't always last. But as the weeks went by, she could see he was different. Strangely enough, he seemed more relaxed as he gave away his money. He spent a few dollars on the members of his family, paying for repairs on his father's house, but the rest went to charity as he began to seek a new focus for his life.

Characteristically, he was once again full of energy and hope, bursting periodically into a repertoire of hymns, more certain every day that they had set out together on a journey of faith. His old friends thought he had lost his mind, telling him so with whatever honesty and discretion they could muster; but Millard had never felt saner in his life. He was beginning to spend more time with his family, and in December 1965, he and Linda and the children, Chris and Kim, set out for Florida in a crowded Continental that now contained everything they owned. They spent a few weeks just being together, and on their way back home they stopped for the night in Albany, Georgia. Millard remembered a couple of old friends,

Al and Carol Henry, that he knew were living on a farm nearby. It was a Christian community with a funny Greek name—Koinonia, or something like that—but he wasn't sure how to spell it, and it took him a while to track down the number.

It was startling to wonder in the years after that exactly what might have happened if he hadn't made the effort. There was no way to know when he got his friends on the phone that this was a pivotal moment in his life. They invited him to come to the farm for a visit, and Millard was drawn to the place from the start. It was nestled in the curve of a two-lane road, where the soil was rich and the land gently rolled, and the peanut fields gave way slowly to groves of pecans. There was a concrete-block house set back in the trees, where the farm people gathered for their midday meal. It was modest fare, served in a community dining room, the residents using apple crates for chairs. One of the men at the table that day was a ruddy-looking farmer with faded jeans, a threadbare shirt, and work boots laced up nearly to his knees.

"That's Clarence Jordan," somebody said, and there was awe in the voice. Soon, the Fullers could understand why. They learned that Clarence founded Koinonia in the summer of 1942, choosing four hundred acres of eroded farmland in Sumter County, Georgia, not too far away from his boyhood home. At the time, Clarence was a Southern Baptist preacher, trained at the seminary in Louisville. He was a tallish man at more than six feet, with a wry sense of humor and a love of good stories. He found a few of those in the Bible, and as he began his study of the Greek New Testament, he was intrigued especially by the book of Acts. The apostles were radical people, he decided—socialists, in fact, committed to sharing everything they owned: *Now the company of those who believed were of one heart and soul, and no one said that any of the things which he possessed was his own, but they had everything in common.*

It was all right there in the pages of his Bible, and Clarence kept wondering in his seminary years whether those ideas were quaint and obsolete, or whether they could work in the twentieth century. There were other notions, too, that he thought were important: the basic ideals of brotherhood and faith, which were evaded every day in the Jim Crow South—rationalized and rendered hypocritical by his neighbors in southwest Georgia and beyond. Clarence was offended by that, and with the help of his friends at Koinonia Farm, he decided that the time had come to make a stand. His neighbors up the road didn't like his ideas very much, particularly when he raised the issue of race—which he did in simple and straightforward ways. When he hired a black man to work on the farm, they ate lunch together, and word quickly spread around Sumter County of white men taking their meals with a Negro.

One day, the Klan paid a call at Koinonia. It was almost dusk, the sun sinking slowly toward the fields in the west, as four or five men disembarked from their car.

"We're looking for Jordan," one of them said.

Clarence smiled and offered his hand, but the Klan delegation was not feeling social.

"We're here to tell you," said the leader of the group, "we don't allow the sun to set on any white man who eats with a nigger."

Clarence, so the story goes, didn't say anything at first. He stole a quick glance at the western horizon, then turned his attention back to his guests. There was an aura of small-town meanness about them. He had seen it before—most often, he thought, among men who were frightened and didn't want to show it. Clarence searched his mind for the right words to say. He understood clearly that the danger was real, for fear was a volatile emotion in the South, and there was plenty of it going around that day.

Finally he smiled and reached out again for the calloused hand of the Klansman. "I'm a Baptist preacher," he said, "and I've heard of men with power over the sun. But until today I never hoped to meet one."

Millard Fuller chuckled when he heard the story, and he thought their visit to Koinonia Farm might turn out to be something special. He had never met anybody like Clarence, who was earthy and irreverent, with a hint of mischief in his pale blue eyes—and yet somehow he seemed so devout. Millard was eager to know more about him, and when lunch was over, he turned to Linda and told her with a mixture of piety and surprise: "I think God has brought us here."

The next several years seemed to justify his faith. The relationship grew between Millard and Clarence, and they began to talk about conditions in the South. Among other things, there was a critical shortage of low-cost housing. They could see it every day in Sumter County, and Clarence suggested that they start building houses—good, solid structures without any frills—that poor people could buy through no-interest loans. In several different places, the Bible was clear: If you loan money to the poor, don't charge any interest. Clarence thought the Bible meant what it said, and without interest payments to drive up the cost, a lot of poor people could afford to own a home.

It seemed like a radical idea at the time, and Millard and Clarence liked to see it that way—as a bold assault in the name of their faith on one of the most basic conditions of injustice. Certainly, the results from the start were dramatic. Lillie Mae Bownes, for example, was one of the first homeowners—a domestic worker by trade, whose husband, Jonas, had a job at the sawmill. They had lived for years in a rundown cabin, where they gathered tin buckets at the sight of a cloud, placing them under the holes in their roof, hoping to catch at least a little of the rain. But the water poured in and the buckets overflowed, and they found themselves padding through the puddles on the floor.

And then in 1968, Millard, Clarence, and a team of volunteers worked alongside them to help build a house. On the day it was finished and they began to move in, Lillie Mae went searching through her mind for the words. "I feel like I'm just kinda flying," she declared, "flying with the Lord—catching the breeze of His good will."

After seeing such moments repeated many times, Millard knew this was an idea he could sell. He had always been a salesman at heart, and he had something now that was worth a lot more than all of that stuff he had peddled in the past.

Back in those days, his obsession with money had almost cost him everything that he valued—his integrity, his family, his physical health. Now, remarkably, those things were restored, and with the help of Clarence, he was beginning to envision a different kind of life, new channels for the energy that was stirring inside him, and the faith that was beginning to build in his heart.

Epilogue. For the first several years, Millard and Linda Fuller, along with Clarence Jordan, built houses for the poor in Sumter County. But after Clarence died in 1969 and was buried in a thicket of pines at Koinonia,

Millard channeled his grief, not to mention his restless resolve, into building on the Habitat idea. His organization, Habitat for Humanity, was formed officially in 1976, and in the 1980s, after Fuller enlisted the support of former president Jimmy Carter, Habitat soon became a household name. By 1996, when this piece was written, Habitat had built nearly fifty thousand houses in forty-eight countries, including twelve hundred communities in the United States.

Over the years, I've had the opportunity to write periodically about Jimmy Carter, a politician whose public agenda is tied inextricably to his faith. There have been many occasions in the course of his career, especially in his work for Habitat for Humanity, where his faith has won him great public acclaim. But there have been other times when those same Judeo-Christian beliefs—and the passion for justice he thinks they require—have led him into the lion's den of controversy. This is the story of one of Carter's most painful and controversial moments: the publication of a book that sharply criticizes the policies of Israel. Even many of his admirers felt betrayed, but Carter, typically, pushed doggedly ahead—certain as always that history and justice would vindicate his views.

The Lion's Den and Jimmy Carter

Jimmy Carter, the Christian crusader for peace, stood before his Brandeis University audience, gazing out across nearly two thousand faces as he prepared to defend his criticism of Israel. It was January 2007, and Carter was promoting his twenty-first book, a treatise on peace in the Middle East with a title that was certain to set off a firestorm: *Palestine: Peace Not Apartheid*. Carter was not the first to use that analogy. At least two other Nobel laureates, Nelson Mandela and Desmond Tutu, had visited the West Bank and the Gaza Strip and compared the travail of the Palestinians to the system of oppression in their native South Africa. And reporters who had covered the Middle East had heard the same conversation in Israel.

As the Carter controversy unfolded, I thought of my own trip in the 1980s. I had been to the West Bank and had seen an old Palestinian man plowing in his field behind a swaybacked mule. A few feet away, Israeli steam shovels were carving up his land, ripping out his olive trees to make way for a settlement, while the old man protested in the only way he knew—by continuing to plow.

A few days later in a hilltop community in the Galilee, I mentioned that scene to a family of Jewish immigrants to Israel, people who had recently arrived from South Africa. They winced at the story and began to talk about their own disillusionment. Though intensely proud of their Jewish heritage, they had come to Israel, they said, primarily to get away from apartheid, a system of injustice that they knew was crumbling. But now they saw the spread of Jewish settlements in the Palestinian territories, with oppression the inevitable price of security. Like Mandela and Tutu, and later Jimmy Carter, they compared these developments—and the denial of Palestinian rights by Israelis—to the system of apartheid they had known in South Africa.

Nevertheless, for many Americans in 2007, the title of Jimmy Carter's book was a shock. Because of the climate in the United States, that low-grade dread and awareness of terror that citizens of this country shared with Israelis, Carter's evocation of the sins of South Africa triggered a rage more intense than he had expected. Alan Dershowitz, a Jewish attorney and law professor at Harvard, accused him of writing "an indecent book" filled with "hyperbole and overstatement" and demonstrating "bias against Israel." Dershowitz said Carter's use of the term "apartheid" was "especially outrageous."

Responding during an interview on *Larry King Live*, Carter at first refused to back away from either the tone or the substance of the book. "The oppression of Palestinians by Israeli forces . . . is horrendous," he said, "one of the worst cases of oppression I know of." Carter said he knew when he wrote it that the book was certain to be controversial. But that, he added, was precisely the point—"to precipitate some controversy . . . to promote debate," particularly within the United States, where the issue, so often, was simply brushed aside.

And yet Carter seemed stunned as the denunciations grew more heated. In response to the book, fourteen Jewish members resigned en masse from the Carter Center's advisory board, withdrawing with dismay and a sense of betrayal from a mission that all of them had admired. They had supported Carter's postpresidential crusades—his battle against the ravages of third world disease, his support of democracy in developing nations, his personal diplomacy to the world's trouble spots. But now with the release of the Palestine book, Carter was suddenly and immediately a pariah. Kenneth Stein, who had once been his Middle Eastern adviser, called the book "one-sided" and "replete with factual errors," and said the title was "too inflammatory even to print." And Deborah Lipstadt, a professor of Holocaust studies at Emory University, where the Carter Center is based, charged that the former president's book "trivialized the murder of Israelis."

In the wake of those attacks, Carter accepted an invitation to speak at Brandeis, the predominantly Jewish university in Massachusetts, and set out to repair at least some of the damage. On January 23, 2007, he began his talk by outlining his reverence for Jewish history—both the Old Testament stories that he had grown up with and essentially memorized in his Sunday School classes and the more recent example of Louis Brandeis, the man for whom the university was named. Carter praised Brandeis, who in 1916 became the first Jewish member of the U.S. Supreme Court, both for his advocacy of freedom of speech and his activist support for the founding of Israel.

Carter spoke also about his presidential decision to create a national Holocaust Museum, with a commission chaired by Elie Wiesel, the Nobel Laureate and Holocaust survivor whom he had long regarded as a friend. "I understand completely," Carter continued, "the fear among many Israelis that threats still exist against their safety and even their existence as a nation. During all these years . . . I have reiterated my strong condemnation of any acts of terrorism, which are not justified at any time or for any goal. I have spent a great deal of my adult life trying to bring peace to Israel and its neighbors, based on justice and righteousness for the Palestinians."

But at Brandeis, as he had in other places, Carter reiterated his criticism of Israeli policies toward the West Bank. Israel's settlements, he said, had taken "choice hilltops, vital water resources, and productive land," and that confiscation, along with a forty-foot security wall through much of the Palestinian territory, "makes the lives of Palestinians almost intolerable."

It seemed clear enough as Carter spoke that he saw the Middle East through a southerner's eyes. He had come of age in the rural South during a time of racial segregation—of second-class standing for a whole group of people, and the easy rationalizations of their neighbors in power. As with many other white southerners of conscience, he could identify with the oppressors as well as the oppressed, and that instinctive, double-edged understanding had made his indignation even stronger. And for Carter, in a deep and personal way, it was all underscored by his reading of the Bible—particularly the Hebrew prophets, who spoke of justice "rolling down like water, and righteousness like a mighty stream."

As Abraham Heschel, the great Jewish theologian and author, once wrote, "The prophet is a man who feels fiercely," and Carter himself had a bit of that passion. The Camp David Accords, bringing peace between Israel and Egypt, had been his greatest achievement as president, the result of his own ferocious lobbying of Menachem Begin and Anwar Sadat. And even when he failed to win re-election his obsession with the Middle East continued. In 1990, he met with Yasir Arafat in Paris and argued fervently that it was time to make peace—time for Arafat to recognize Israel and renounce terrorism once and for all. But he also spoke of Palestinian suffering, indignities he had seen firsthand, and he told the chairman of the PLO: "This is an obsession with me." Arafat and Carter talked often after that, and three years later when the PLO recognized Israel in the Oslo accords, the historian Douglas Brinkley, among many others, thought it was a monument to the tenacity of Jimmy Carter.

"Carter," Brinkley wrote, "pressed harder and more consistently for a political solution to the Arab-Israeli impasse than any other diplomat on the world stage. Even when he had no official role, he never let up. . . . Carter had been ruthless in the pursuit of peace."

When Brinkley wrote those words in *The Unfinished Presidency*, a book that was published in 1998, the public understanding of the former president was still very different from the portrait of stubbornness Brinkley sought to unveil. Ever since the 1980s, when Carter, as former president, began his heralded work for Habitat for Humanity, what most people saw was his Christian compassion; for there he was in the hot summer sun, sweating alongside a low-income family, helping with his own skilled carpenter's hands to build them a house.

I worked twice with Carter on those kinds of projects, and the one I remember most clearly was in Watts. In the heart of the nation's most famous ghetto, Carter and several dozen other volunteers worked with the family of Toni Miller, a single mother full of dignity and pride who wanted a stable home for her children. When the house was completed, Carter presented Miller with a Bible, and the new homeowner, who had carried herself all week with reserve, became choked with emotion and unable to speak. A tear drifted softly down her cheek, and when her son reached out to brush it away, Carter, also visibly moved, reached out gently to touch her on the arm. It was, said Miller, a moment that added new meaning to her life.

For Carter, such occasions were never just photo-ops, a feel-good moment to share with the world. They were part of a commitment that came from his core. "How many of us," he asked one audience of Habitat supporters, "have done something for other people that caused a real sacrifice for ourselves? One of the most disturbing things in the Bible was when Jesus declared late in life, 'Inasmuch as you have done it unto the least of these my brethren, you have done it unto me.' What that means is that as we are aware of hunger, homelessness and other human needs and do nothing about them, that is an expression of our actual attitude toward Jesus Christ."

According to the people who know him the best, that in part is the real Jimmy Carter—a latter-day New Testament apostle who sees the panoply of human needs squarely in the light of his own Christian faith. For many Americans, it's a warm and reassuring reality, but it is also only one part of the story, one piece of the character of a complicated man. In addition to his work with Habitat, or his fight against the scourge of third world disease, Carter has been a battler in the cause of peace. That mission, ironically enough, has provided a glimpse of his difficult side: his stubbornness, tenacity and, some critics say, an arrogance undergirding his will to succeed.

In 1994, for example, he set out essentially on a one-man mission to head off a war on the Korean peninsula. He managed to persuade the North Koreans to abandon work on their nuclear program but then insisted on announcing that accomplishment himself—on CNN, before the Clinton administration had approved it. When Clinton grew angry at Carter's presumption, Carter fired back, incensed by Clinton's ingratitude. The strain between them lingers even now.

Even some of Carter's friends will acknowledge that the pattern has been a problem for him all along—a combination of certainty and self-righteousness that leads him periodically into pointless disputes that a subtler, more nimble politician might avoid. James David Barber, in his ground-breaking book *The Presidential Character*, writes about how Carter in his early career campaigned with "a rhetoric of indignation." He attacked the motives of his political opponents and presented himself as the upright alternative, a politician, at last, who could survive the moral scrutiny of the people. And the image, of course, was based on the truth, for Carter *was* more ethical than most politicians. But even as president, there were times, it seemed, when he was blinded by the light of his own integrity—and his own particular understanding of the truth.

"Jimmy Carter as a person," said William Greider, former national editor of the *Washington Post*, "is so immensely confident of his virtue and good intentions; that's the anchor he has. But . . . people can't see into his heart."

Instead, what many people have seen is a kind of tone-deaf arrogance as Carter, on occasion, has gone his own way and said the things he thought needed saying, without a clear view of how they might be perceived. That was obviously true with his Palestine book.

For reasons that are easy enough to understand, Carter was certain of his views on the Middle East—especially the long and brutal standoff between Israel and Palestine. In the years since his presidency, he had been to the region many times and had seen the suffering of Palestinians firsthand. In *Palestine: Peace Not Apartheid*, he quotes the Israeli human rights organization B'Tselem, which criticized Israeli policies, including the demolition of Palestinian houses: "Israel's policy of punitive demolitions constitutes a grave breach of international humanitarian law, and therefore a war crime. Through a variety of legal gymnastics, Israel's High Court of Justice has avoided judicial scrutiny of the issue, serving as a rubber stamp for Israel's illegal policy."

Carter also criticizes Palestinian excesses, writing, for example, about suicide bombers: "Some Palestinians have responded to political and military occupation by launching terrorist attacks against Israeli civilians, a course of action that is both morally reprehensible and politically counterproductive. These dastardly acts have brought widespread condemnation and discredit on the entire Palestinian community—and are almost suicidal for the Palestinian cause."

But throughout the book, Carter's impatience with Israel is clear. On page after page, he criticizes "the minority of Israelis" who put West Bank settlements ahead of peace. "The bottom line is this," Carter writes. "Peace will come to Israel and the Middle East only when the Israeli government is willing to comply with international law and withdraw from the Palestinian territories. In the eyes of

Carter's critics, his distribution of blame was fundamentally unfair and essentially unsympathetic to Israel. As Emory's Deborah Lipstadt notes, the book makes only two references to the Holocaust and not many more to the specter of Iran—a country whose president, Mahmoud Ahmadinejad, is a Holocaust-denier on the brink of obtaining a nuclear weapon. Because of the terrors associated with such a possibility, Carter's pointed criticisms of Israel seemed outrageous to many Jewish leaders, and their anger, of course, was sealed by Carter's choice of title.

Far from the sparking the debate he had hoped, his apartheid reference, at least for a time, quelled any possibility of civil discussion. Carter himself became the focal point of debate, accused by his critics of everything from anti-Semitism to intellectual dishonesty. And yet he is, as one scholar put it after visiting the Carter Center in Atlanta, "a tough old bastard." With characteristic stubbornness, he soldiered ahead and defended his views, while trying to reach out to the Jewish community. One of the high points was his visit to Brandeis, where he was received in general with civility and respect. Two days later, one student told the *Jerusalem Post* that Carter's speech had "the potential to change the climate" when it came to discussing the policies of Israel. "Wherever you fall on the spectrum," the student, Shayna Weiss, continued, "it's important to see the human consequences of your decisions."

As the controversy rumbled through the winter and spring, there were a few scattered voices in Carter's defense. Paul Findley, a former Republican congressman from Illinois, wrote a column in the *Chicago Tribune*, declaring that "at the age of 82, Jimmy Carter entered the lion's den. . . . He deserves a hero's praise." And Chris Hedges, defending Carter in the *Nation*, maintained that if anything the former president didn't go far enough. "Carter's book exposes little about Israel," wrote Hedges, a former Middle East correspondent for the *New York Times*. "The enforced segregation, abject humiliation and spiraling Israeli violence against the Palestinians have been detailed in the Israeli and European press and, with remarkable consistency, by all the major human rights organizations. . . . The bleakness of life for Palestinians, especially in the Gaza Strip, is a mystery only to us."

For Carter, it was a mystery he intended to dispel, and he was convinced by the winter of 2007 that he had achieved part what he set out to do: He had forced a debate in the United States on the wisdom and justice of Israel's policies—policies that he thought were an obstacle to peace. To the extent he succeeded, it was probably true that only Carter could have done it. There were not many American leaders with the nerve—or, some might say, the self-righteous certainty of his own point of view—to plunge headlong into those troubled waters, risking his reputation in the process. But the debate that Carter set out to provoke lay, in a sense, at the heart of his legacy—the passionate pursuit of justice and peace, bolstered by the stubborn depth of his resolve.

It was, of course, a controversial legacy, made more so by the Palestine book. Even some of Carter's former admirers, who had once been plentiful in the Jewish community, believed he had damaged his standing in history. But it was a risk that Carter seemed willing to take, for he had long since rejected the role of elder states-man, the more traditional stance of holding himself somehow above the fray.

It would have been easy for him to do it—to play it safe in the closing years of his life, while waging his battles against poverty and disease—and with the exception of the far political right the admiration would have been overwhelming. Even in the midst of the Palestine controversy, Nicholas Kristof in the *New York Times* wrote about a visit by Carter to a village in Ethiopia, a scenic place with thatched-roof houses and a swift-flowing creek, but a place where the people were suffering from diseases most of the world had never heard of. The primary scourge in this particular village was a fly-borne malady called river blindness, and Carter was there to help provide a cure.

That had been a primary mission of the Carter Center, attacking diseases in the poorest places in the world, and for Carter himself the relief of that suffering had become a part of his definition of human rights: the right to be free not only from political oppression but from the crippling tyranny of sickness. In his column for the *Times* Kristof praised the results the Carter Center had achieved—the near eradication, for example, of the guinea worm plague that had afflicted hundreds of villages in Africa.

"At the end of the day," Kristof concluded, "this one-term president who left office a pariah in his own party will transform the lives of more people in more places over a longer period of time than any other recent president."

But despite such accolades and acclaim, Carter somehow could never play it safe, could never bring himself to stay clear of the controversies of the day. The last time I saw him, at the Carter Center in Atlanta, he was closing in on his eighty-second birthday, and I was struck by the first intimations of frailty—a stoop to the shoulders, a thinning of the hair. It seemed to me that all of that only made him more impatient, more determined to finish the work he had started, and the Middle East, of course, had always been near the top of his agenda. He made it clear as we talked on that morning in June that he still believed in the possibility of peace, for he had seen the yearning in every trip to the region—the ordinary people, Israeli and Palestinian, who hoped against hope for an end to the killing.

And of course there was also the matter of his faith. When he came to Brandeis, he spoke with feeling about "the Hebrew scriptures that I have taught on Sundays . . . since I was eighteen years old." In the English translation of those scriptures, he said, "the word 'justice' is mentioned 28 times and the word 'righteousness' 196 times." In the Middle East, he believes, those two qualities are prerequisites for peace, and an Israel reconnected to its "finest ideals" can still lead the way. Despite the provocative title of his book, and the predictable pain and outrage that followed, that, I'm convinced, is the message Jimmy Carter was seeking to convey.

PART III

Soundtracks

Sometime late in the 1960s, I began to get interested in country music. Part of it was the fact that I was living and going to school in Nashville, and eventually, by a kind of osmosis, I found myself ruminating on the lyrics— particularly those of the great <u>Johnny Cash</u>, who seemed to be, even at the time, <u>a powerful force of reconciliation</u>. I wrote about Cash several times, and the piece that follows, written in 2003, was published on the sad occasion of his death. It is my tribute to an American icon.

The Man in Black

It stands there on the left, a mile or two beyond the tacky frontiers of runaway suburbia, looking like an antebellum prop on a movie set. Unlike most recording studios in Nashville, which are jammed together in a spruced-up swatch of urban renewal turf, the House of Cash rises stately and alone against a backdrop of rolling Tennessee pastureland.

The grass is still bent from the dew, and the sound of a mockingbird echoes faintly across the hillsides as Johnny Cash's Cadillac glides into the parking lot. It is eight thirty in the morning, a time of day that he would have dreaded a few years back—during the seven or eight years when he would begin each day by gulping a handful of amphetamines. He wasn't too particular about the dosage, two or three at a time, ten or fifteen milligrams a pop, dexedrine, benzedrine, dexamyl. It didn't much matter as long as they did their thing—as long as they helped him get from one concert to the next on the long road trips, and then, finally, as long as they helped him exist from one miserable morning until the one that followed.

The side effects were predictably squalid. He would pace the floor until the desolate hours of semidawn, until finally barbiturates would bring him down and lull him into a nightmarish sleep. He developed a nervous twitch in his neck, and apparently in his brain as well, judging from some of the things he did as his metabolism ran its tortured course from uppers to downers and back again.

He was arrested and jailed seven times, on charges ranging from public drunkenness to buying drugs from illegal sources. On one of his stops in jail—in Carson City, Nevada—only an impromptu rendition of "Folsom Prison Blues" managed to pacify an unglued lumberjack whose avowed intention was to strangle his more famous cellmate.

He once crashed through a warning gate at a U.S. Navy bombing range and drove four miles across a live mine field in the Mojave Desert. He drove tractors over cliffs, wrecked half a dozen expensive cars, and tore up his marriage. Yet somehow he managed to survive until 1968, when, as Kris Kristofferson puts it, "he got him a good woman" and found himself reintroduced to Jesus.

That reintroduction became a bedrock for him, and in the process it gave his music a sense of mission that grows stronger and stronger as time goes by. Whether it's singing protest songs about the plight of Indians or doing free shows in racially tense prisons or donating time and testimonials to Billy Graham's crusades, Cash is essentially giving expression to a brand of back-home Christianity that is far more subtle than most people might expect.

"Yeah, I guess that's true. That is what I'm trying to do," he agrees, as he munches on an apple in his wood-paneled office, his features ruddy and relaxed, and his trim, two-hundred-pound frame draped into an easy chair.

Cash does not give many interviews these days, but when he does, he participates fully and shows no traces of superstar pre-tensions. In the early stages, in fact, his voice will display just a hint of the butterfly tremors that are there around the edges when he walks on stage before five thousand people. But launching into an answer is like launching into a song, and his presence becomes certain and commanding as he begins to discuss, say, the relationship between his religion and his legendary concerts at several dozen prisons.

"The only prison concert I ever got paid for," he explains in a baritone voice that's as rich and ringing up close as it is on record, "was the one I did in Huntsville, Texas, in 1957. I took the show to the other ones free, I hope, as my Christianity in action. I don't usually talk about that, and I wouldn't now if you hadn't asked me. I don't think a Christian oughta brag about his deeds, and anyway it's something that's meant a lot to me."

He peels off another chunk of apple with his black-handled pocketknife and then begins warming to the subject. "There are a lot of people who don't understand what's happened to me," he says.

"They say Cash used to be tough and now he's soft. The truth is I'm a lot tougher now. What those people don't understand is that the old Johnny Cash would have literally died in sixty-six or sixty-seven if it hadn't been for faith.

"Faith is the foundation of everything I do. It's what I am. It always has been, really. There was just a time when I wasn't living it very well."

Cash does not usually begin such monologues on his own. He is not a heavy-handed proselytizer, for he understands full well the tedium of holier-than-thou sermons. But his Christianity is a serious thing, as are the morals and values that have been tied up with it ever since his boyhood days in Dyess, Arkansas.

He grew up in a five-room, wood-frame house in the sultry cotton country of the delta. The depression was in full force, but his father, Ray Cash, always seemed to make enough of a crop to feed his own family and to bail out needy neighbors as well.

Dyess, as it happened, was a New Deal experiment—a socialistic farmers' cooperative with a store, cotton gin, and cannery that belonged to the farmers themselves. According to the plan, the co-op members would bring their edible crops to the cannery, and after the processing was completed they would get back eight of every ten cans. The other two would be sold to keep the project going, and if there were any profits at the end of the year, the co-op members would divide them.

The work-weary farmers didn't give much thought to economic theories. But young John Cash was deeply influenced—permanently, as it turned out—by a curious meshing of the Protestant work ethic, a Golden Rule empathy for people in need, and the gritty fundamentalism of an Arkansas Church of God.

All of that has stamped his music with a distinctive tension, a creative tug-of-war between toughness and sentimentality, idealism and earthiness that has enabled him to reach an impressive array of people and emotions. He could stroll onstage at San Quentin, for example, and sing a few old spirituals like "Peace in the Valley," tugging on the heartstrings and the latent, laid-away softness that does not usually show itself behind the walls of a prison—and then he could break suddenly into one of the most ruthless and hard-hitting prison songs that many of the inmates had ever heard, "San Quentin, I Hate Every Inch of You."

Cash saw no contradiction between the feelings expressed in the spirituals and in the prison songs, or for that matter between the various kinds of stages where he was asked to play—from Richard Nixon's White House to the Ryman Auditorium to the annual folk festival in Newport, Rhode Island. It all fit together deep in his instincts, and to understand how, it helped to spend an unhurried hour or two in his tastefully posh, second-floor office at the House of Cash.

The trappings around the room could tell you a lot—a Holy Bible in the middle of a heavy oak coffee table, and next to it a paperback collection of Appalachian protest songs, *Voices from the Mountains.* On a table off to the side is a stack of testimonial books from born-again Christians, and on the wall behind his desk are five color photographs that he took himself. Three are close-ups of his family—his second wife, June, and his young son, John Carter; and then a pair of nature shots that may or may not be intentionally symbolic—a hummingbird hovering near a dew-covered blossom, and a gnarled and wind-blown cottonwood tree, clinging to life in a New Mexico desert.

Still another photograph, less predictable than the rest, leans next to the desk in a stained wooden frame. It's an autographed enlargement of a Bob Dylan album cover, with an inscription that reads, "To John and June, Love, Bob Dylan."

It turns out that Dylan and Cash go back a long way, to the 1960s when the fans of folk and the fans of country found themselves on opposite sides of a chasm—one group focusing on the nation's shortcomings, the other on its promise. The folkies were younger and luckier. They had that crucial combination of intelligence, sensitivity, and economic security that made it possible to question the status quo; and when they did, in a time of war and civil rights protests, they found a lot of answers that were not very satisfying. The fans of country, meanwhile, had come out the other side of a ferocious depression and a couple of wars with their patriotism stirred and their standard of living on a steady path upward. They not only believed, they *knew* that things in the country couldn't be as bad as its critics were contending. They became increasingly defensive and bitter, and before the shouting match was over it brought out some of the ugliest instincts that both sides had to offer.

At least that was generally true. But there were, of course, exceptions, and Cash was among them. He saw no problem in focusing on problems as well as prosperity, believing that the commonality of the American experience went deeper than even the most serious of political divisions. He came at that understanding through his musical intuitions, and the process began in earnest back in 1962, when Columbia Records released an album entitled *The Free-Wheelin' Bob Dylan*.

It contained some of Dylan's best-known originals—"Blowin' in the Wind," "Don't Think Twice" (which Cash later recorded), and a bitter protest anthem called "Masters of War." All of them were done in Dylan's peculiar, talking-blues style that soon turned the folk world on its ear.

Cash, however, heard the album a little bit differently from most of Dylan's other admirers. "I didn't know him back then," he remembers, casting a glance at Dylan's likeness, "but I liked the album so much I wrote him a letter—got his address from Columbia Records [which was also Cash's label] and I congratulated him on a fine country record. I could hear Jimmie Rodgers in his record, and Vernon Dalhart from back in the twenties, the whole talking-blues genre. I said, 'You're about the best country singer I've heard in years.'

"He wrote back and seemed kind of flabbergasted," Cash continues. "He said, 'I remember one time back in Hibbing, Minnesota, in 1957, you were there and I was one of the people out there listening.' He said, 'All during the fifties, it was you and Hank Williams.'"

The letters were the start of a steady correspondence that cemented a sense of soul brotherhood even before the two singers met at the Newport Folk Festival in 1963. Theirs quickly became one of the most remarkable friendships in American music, and in some ways one of the pivotal expressions of Dylan's humaneness and Cash's Christianity.

Both performers recognized that the political divisions between their fans were far from frivolous, tied as they were to such issues as war and peace and residues of prejudice. But in their music at least—and therefore in the deeper and instinctive aspirations of the people who listen—the two performers sensed a similar groping for the same universals. In addition to Dylan's nonpolitical songs of rambling, Cash could identify strongly with a peaceful anthem like "Blowin' in the Wind." He had recorded his share of songs just like it, and some that were even more obviously angry.

One of the angriest is "The Ballad of Ira Hayes," the story of a marine in World War II who had helped plant the flag on Iwo Jima hill. The photo of Old Glory on the rise became a classic, but as the song says, Hayes was "just a Pima Indian." He returned to the reservation, where jobs were scarce, and without either work or hope, he became a drunk. One night as he staggered home he passed out and drowned in an irrigation ditch with barely two inches of water in the bottom.

Cash recorded a whole album of songs about such Indian tragedies, but he also wrote and sang about other subjects that struck far closer to home for most of his audience. During the height of the protests against the war in Vietnam, he wrote a song called "What Is Truth?" offering a blunt chastisement of those who were closing their minds to the young.

The odd thing was that the song was a hit on the country charts, and the reason, Cash thinks, is that even in his most protesty songs, he never traveled far down the road to ideology—never let his music depart from its basically Christian, humane roots to become the political property of any one faction. But the factions didn't understand all of that, and they worked very hard to claim Cash as their own. Richard Nixon invited him to appear at the White House and, through H. R. (Bob) Haldeman, asked him to sing two of the most conservative songs of the era—Merle Haggard's "Okie from Muskogee" and a reactionary recitation called "Welfare Cadillac," written on a whim by an amateur songwriter named Guy Drake.

Cash politely refused to sing either song, much to the delight of his growing following of college kids. But much to their simultaneous disappointment, he pointedly refrained from criticizing either Nixon or the songs themselves, explaining instead that he didn't know "Welfare Cadillac," and that he was sure Nixon would soon invite Haggard himself to sing "Okie from Muskogee."

"I try not to become involved in politics," Cash explains today, and in a narrow sense that's certainly true. But in a larger sense it isn't, for Cash began to understand that people saw him as a reconciling force—a person whose music and presence could somehow reach beneath the anger and divisions.

The crowning symbol of that new mission became his television show on ABC. It began in the fall of 1969, and during two seasons it lasted Cash managed to plug such country artists as the Statler Brothers, Charley Pride, and a struggling young songwriter named Kris Kristofferson. But equally significant in his own mind was his attempt to introduce his country fans to the folk artists many of them might have expected to despise: Bob Dylan, Pete Seeger, Arlo Guthrie, and Judy Collins, to name a few.

"A lot of people got their first look at American folk on my country show," Cash remembers. "I thought at first we might get some flak for it, but we didn't really. I saw that country and folk had a lot in common."

There was nobody any better at proving the point. Many nights during the time of trouble in the country, Cash would wander onstage at the Grand Ole Opry, the late-night crowd moving toward the point where fatigue gives way to a round rebel yells. Clad in his ruffled white shirt and Lincolnesque dress suit, he would run through a kind of autobiography in song: from lonely-times ballads like Kristofferson's "Sunday Morning Coming Down" to the gospel songs of his later years, delivered in a voice that sounds as if it's welded to the lyrics.

During one of those appearances, on March 15, 1974—the last performance of the Grand Ole Opry before it moved to its slick new quarters at Opryland—Cash paused briefly in the middle of his set and ad-libbed an introduction to a pair of new songs. The first of the two was also the oldest, a personal anthem called "Man in Black," written in 1971 before a concert at Vanderbilt University. It was intended to be a statement of his political philosophy, and as the spotlight narrowed and focused on his face, these were the words he began to sing: *I wear the black of the poor and the beaten down, / Livin' in the hopeless, hungry side of town.*

As the lyrics poured out, the old men with wrinkled faces and the scabs of fresh razor nicks sat ramrod straight and squinted toward the stage as if it were crescendo time in the preacher's sermon. The good ole boys decided to ease off for a while on the rebel yells, and the ladies with the piled-up hair and the Instamatic cameras let their flashbulbs lie temporarily still.

Cash had gotten inside them the way he always does. But then, to underscore the point that he was still one of them, he quickly shifted gears and moved into a song called "Ragged Old Flag." It was a poignant pledge of allegiance, the story of an old man sitting in a small-town square, gazing at the tattered flag that flies above the courthouse and speculating about all the things that it and the country have been through together.

"I don't like to brag," the old man tells a stranger, "but we're mighty proud of that ragged old flag."

It was a triumphant night for Johnny Cash, one of many as he built on a legacy that would only grow larger and stronger with the years. And so it was no surprise that on the day of his death, September 12, 2003, the radio was overflowing with his songs. There was Cash himself singing "Folsom Prison Blues," and Emmylou Harris with perhaps his finest ballad of heartache, "I Still Miss Someone."

But even more poignant was his daughter Rosanne singing "My Old Man," the haunting tribute she had written for her father. She freely acknowledged his limitations: *He believes what he says he believes, but that don't make him a saint.* But then at the end of every verse, she always returned to the same affirmation, tender and simple and straight from the heart: *How I love.my old man.*

She was singing, of course, from the heart of us all.

The more I listened to country music, the more I realized (more slowly than some) that music is a part of the national story—a tool for journalists or the writers of history if we would only pay close attention. That seemed to be true not only for country but rock 'n' roll as well, as I tried to say in this article written in 1976. Originally published in Country Music *magazine, and co-authored with the great music writer Michael Bane, the piece was later modified into a chapter in the book* Watermelon Wine. *The version of it here is a combination of the two.*

Southern Rock:
The New Good Ole Boys

The South's gonna do it again.
—Charlie Daniels

A late winter's night in Nashville, and the city auditorium is jammed to the gills. Every high school and college student within a hundred-mile radius appears to have migrated in for a concert by the Marshall Tucker Band. The atmosphere is giddy, and if it weren't for the wafting faint smell of burning marijuana, you'd swear the place had the feel of the midnight madness at Ernest Tubbs's.

Bass player Tommy Caldwell surveys the scene, flashes one of his patented grit-eating grins, and moves toward the microphone with a country boy's swagger. He still has some of that kick-over-the-barstool stage presence that he and the other Tuckers developed in the sleazy southside clubs of Spartanburg, South Carolina—back in the days before the Tuckers had become, along with the Allman Brothers and the Charlie Daniels Band, the prime practitioners of southern rock. But the days of dodging beer bottles and eking out a living are behind him now; the crowds are friendly and raucous, and Caldwell knows when he has them in his hand.

"We gon' do a song from our first album," he says, grabbing the mike stand and planting his feet as if he plans to be there a while. "We got some guy that's gon' play fiddle with us from Nashville.

Don't know if ya'll know who he is, but it looks like ole Charlie to me."

As the crowd erupts into war whoops and rebel yells out strolls Charlie Daniels, looking like a friendly, fiddle-playing grizzly bear, only bigger, his cowboy hat pulled low over his eyes and his fiddle bow cocked at the ready. With the amps turned up full blast, he and the Tuckers launch into the hard-rocking, country-flavored beat of "Fire on the Mountain"—the faithful surging toward the stage and crushing together like rebel sardines, the girls, often as not, perched on the shoulders of their shaggy-haired dates, clapping and swaying and calling for more.

It continues that way for about three hours, which is a pretty standard show these days when groups like the Marshall Tucker Band or Charlie Daniels and company are touring their native Southeast. And although frenzy has been a staple of rock 'n' roll camp followers ever since the early days of Elvis, there is somehow a difference in quality between the chemistry of today's southern rockers and, say, the drug-cult, guitar-smashing antics of Alice Cooper.

Southern rock, at its best, is something more than rock that happens to be played in the South, and its fans are reveling in something more than the sound of the music. They may not understand it fully, may not have sorted out all the pieces, but the people on stage understand it very well. They are people like George McCorkle, the affable, slow-talking rhythm guitarist for the Marshall Tucker Band, who finds himself, at the reflective age of thirty, intrigued by the substance of the music he's been involved in ever since he picked up a guitar.

"After a while," he says, sitting backstage before the show, his elbows propped on his knees, "you get older and your music matures. You start playing your roots—country, blues, or whatever. It's what you grew up with and you can't escape it."

That's the view of a lot of southern rockers. They see their craft as a fusion of very old musical forms, with roots running from Smoky Mountain hillbilly pickin' to the crystal-clear notes of Kentucky bluegrass to the hard-edged bar blues coming out of Memphis. It's logical that it would be that way, for rock 'n' roll began as a distinctly southern hybrid—an Elvis Presley–Carl Perkins blend of black man's blues and white man's country.

In the early days, Perkins and Presley managed to hold onto

their original audiences, with Perkins's "Blue Suede Shoes," for example, hitting the top of both country and rhythm and blues charts. Quickly, however, rock began to develop a more youthful audience of its own, and eventually, after a trip across the ocean and back, it struck out in assorted electrified directions that bore little resemblance to the point of origin.

Today's southern rock—at least as practiced by the Marshall Tucker–Charlie Daniels–Allman Brothers axis—is essentially an attempt to recreate and refine some of the original fusions in a modern-day setting, turning loose all the amps and volume of the West Coast heavy metal rockers, but blending in the craftsmanship of old-time blues and country. It is no accident, the southern rockers say, that all of this is happening at a time of peculiar goings-on in the South. For southern music—whether blues, country, or barroom boogie—has always been a barometer of the society in which it thrives. And so it is today, as the South emerges from twenty years of turmoil, and the young people who were estranged from their region and heritage during the years of upheaval begin to realize that once a few key sins are purged, theirs is not, in fact, a place to be ashamed of.

"Barriers have broken down between groups of people, just like between categories of music," George McCorkle affirms, making an instinctive, on-target connection between music and sociology. "Kids aren't ashamed of country anymore, and they're not ashamed of blues. And when you mix it all together and the music gets to cooking, it's a pretty damn exciting thing to be around."

The philosophizing jogs something in McCorkle's memory, and he lets loose a country boy's soliloquy on the early days in Spartanburg, and how even today he loves to go back and play country music or whatever he feels in the beer-spattered clubs where the whole trip began. "It's all what you grew up with," he says by way of concluding the conversation. "It's southern."

With that he excuses himself politely and threads his way to the tuning room where Daniels and the rest of the band are belting out bluegrass harmonies to some straight and unamplified country picking.

He ducks inside, escaping a backstage chaos that rivals the scene in the auditorium itself. There are dozens of groupies, resplendent in faded jeans and braless T-shirts, including one that proclaims, in big block letters, "AIN'T IT GREAT TO BE ALIVE AND IN TENNESSEE." And in a sort of odd and homey counterpoint, there are also a goodly number of wives and children, licking their fingers and munching away on a tableful of barbecued ribs—mingling in the process with reporters and record company people who are putting away awesome quantities of Budweiser beer.

It's weird and dizzy, but it has, nevertheless, all the feel and fervor of an old-time family reunion.

The family headquarters these days is in the sleepy southern outpost of Macon, Georgia. The city is, at first glance, the ideal sort of place to be from—a faded childhood memory of fried-chicken picnics and hand-cranked peach ice cream, all on a manicured lawn without ants. The gentility of the Old South rustles up and down the tree-shrouded streets like the first breeze of a July afternoon.

But the beat of the New South is becoming more and more prevalent, especially in a converted slaughterhouse over on Cotton Avenue. That particular slaughterhouse, along with the brownstone next door and a well-appointed studio just across town, are the home digs of Capricorn Records, one of the largest independent record producers in the world and the prime evangelist of southern music. From this casual home base have flowed the frenetic, white-boy blues of the Allman Brothers and the down-home country funk of the Marshall Tucker Band, the hard-edged bar boogie of Wet Willie and the sweet southern soul music of Otis Redding, all to the tune of some twenty-five million record albums in 1976 alone.

Capricorn Records, headed by a shrewd and chauvinistic southerner named Phil Walden, has ramrodded the revival of southern music into something of a national mania, leaving the sleepy streets of Macon littered with a few long-haired millionaires along the way.

"But this is not a new phenomenon," Walden insists, as he leans back in his overstuffed chair and surveys his eighteenth-century broad-topped desk. "The music has always been here. The phenomenon is that it's being done down here. People—musicians—are remaining in southern communities to record and perform. We've got a base here now."

The base was a long time in coming, for the South has always been slow and cautious in its flirtations with technology. But the music itself, like the other resources springing naturally from the land and its people, has been around for centuries—spreading inexorably from the point of creation to the eager consumers elsewhere in the land.

Walden maintains, in fact, that almost all of American music is traceable to the South, and he may be pretty close to right. From the simmering poverty of Appalachia came the eloquent statements of hillbilly music, eventually flowing down from the hills into a booming city called Nashville and a collapsing auditorium called the Ryman. From the Carolinas and the scrub palmetto flatlands of Florida, traditional Scotch-Irish folk music mutated (with the help of the Kentucky-bred influence of Bill Monroe, among others) into the mandolin wind known as bluegrass. In the urban melting pots of Memphis and New Orleans a whole new class of citizens—blacks fleeing the farms after the Civil War—found a world even more appalling and gave poignant voice to that world with the blues and, later, jazz.

Nor were the musical forms content to remain separate. In a society generally painted in hues of black and white, the music knew very little color. Jimmie Rodgers, the first hillbilly superstar, took both his guitar and his singing styles from the black railroad workers in Meridian, Mississippi, and is best remembered today for his yodeling interpretations of the blues. And on the other side of the line, Lillie Mae Glover, who sang the blues as Memphis Ma Rainey along Beale Street in the twenties, remembers that one of her most requested numbers was a hillbilly lament called "Heart Made of Stone." That song, she says, had soul.

The blues and hillbilly music came together once and for all one afternoon in 1954, when a small-time Memphis record producer named Sam Phillips, an Alabamian by birth, and an unknown Mississippi singer named Elvis Presley decided to try something a little bit different. What they tried was infusing the black soul of the blues, with its overtly sexual imagery, into a harmless little hillbilly song sung by the former truck driver from Tupelo. What Phillips and Presley and ultimately the rest of the world got was rock 'n' roll. The explosion that followed quite literally rocked the world, and southern music, more than ever before, had gained widespread acceptance.

But there was more to come. Over in Nashville a couple of Kentucky-bred kids, Don and Phil Everly, came up with a song called "Bye Bye Love," written by the incredibly successful songwriting team of Boudleaux and Felice Bryant. The Bryants had already offered the song to more than thirty artists, including Porter Waggoner, but none had displayed much interest. In the hands of the Everlys, however, "Bye Bye Love" became a watershed hit, quickly soaring to number one on both the pop and the country charts.

Meanwhile, equally potent forces were beginning to stir in slow-moving Macon. Over a sink full of dirty plates at the Greyhound Bus Station, a dishwasher named Little Richard was busy writing a song called "Tutti Frutti" and would soon do a little world-shaking of his own. And while Elvis, Little Richard, and the Everlys got ready to rock through the fifties, another black Macon singer by the name of James Brown was already laying the groundwork for the next great musical step—the modem-era soul music that would soon become the Motown sound of Detroit.

By the end of the musically frenetic decade of the fifties, another Macon figure was beginning to make himself felt, at least in a tentative way. A teenaged Phil Walden had wandered across the railroad tracks separating genteel Macon from the funky black beer clubs and the gritty black soul music and was soon managing a black band of his own.

But Walden's band kept being clobbered in local talent contests by yet another Macon soul singer—a fellow by the name of Otis Redding—and Walden, whose opportunistic streak had matured at an early age, decided to shift allegiances. He became Redding's manager, booking him into clubs and college auditoriums, and the two men were soon riding the crest of a soul music tidal wave. Walden and Associates rapidly attracted other soul acts, including Clarence Carter, Sam and Dave, Arthur Conley, and Percy Sledge, and the Macon offices were no longer quite so quaint or quite so far removed from the mainstream of music.

And the mainstream was about to take a quantum step closer to Macon. In 1969, Walden went to Muscle Shoals, Alabama, to hear a sessions musician named Duane Allman. Walden was impressed and suggested that Allman get together a band and move to Macon. The rest is history. Duane Allman did exactly that, and southern rock had come of age.

It's a sad sort of irony that the Allman Brothers Band developed a Hollywoodish image in the mid-seventies, thanks to the jet-set antics of Gregg Allman—his on-again-off-again marriage to Cher

Bono and his prosecution testimony in the cocaine trial of the group's former manager.

The Allmans split up in 1976. In the end the pace was just a little too fast, the living just a little too high, for a bunch of southern kids who stuck it out on the home front, touring incessantly and turning on the locals with a different kind of music. But nothing could detract from the importance of the music. At the white-hot core of the Allmans' sound was the vital interplay between blues and country, a musical mirror of the central tension of southern life, the interaction between black and white. Allman music at its best is a sometimes subtle, sometimes overpowering blend of black urban blues—in the vocals of Gregg Allman—and the bluegrassy strains of old-fashioned country—in the vocal and guitar work of Richard Betts—with just enough jazz and hard-edged rock 'n' roll to keep the whole mixture cooking.

Beneath Gregg Allman's electrified bar blues (and he had one of the finest white blues voices in the country), there's always the slightest hint of a bluegrass guitar, a tiny reminder that blue skies are just ahead. Beneath even the most folksy of Richard Betts's country compositions are the underlying pain and loneliness of the blues. And somewhere between the two poles of black and white, urban and rural, blues and country, lies the soul of southern music.

There was a time, says Betts, who grew up picking bluegrass and listening to Hank Williams in the sun-blasted heartland of central Florida, when being from the South was anything but an asset to an aspiring rock 'n' roller. "For so long," he explains in his easy drawl, "the scene was either in England or in New York or L.A. For so long, southern groups had to copy that sound. The Allman Brothers were the first group to say, 'Fuck it, we're gonna stay in Macon.'

"It's really interesting," he continues. "People are starting to realize that southern music is something really good that they've overlooked for a long time. It's not anything new. It's just being discovered. It's almost like a cultural thing started happening."

The cultural thing, he believes, was a southern coming of age. The central tension may still be around, but there has been a profound, even radical reordering of the interplay between black and white. And it came at a time when the South was being hit with all the other mind-bending, homogenizing, fabric-tearing forces that were being unleashed in the country at large—from the proliferating influence of television to the bloody street battles over Vietnam. Through it all, the South was changed. But it was not changed altogether, and that fact is demonstrated most graphically in the music and self-conscious southernness of Tennessee's Charlie Daniels.

Daniels is not a Capricorn act (he's on the Epic label), but he cuts most of his records in Macon, and before a recent session he grabbed a few minutes to talk about his peculiar career. It was morning, which was not exactly his favorite time of day, and he looked a little bleary around the eyes as he ambled into a vacant side office at the Capricorn studios. As he settled himself on the vinyl-covered couch, the belly snap popped on his cowboy shirt, displaying some ample padding about the midsection. He ignored the futile chore of resnapping, leaned back, and occasionally spit excess tobacco juice into a worn-out Styrofoam cup.

Daniels is widely thought of as the most overtly southern of all the southern rockers, and there is very little about his conversation, his music, or his general appearance to belie that impression. All, in fact, seem as homegrown and country as in the days when his affiliation with tobacco was considerably more strenuous than it is today—when he picked it for a living in the sunny flatlands of central North Carolina.

He concluded, not surprisingly, that there must be an easier way, and eventually he struck out for Nashville, seeking fortune and maybe a little bit of fame as a sessions musician in the city's armada of recording studios. He hit town in 1967 and played on some memorable albums (Dylan's *Nashville Skyline*, among others), but he never quite made it as a part of the Music Row in-crowd. Almost by default, he decided instead to become a star.

It took a few years, and some experimentation with sounds, for the Nashville producers were steadfastly intolerant of the decibels and rough edges that make his music distinct. So he fled to Macon and cut an album called *Fire on the Mountain*. It sold a million dollars' worth of records, chiefly on the strength of two country-sounding singles that have become, through the sentiments they express, the rallying anthems of the southern rock movement.

The lesser known of the two, especially outside the South, is a song called "Long Haired Country Boy"—a heartfelt description of a shaggy-headed good ole boy who, like Daniels, has lived through civil rights, Vietnam, rock 'n' roll, marijuana, post-Beatlemania, and all the rest, and has emerged with a curious combination of values and life-styles. The trappings are different: he smokes marijuana and lets his hair grow long, while his counterparts of ten or twenty years earlier might have been more into duck tails and beer. But something more basic and southern is still intact—an attitude, a sort of live-and-let-live affability that is tinged, nevertheless, with defiance: *If you don't like the way I'm livin', you just leave this long-haired country boy alone.*

"Yeah, that's kind of my philosophy of life," says Daniels with a tug at his sandy-blond whiskers. "I ain't got no image to protect or none of that bullshit. We don't wear no rhinestone Nudie suits; we don't have to worry about nobody knowing that we drink or smoke dope. I don't give a damn, you know? The kind of people we appeal to don't give a damn. I ain't worried about the Baptists banning us, because they don't come to see us anyway. We're kind of a hard-livin' bunch of people. I think that reflects in our music. We just are what we are."

That I-am-what-I-am-and-if-you-don't-like-it-don't-mess-with-me kind of defensiveness is probably one of the more staple characteristics of the southern psyche, and has been ever since the days of the Civil War. It can be directed from person to person, or from classes of people to classes of people, or even (as has happened a lot during the past hundred years) from the South as a whole toward the rest of the country.

Too many times, of course, it has gotten tangled up in defense of the wrong sorts of causes—slavery and segregation among them—but it always went deeper than the causes themselves, and it has in fact outlived them. The remorseful, guilt-ridden South that danced through the fantasies of homegrown liberals never really materialized, but what has begun to show itself instead is something considerably more substantial: a growing combination of pride and resentment, nurtured in part by the racially integrated order that is beginning to take hold in most of the South. We've been through a lot, people are saying, and have been compelled to change whether we wanted to or not. In retrospect, a lot of southerners are glad about that, but they can't help noticing that serious problems elsewhere became forgotten, somehow, in the moralizing over theirs; and all of it has left them feeling more southern, and prouder of it, than they ever had before.

When Charlie Daniels recorded his "Fire on the Mountain" album, he put some of those feelings into a song that became—particularly in the South—the biggest hit he ever had. The verses in "The South's Gonna Do It Again" were essentially a celebration of the vitality of southern music, but the chorus that gave the song its title was much more general, a reaffirmation of a new southern pride.

In 1976, it was that kind of risen South spirit that led many southern rockers to an ardent support of Jimmy Carter's presidential candidacy. Daniels and the others did several benefit performances each, seeking to raise money for the Carter campaign, and in gratitude Carter invited them to play at his inauguration.

It was a peculiar scene at a presidential ball—the big-band sounds of Glenn Miller or Tommy Dorsey giving way abruptly to the foot-stomping, whoop-em-up beat of southern country funk. "I never supported a politician before in my life," said Daniels. "But I was around Carter a little bit, and I said, 'There's an honest man.' He was the first honest politician I ever met."

Reminded, however, that there were people who look askance at Carter because he's from the South—who still associate the place of his birth with some dark and murky characteristic that can't be trusted—Daniels replied with a spit in the direction of his Styrofoam cup: "It's time people quit thinking that." Then after a pause: "Damn those sons of bitches. I don't owe 'em nothin.' I'm proud of it. Proud of being from the South."

Charlie's irritation comes and goes, depending on his mood. Catch him at a better time, or when he's not being confronted with all the narrow-minded opinions that have been directed at his region, and he's one of the gentlest and least pretentious people you would ever want to meet. But whatever his frame of mind, his pride in the South and his music remains intact. And that kind of pride is what gives southern music its evangelical air.

There is a shared sense of place that links musicians and audience before the first note is played. The music is part of the landscape, tangible as Georgia red clay and pervasive as Smoky Mountain mists. There are times (especially in the music of Charlie Daniels, Richard Betts, and the Marshall Tucker Band) when the sound is downright country—a testimonial to the renewed power of tradition among a generation in which you might not expect it.

But even more obviously, the music of Daniels and the others represents the sound of change—the intertwined preoccupations with roots and with experimentation that have dominated the recent history of country music (just as a profound combination of nostalgia and future shock has dominated the lives of those who listen). Some of the musical changes have been highly creative, others strictly commercial. No one knows where the whole thing will lead, chiefly because, if you hang around recording centers such as Nashville, you realize the music—like the country as a whole—seems to be heading in multiple directions, all at one time.

The preoccupation with the roots of southern music was not at all limited to rock and country artists, nor did it simply rise and fall in the 1970s. In the 1990s, on assignment from the Oxford American *magazine and the weekly newspaper* Creative Loafing, *I had the good fortune to profile a rising jazz band from North Carolina with the unlikely name of the Squirrel Nut Zippers.*

Old-Fashioned Notions
of Love and Music

The crowds are bigger now than they were. In Nashville at the end of their most recent tour, there were maybe five hundred people at Performance Hall #328, a cavernous room with cement floors and bare brick walls and a scattering of chairs that nobody uses—not on this particular night at least, for when the Squirrel Nut Zippers hit the stage, almost nobody wants to sit down.

Their music is a little bit hard to define. In the end, it's jazz—exuberant echoes of the twenties and thirties, of Calloway, Ellington, and all the rest, but there are other old ghosts that are in there as well. In the guitar of James Mathus, there's the bluegrass twang of Bill Monroe, mixed and muted by the sound of delta blues, and some people say they can hear Robert Johnson and the Dixieland brass of New Orleans and maybe a little bit of Al Casey from Harlem. But whatever it is that goes into the mix, the Squirrel Nut Zippers have made it their own. They are young musicians from Chapel Hill, many of them veterans of the rock 'n' roll bands that abound in the area, but now they have fallen in love with the past. In the process, they have found something new, something fresh and undiscovered for many of the people who turn out to see them, and whenever they perform anywhere in the South—still the cornerstone of their success—the dancing breaks out in every corner of the room.

By 1997, they had done two albums, with a third on the way, and played at the Olympic games in Atlanta, on the radio show, *A Prairie Home Companion*, and at the second inauguration of Bill Clinton. That was the part that worried them some—this cult-figure fame they were starting to achieve—for they could see already that it might be a distraction. Not that any of them hated the acclaim, and certainly not the money that began rolling in. But when people started saying they were the South's hottest band, there was, in the accolades and the praise, a whiff of the dangers that could well lie ahead.

They remembered the innocent days at the start, back in 1993 when they played for their friends at a Chapel Hill pub. Katharine Whalen, one of the group's lead singers, dressed herself in white that night. "It was a virginal experience," she said. There were a few dozen people packed into the club, many of them sitting on each other's laps, nobody knowing quite what to expect. By the end of the night, they were screaming for more, and the Squirrel Nut Zippers did their best to oblige. They knew only twelve songs—an old string-band tune from the Skillet Lickers and a couple of Billie Holiday covers and a handful of others they had written themselves. It was not cool jazz—not cerebral or restrained. There was a passion that seemed to explode from every note—a joy they'd discovered in an attic full of records, from Bill Monroe to Bourbon Street jazz, and a chemistry that came from doing something different. It was a feeling, they said, that they didn't want to lose.

"It could stop being fun," Katharine Whalen worried, "if it becomes too popular, if people start talking about 'the scene.'"

But so far, so good. As the 1990s headed to a close, they were no longer playing for tips in a hat, but the innocence of it was still intact. They were playing their jazz, and delighting themselves every minute of the way, and their plan for the future was simply to continue.

It began as art for the sake of itself. Jimbo Mathus, as he's known to his friends, had fallen in love with Katharine Whalen. They had an old house near the Durham County line, creaky and sprawling, with an upstairs balcony, an elm tree in the yard, and an upright piano installed in the parlor. The place was perfect except in the winter when the wood stove was never any match for the cold. But to Whalen and Mathus, it felt like home. Mathus was a native of the Mississippi delta, and he grew up loving everything that was old, especially old music. His father once played for Flatt and Scruggs, and as Jimmy came of age in the 1970s, his first real crush was the bluegrass guitar.

He was also fascinated by the blues—the pain and passion of Howlin' Wolf and Blind Lemon Jefferson—and later as he got more serious about it, he studied the subtle technique of Robert Johnson. There was something in the chords—the flatted notes, the diminished voicings—that clearly foreshadowed the great Duke Ellington. The whole evolution seemed to be right there.

"I can hear it now plain as day," said Mathus, and when he talked to Katharine about it, his blue eyes dancing, she began to feel for the first time in her life that she had met somebody a lot like herself. "We were raised to have enthusiasms," she explained, and in the twenty-something world where both of them lived, that quality was rare. Everybody was cool, seldom given to the passionate fascinations that she and Mathus both saw as routine.

Katharine was an artist. She came from the mountains of North Carolina, where she grew up in a cabin that her father had built from a Foxfire kit. Her grandmother Kate Bertram, for whom she was named, ran the family farm, raising the meat and vegetables on which they survived. There were many things about that life she admired—the sense of independence and the gift for self-expression that seemed to be all around. Everybody read books and listened to music, and Katharine herself became an oil painter. Later, when she married Jim Mathus and they moved in together, they made some puppets and put on shows for their friends at the house, and soon after that, she took up the banjo. She didn't want to play it the Earl Scruggs style, picking with her fingers the way most people did. She was drawn instead to the percussive strumming of the old jazz bands, which was rooted in the African history of the instrument. She had never been a serious musician before, and Jim helped her learn. They listened to old records and studied the style, and in the summer of 1993, they decided it was time to include a few friends.

They thought first of Ken Mosher, a Chapel Hill musician who could play anything. He worked at a restaurant where Jim was a busboy, and their friendship gradually evolved into music. Through Mosher they met Chris Phillips, a drummer, and the group quickly grew and took on a shape. The first twenty practices were all at the house—parties essentially, or potluck dinners, where Jim and Katharine would fry up some chicken, and Mosher brought the ribs, and they would eat and practice and write a few songs. Mosher was the catalyst for much of what they did—a man of talent and very little ego—and the personal chemistry that began to develop left its distinctive imprint on the music.

They knew as the summer was nearing its end that they were onto something good, and they decided it was time for the group to have a name. On a cool, velvet night when practice was over, they were lying around on their cars, staring at the stars, and Katharine remembered an early conversation, when she and Jim were new lovers, talking about life before they had met.

"What kind of candy did you like?" she had asked.

"Squirrel Nut Zippers," he replied with a grin, and he described with a sense of nostalgia and awe that offbeat brand of caramel and nuts. Katharine was charmed, and the thing she remembered most was his accent, the sweet delta twang he had never quite escaped. Thinking back on the moment, she thought the name held promise for the group. The candy, after all, was quirky and distinctive, just like the music, and it carried her husband straight back to his roots— to a boyhood spent in the Mississippi delta, where he first fell in love with the music of the South.

With their name now chosen and more than three months of rehearsals behind them, they decided they were ready to take the show on the road—at least as far as Chapel Hill. Katharine especially had to be a little nervous. She had been cast in the summer as one of the singers, and she had never performed in public before. But the first show came, in November 1993, and then the reviewers cut loose with their praise. There was a "fundamental joy," as one critic wrote, that set them apart, and within a few weeks of their first public show, everything seemed to be moving at a blur.

The recording offers came right away, and within a year they were under contract with Mammoth, a small but aggressive Chapel Hill label specializing in alternative music. They began to tour all over the South, hitting the road for two weeks at a time, then return- ing to North Carolina to write. They were no longer doing many covers, turning instead to their own creations—rollicking originals like "Wash Jones," which Mathus wrote about a character out of Faulkner, and the bass player Don Raleigh's "Anything But Love," which was chosen for the soundtrack of a movie.

More than any of the others, perhaps, Katharine Whalen was taken by surprise. In the first few months, she had thought of their music as an exercise in creativity that was an end in itself—like the painting and the puppets and other things they had done. Their first live show in Chapel Hill, with all their friends crowding into the bistro, seemed like a perfect capstone to the project. But now she could see that it was something else altogether—an experience that had a momentum of its own, and the only question now was how far it would take them.

Tom Maxwell didn't know the answer to that, and he didn't really care. As one of the finest musicians in the group (he played guitar and often sang lead), he felt like a kid at the age of thirty-one—a musical pilgrim on a journey to the places he had only read about.

The first of those was New Orleans. Mathus had been there before, but Maxwell had not and neither had Mosher. Not long after the Zippers' first album, which they decided to call *The Inevitable*, the three of them set out for Louisiana. Maxwell at first could hardly believe it, walking the streets that Louis Armstrong had walked, eating, drinking, "absorbing the beautiful menace of the city." There were brass parade bands playing all around, and little clubs in the Quarter where ancient black men made music so pure, so exuberant and free, that Maxwell and the others had to be a little humbled. As Mathus put it, "It showed everybody how far we had to go."

But if that was true, New Orleans seemed to be a good place to start, especially when they found an old studio at Esplanade and Chartres on the northern boundary of the Quarter. It was a mansion, really, with marble floors and a hanging garden and a third-floor balcony with a view of downtown. The recording equipment was downright historic. There was a mixing board made for Jimi Hendrix and speakers from the Abbey Road studio in London, and the combination of nostalgia and elegance was so breathtaking that the band decided they had to record there. They descended on Kingsway Studio, as the facility was known, in October 1995 and cut their second album—a well-named collection of twelve new songs they simply called Hot.

To Mathus, looking back, the whole experience was a turning point for them. For one thing, they did the record live—everybody in the studio at once—which made it more edgy, more authentic and urgent, than it might have been otherwise. But more than that, the trip to New Orleans was a chance for the band to absorb something new—to encounter Dixieland jazz in the place of its birth, to see for themselves what the masters could do. Their feeling for the music went deeper after that, and their own ambitions were a little more intense.

"I believe in experiences," Jim Mathus said simply. "You absorb them. They trickle out."

Not long after the New Orleans experience the group made a pilgrimage to the outskirts of Harlem. They went to see Al Casey, who had played guitar for the great Fats Waller. Maxwell especially was a Waller fanatic—awed by the delicate interplay of his band. Waller was a keyboard artist, one of the dazzling Jazzmen of the thirties, and for nearly a decade, beginning in 1934, Al Casey was with him every step of the way. Waller died in 1943 on a train to Kansas City, but Casey played on, and more than fifty years later he was still going strong—living comfortably in upper Manhattan and performing with his band, the Harlem All-Stars.

When the Squirrel Nut Zippers discovered this fact, they decided immediately to go and look him up. It was one of the great perks of being in a band, this astonishing possibility of meeting with their heroes, and the Zippers were nervous when the day finally came. It was an April afternoon about three o'clock when they made their way to his New York apartment. Casey was waiting there with his wife, sitting in an easy chair in his slippers. He was eighty years old, but gracious and alert, getting ready, in fact, for a gig that night in a New York club.

The conversation was awkward at first, but Maxwell managed to break the ice. He talked nonstop about the days of Fats Waller, reminding Casey of things he had long since forgotten. Before it was over, the old jazzman had pulled out his scrapbook, showing off pictures with Lena Horne and Billie Holiday—and then in the midst of it all, it hit him. He was now the only one left.

"He shed a few tears," Jim Mathus remembers, and an unlikely bond was forged in the moment. A few weeks later, they played together in a New York club, the Zippers and Casey at a place called Tramps, and Mathus says it was magic. There was Casey at the age of eighty, playing "the sweetest, most beautiful music you could hear—like a Buddha playing jazz." Suddenly, for Mathus the whole thing was clear: Al Casey had simply gotten better with the years. It was apparent from the way his fingers hit the strings that he loved the music even more than when he started. For the band as a whole, it provided a final piece of perspective—a parable against the day when they might get jaded, when the distractions that are a part of life on the road might try to steal center stage from the music.

Certainly, the possibilities were there. There had been some tensions and strains within the group—personnel changes, which were always hard, and business decisions that they all had to make. How much should they tour? What places should they play? How big, in the end, did they really want to be?

"We have fought and bickered about those things," Katharine Whalen admits. "But never about music. From the day we started, that part has been effortless."

That was clearly true on their final tour of 1996, when they set out on a trip through the musical hotspots—New Orleans, Austin, Memphis, and Nashville—and a handful of other cities in between. One of Tom Maxwell's favorites was Houston. On the afternoon before they performed, he went looking for the civic auditorium where Johnny Ace had died more than forty years before. Ace had never been a musical star. He was born in Memphis and played piano for Albert Duncan and Bobby Blue Bland. Later, he had a few hits of his own, most of them modest, before the Christmas Eve night in 1954 when he killed himself playing Russian roulette. Maxwell found the dressing room where it happened, and stood there trying to imagine the scene—the look in the eyes, the spinning of the chamber which came up full. It was the first great tragedy of the rock 'n' roll era, and in Maxwell's mind, the dressing room was a shrine—much like the studios in Memphis where Elvis Presley had made his first records: an old blues song from the Mississippi delta and a bluegrass anthem from Bill Monroe. Everything seemed to be so connected. That realization was always the key—the precious understanding that could never be lost.

"It keeps us starry-eyed," said Maxwell, which meant at least they were still having fun.

And so they hit the stage in Nashville, the last stop before the Clinton inauguration ball. A few hours earlier they were weary from the road, subdued as they were waiting for the show to begin. But suddenly, it appeared, they were feeling pretty good—Jimbo Mathus with his little-boy grin and the cowlick swirling through his chopped-off hair, and Je Widenhouse blasting his trumpet from his place on the side, and Katharine Whalen, lovely as always, in her faded white dress that was slinky and camp. As they moved through the set, the people in the crowd began to recognize the standards—"Hell," "Lover's Lane," "Anything But Love"—and within a few minutes, they were borderline rowdy. People were screaming between every song, singing, dancing, strangers grabbing one another in the aisles.

> *Grab your drink and clear a space*
> *I think it's time to torch this place.*

As Mathus and the others shouted out the lyrics, the lights flashed and the drums pounded and the audience crushed its way to the stage. And then suddenly it was over, and the encores were done, and the bus was waiting in the alley outside. It was a beautiful night, chilly and crisp, with a three-quarter moon and a few fluffs of clouds, and Mathus, immediately, was coming down from his high. The adrenalin, he said, was part of the fun, but he was looking forward now to the break—a time to visit his home in Mississippi, which was still the center of his musical universe. He wanted to pay his respects to the family of Charley Patton, one of the late bluesmen of the delta, and maybe cut a tribute album in the spring.

It seemed unlikely in the middle of a show, when the energy was flowing and the crowd seemed to teeter on the edge of a riot, but for the Squirrel Nut Zippers, this was a serious mission they were on. It may have been simple enough at its core—a story of friends and a love of old songs—but they felt a responsibility to the past. It was like the old house where the group was born. They did a few things to freshen it up—added some plumbing and a little bit of paint—but it still felt old.

"We're drawn to old things," Katharine Whalen explained, "not to polish them up, but to make them accessible. That's the way we feel about performing. We want our values to show every time—our old-fashioned notions of love and music. If this experience stops being about that, something, I'm sure, would make it fly apart."

Epilogue: Eventually, as is often true in popular music, the band did fly apart, cutting its last album in 2000, having endured, as Katharine Whalen feared, a barrage of business disagreements and personnel changes. Before the end, however, the Zippers sold more than two million records and left their own distinctive legacy in the world of southern jazz.

Not long ago, at a basketball game at Vanderbilt University, Emmylou Harris and Marshall Chapman sang the national anthem. In addition to being good friends, these two performers have come to embody the best of country music. Among other things, they understand its history—how the music gave voice to the vagaries of life in a way that made sense to ordinary people. They also understand the relationship between the music of Nashville and other forms, having absorbed a subtle variety of influences while also remaining true to themselves. As I thought about their performance at the basketball game, I remembered profiles I had done of both singers—short pieces written in the 1990s, when country music seemed to be losing something precious. Harris and Chapman, however, were not part of the problem, as I tried to say in both of these stories, expanded here from their original versions. First, Emmylou:

Country Queens

Cowgirl's Prayer

She's on the road again to promote her latest labor of love. They are all that way for Emmylou Harris—these albums she has crafted for the past twenty years. Her most recent, *Cowgirl's Prayer*, was nearly eighteen months in the making, and the critics have agreed that it's one of her best—a heart-rending mixture of pure country ballads, with a little bit of Cajun and gospel and rock 'n' roll. She has never been one to worry about the boundaries, and in the musical climate of the 1990s that may be part of her problem. Harris has reached a curious point in her career. Her place in country music is secure. There is probably nobody in the past several decades who has done more than she has to keep it alive, to nourish the heart and soul of that tradition.

She has been a student as well as an artist, finding threads of continuity in disparate performers, from the Louvin Brothers to Bruce Springsteen. She has recorded their songs and made them her own, paying more attention to art than demographics, and the result is an impressive body of work. But lately, there's a problem. Since the late eighties, despite her energy and the widely acknowledged quality of her work, she's found it hard to get her songs on the radio.

Commercially at least, she doesn't have to worry; her sales are steady enough to make a good living. "I'm luckier than most," she says. "My audience doesn't live or die by the radio."

Still, there's a pain that goes with rejection, and she feels it most when she thinks of the songs—the creations of composers like Leonard Cohen, who wrote the title cut for *Cowgirl's Prayer*. Cohen is a writer of stunning finesse, and the beauty of his words—the story of a girl and her runaway horse—is crystallized in the voice of Emmylou. She says she falls in love with good songs, and perhaps with Cohen's even more than most. Linda Ronstadt sent it to her in the mail, a haunting rendition by the pop singer Jennifer Warnes, and Emmylou was deeply affected from the start.

"It's the kind of music that enriches my life," she says, "and it's a shame that these songs that say so much are less and less likely to be on records. Certainly, they're not played on the radio, which is becoming so caricaturish and shallow. Until we get a different kind of format, I'm concerned where country music is going."

The anger flashes for a moment in her voice, but it seems to subside when she talks about herself. "I'm not really sure," she says with resignation, "that country music and I, right now, are compatible."

If that is true, her producer, Allen Reynolds, says he understands why. "For Emmy," he explains, "music is more than a matter of commerce." At least since the early 1970s, it has been the defining love of her life, and at a time when radio is becoming more cautious, more predictable and narrow and indifferent to art, she refuses to bend with the demographic winds.

It hasn't always been that way, for Emmylou Harris came late to country music—to those heart-breaking harmonies with the voices intertwined and lyrics so clear and honest and real. There was a time, she says, when she couldn't quite hear it. She came from an upper-middle-class family, born in Birmingham, Alabama, and she later studied drama at the University of North Carolina at Greensboro. But she left the school after three semesters, having already started to sing, and she began to play little clubs in Washington, doing folk music mostly—the songs of Joni Mitchell, Bob Dylan, or Joan Baez. By then, she was dabbling in the old stuff too, developing an ear for Bill Monroe, and maybe on nights when the crowds were small, which seemed to happen a lot in those days, she might do a ballad from Kitty Wells. But she says she never really listened to the music, never really let herself feel it in her bones, until the rainy night in 1971 when she met Gram Parsons.

Parsons was a rebellious refugee from Harvard University and Waycross, Georgia. He had been a rock 'n' roller for most of his life—a singer with the Byrds, and later with the Flying Burrito Brothers—but a piece of his heart still belonged to country music. It was the music he knew in small-town Georgia, the songs of Merle Haggard and Kitty Wells, and by the early 1970s, when he met Emmylou, he was determined to cut his own country album. He took some delight in the shock value of it, a shaggy-haired rock 'n' roller like himself sounding just as raw as Haggard and the rest. He was looking for a girl to sing some duets when he met Emmylou in a bar called Clyde's. It was a singles club in the heart of Georgetown, and she played there a lot. On the night when Parsons came in to hear her, she says there were maybe three people in the place, but Parsons seemed impressed with what he heard, and on one of her breaks, the two of them headed off to the basement.

They began to work up some songs, sitting there together on the kegs of beer, and for Emmylou, it was magic. There was something inexplicable in the blend of their voices. Gram's was flawed, cracking sometimes as he strained for the notes, but it was also strong and full of heart, and when Emmylou sang the harmonies for him, she knew it didn't get any better than that.

They made a couple of albums together, the second of which, *Grievous Angel*, was widely hailed by the critics as a breakthrough record—one of the greatest country albums ever made. But Gram had a wild and self-destructive streak, and in 1973 he died—apparently from the effect of too many drugs. For Emmylou, there have been other moments of tragedy and pain—broken hearts and marriages that didn't work out—but few things have hit her with the force of that death. Not long afterward, she sat down and wrote a tribute to Parsons, a soul-wrenching ballad called "Boulder to Birmingham," in which she sang about the longing just to see his face.

She has said many times in the years since then that she loved Gram Parsons as a musician and friend—but perhaps even more, she treasured the gift of music that he left her. She built her career on the strength of that gift, and by 1975 her solo records were beginning to take off—to the sound of rave reviews all around. "Listening to her sing," said Marshall Chapman, "is kind of like getting a sneak preview of heaven." But there were others who argued that her choice of material was even more distinctive and important than her voice. She found country songs in the strangest places—from the urban rock 'n' roll of Bruce Springsteen (she says he reminds her a lot of Hank Williams) to the old-fashioned ballads of Stephen Foster.

John Rumble of the Country Music Foundation says he used to see her often in the musty stacks of the foundation's library, searching out the history of assorted country songs. But she also admired the contemporary writers, and many's the time, says Allen Reynolds, when a group of them would gather to play at her house.

"Emmy is so tuned in," he says. "She keeps up with new artists, and goes way out of her way to help them. I've seen her do it time and time again."

Reynolds and many others in Nashville maintain that Harris has become a symbol of country music artistry. But even as her status has grown more secure, her commercial standing in the industry has slipped. By the 1990s, she never had number-one records anymore, and it had been a few years since she had cracked the top 40. Partly, it was a matter of her own indifference, for when she formed a new band in 1990 and asked Allen Reynolds to be her producer, their first major project was a live country album. Live albums rarely get a lot of airplay, but Harris was determined to do it anyway.

She wanted to perform at the Ryman Auditorium, legendary home of the Grand Ole Opry before it moved to its slick new quarters. There was something mysterious about the building, she said, something in the feel of the hillbilly dust, and she was a little awestruck when she first took the stage. She knew that Hank Williams had once played there, and Roy Acuff and Bill Monroe, and it was an eerie feeling as she gazed through the lights at the stained-glass windows and the benches that still resembled old pews. She knew she was taking a chance with this one—doing an album of songs she had never performed, and doing it live with no time to rehearse. But she also cherished the feeling of fear, the feeling that she was pushing the music to its limits.

She rocked her way through "Lodi," one of her favorites from Credence Clearwater, then a sampler of Springsteen and Bill

Monroe, before coming to a heartbreaking song from the sixties. In a sense it was the epitaph of the decade, a mournful tribute to "Abraham, Martin and John," written by an Alabama songwriter by the name of Dick Holler. Holler's only other hit had been a novelty song—"Snoopy vs. the Red Baron"—but he had been in New York for a recording session when he learned of the assassination of Robert Kennedy. In his private moment of astonishment and grief, he sat down alone in his hotel room, and the simple words poured out in a rush—his tribute to the Kennedys and Martin Luther King Jr. and a final, bewildered note of affirmation:

Didn't they try to find some good for you and me?

In her unrehearsed rendition at the Ryman, Emmylou delivered the song with a feeling more raw than the original recording by Dion DiMucci. It was, perhaps, the high point of an album that won her a Grammy but was totally ignored by country music radio.

The same fate seemed likely for *Cowgirl's Prayer*, when it hit the stores in 1993. It quickly started winning its share of acclaim, while the radio programmers looked the other way. On the surface, their indifference was hard to understand, for most of the cuts were clearly in the mainstream. There was a hard country-rocker called "High Powered Love" and a heartbreak ballad called "Lovin' You Again." But there were also some songs that plowed new ground. Many of the arrangements were folky and spare, and the some of the lyrics even shaded toward gospel—an unpredictable mixture overall, with a feeling of coherence that's a mystery to Emmylou.

"The more records I do, the less I know about it," she says. "You just respect what an album seems to be becoming. Allen Reynolds and (co-producer) Richard Bennett have a good feel for that. They respect the mystery of the whole process, which is the thing that makes them so good to work with.

"Allen is a very song-oriented producer, and my career progresses one song at a time. I'm always drawn to the lyrics first. People know how hard life is. They need music that will give words and expression to the feelings they have. That's what country music is about. It has to be more than entertainment or escape."

And what if the radio won't play it?

Emmylou says it bothers her some, but she also knows she's not alone. Willie Nelson, Merle Haggard, Johnny Cash—all of them known for their integrity and substance—have all joined the ranks of the radio rejects. Maybe it's simply a matter of image, she says, too many gray hairs for the "young country" playlists. But whatever the reason, Harris and the others say they try not to worry.

"It frustrated me for a while," she admits, "but it's a natural thing that happens in a long career. You compete with yourself and your own oldies. I really don't give it a lot of thought anymore. The important thing is to be passionate about the music."

That's the good news for Emmylou. Out on the road, even when her voice is fragile and tired, hoarse from the string of one-night stands, she whirls and dances in the soft blue lights, and the old lover's fire still burns inside her. You can see it in her smile, and hear it in the aching beauty of her songs. When it comes to the music that's defined her life, nobody feels more passion than she does.

Marshall Chapman, who, like Harris, came of age in the sixties and seventies, has always been part rock 'n' roller, part country queen. She has also emerged as one of Nashville's most gifted writers.

Sweeter with the Years

There are two different versions of the Elvis story.
According to the first, Marshall Chapman was seven years old, growing up in Spartanburg, South Carolina, when Elvis Presley came to town. He was playing on a package show out of Nashville, an opening act on a tour of country stars, but already the word was beginning to spread. The Chapman family's baby-sitter and maid, Lula Mae Moore, took little Marshall by the hand and led her down to the Carolina Theater.

They climbed the back stairs to the all-colored balcony, steamy and packed, to catch a glimpse of this picker from Memphis who sang country music as if he were black. "When he came on, it was like an explosion," Marshall said years later. "The whole place just shook." The story, undoubtedly, will ring pretty true for people who have seen Marshall Chapman on stage. During the thirty-plus years of her career, she has built a cult following as one of Nashville's cutting-edge performers.

But in terms of her earliest inspiration, there's another whole version of the Elvis story, which is offered these days by some of her friends. It's different in detail from the one in her press kit, but in its own way it's at least as revealing. In this one, too, she was seven years old. It was a Spartanburg Sunday, and the family was gathered around the television set. Her mother was knitting, and her father was hidden behind his Sunday newspaper, when Elvis Presley flickered on the screen. Mrs. Chapman tried to say something nice. She talked about the young singer's eyes and the emotion that shimmered in his Mississippi voice. "But those sideburns," she said with a frown.

Marshall, meanwhile, was simply transfixed, and at the age of seven, she dove headlong into the first great wave of rock 'n' roll. It wasn't just Elvis. As a teenager she was drawn to the black singers, too—Jackie Wilson, Maurice Williams, and all the rest. She bought their records and saw them whenever they came to town—joining other whites, in the latter days of segregation, in the sweltering balcony of the Carolina Theater.

Eventually, she began to think about performing, but first came college. She left Spartanburg for Vanderbilt University, where she majored in French. But the Vanderbilt campus was just a few blocks from Music Row, a part of Nashville that began more and more to command her attention. She was already a closet country music fan, having listened as a kid to the Arthur Smith Show as it beamed out of Charlotte. It was easy to make fun of the cornpone humor, but the music was real, and in songs like Arthur's "Guitar Boogie," the first million-seller on the country charts, she could hear the antecedents of rock 'n' roll.

When she left Vanderbilt in 1971, she took her degree and went to work as a waitress at the Red Dog Saloon, a basement bar on the fringe of the campus, where she bided her time, waiting to begin her career as a singer. It was not exactly what her family had in mind. Her father, James Chapman, was a textile magnate, the president of Spartanburg's Inman Mills, and he expected great things from his impressive young daughter. She was six feet tall with soft blond hair and a winning smile, and she was smart enough to hold her own with anybody. "He thought I would get the music business out of my system," says Marshall today.

But then in 1976, she signed with Epic Records, and her debut album, *Me, I'm Feelin' Free*, was a hit with critics all across the country. It was about that time that the crowds grew larger at the Exit Inn and all the other watering holes around Nashville whenever Marshall Chapman showed up to play. But there were warning signs even from the start. Her record label didn't really believe. They saw her as rock 'n' roll, not country, and in a business where everybody has to have a niche, she simply didn't fit. "Marshall Chapman was too cool and real for Nashville in the Seventies," writes Alana Nash, a nationally known music critic and author. "Not to mention too bluesy, too irreverent, too original, too powerhouse and too tall." After only three albums, the label cut her loose, and it marked the beginning of a difficult time. Her career was on the skids. Her father died, and there was also a suicide in her band.

Marshall, meanwhile, was living wild, perhaps in a flight from too much pain—or maybe, she says, she was just trying to be what people expected: a rock 'n' roller on the edge. Whatever the reason, there were too many boyfriends and too much booze, but it's the blessing and the curse of a songwriter's life that hard times often make good lyrics. It was true for Marshall in the 1980s. She wrote her songs of disillusionment and hurt, tempered most often with irony and humor. Soon other singers began to take notice, and her songs were recorded by a whole host of artists, from Joe Cocker and Dion DiMucci to Conway Twitty and Emmylou Harris.

By the end of the eighties she was making good money—"BMW money," as one friend put it—and she also discovered that her life was growing calm. She found a good man, a Nashville doctor by the name of Chris Fletcher, and she was recording again on her own record label.

It was about that time that the letter arrived. The warden at the Tennessee Prison for Women, Eileen Hosking, had long been a fan, having heard Chapman play at the Bluebird Cafe, a songwriters' Mecca on the south side of Nashville. After one of those performances, in March 1989, the warden wrote Chapman and asked her to do a show at the prison. Marshall read the letter and put it aside, and there it sat for the next three years. It wasn't the fact that the prison couldn't pay. She was used to that in a town where benefit concerts are common. But there was a line near the bottom that left her queasy. "Quite frankly," the warden felt compelled to admit, "I have no idea how you would be received."

For Marshall at the moment, the possibility of being hooted from the stage by a room full of prisoners was a little too daunting for her to confront. And yet somehow, she couldn't dismiss it, couldn't make herself throw the letter away. Finally, she paid a visit to the prison. She went to the cells and talked to the women, then went to the gym where they wanted her to play. It was musty and old, but when she snapped her fingers the acoustics seemed right. "I thought, 'Wow, we ought to record it,'" she said.

And so they did, and the album that resulted was one of her best. It had its raw and ragged moments, as live albums do, unless they've been sanitized later on. But there was something electric as Chapman rocked her way through the set. Predictably enough, there were hard-living songs of love gone bad and boyfriends hanging around like a debt. But the most haunting moments on the album were the soft ones—the winsome ballads of childhood memories and the passage of time, and feelings that only grow sweeter with the years. More and more, that was the story of Chapman's own life. Songs once born in rebellion and pain now seemed to come from a different source.

The title of her album, released on Jimmy Buffett's Margaritaville label, was *It's About Time . . .* , a reference, in part, to the Tennessee prison. But it was also a reference to her own frame of mind. On the final cut, she sang of that double-edged time now beginning to fade, when "every night was now or never, and the road just seemed to go on forever." The prisoners hung on every note, and it was a reminder of the literary dimension of the music. For most of her career she had seen it that way: Country songs were the poetry of the people, telling the stories of everyday lives with a poignancy equivalent to other literary forms.

Chapman soon discovered other writers who agreed. On an October evening, not long after her prison album, she was a one of the headliners at the Bluebird, sharing the stage with Matraca Berg, a gifted country music performer, with a magical voice and a song-writer's gift for turning a phrase. But on this particular night, there was an unexpected twist. The two singers were appearing with a pair of southern novelists, Lee Smith and Jill McCorkle, whose stories seemed to fit with a good country song.

Even the audience was littered with stars, songwriters Kim Carnes and Rodney Crowell and a handful of authors passing through the city for the annual Southern Festival of Books. They cheered the stories interspersed with the songs, a rocking interplay of comedy and pathos, and the mood turned serious near the end of the show when Chapman sang one of her signature ballads. "Good-bye Little Rock and Roller" told the story of a girl and her dreams and life on the road in a rock 'n' roll band. But eventually the road brought the girl back home, and she found herself married with a daughter of her own, and felt her hopes giving way to her child's.

> *And then one day her baby girl*
> *Walked outside to find her world.*
> *She never dreamed she'd see the day*
> *She'd be fightin' back the tears to say,*
> *Good-bye my little rock and roller,*
> *Goodbye.*

Not long after that performance was over, Chapman sat down to write her first book. It proved to be a best-selling memoir called, appropriately enough, *Goodbye Little Rock and Roller*, and immediately there were rave reviews all around. Emmylou Harris called Chapman "a true American original"—a writer "who talks about the South and rock 'n' roll in a voice that is funny, poignant, and authentic." And Jill McCorkle declared: "I absolutely love this book. It's *To Kill a Mockingbird* with 'Great Balls of Fire' playing in the background."

Chapman herself said the book was just a start, a musician's dive into the literary world that was already suggested by many of her songs. She said there was more where that came from.

In addition to country, rock 'n' roll, and jazz—and all they reveal about the soul and psyche of our part of the world—I have been fascinated through the years by the music most often known as folk, especially those protest anthems from the 1960s, when singers such as Bob Dylan and Joan Baez added their voices to the fight for simple justice. In many ways, it was a form of music that came and went, at least in terms of the cultural mainstream. But a few years ago, I had the opportunity to profile Si Kahn—a disciple of Pete Seeger's and some of the other great folkies, and an unapologetic throwback to those tumultuous years when the power of music took hold of his life, as well as the troubled life of the country.

With Music and Justice for All

Some people say it has its roots in the mountains, this music he has made for twenty-five years. Si Kahn will tell you there is some truth to that. Long before his work as an organizer brought him to Charlotte, North Carolina, the base for his assault on social injustice, he had a little cabin in the north Georgia hills. It was a sawmill shack with a ramshackle porch, where his neighbors would come—it seemed like every day—to play their banjos, dulcimers, and fiddles, maybe an autoharp or guitar.

Kahn himself would join in the music. He had been writing songs for the most of his life. His first-grade teacher once sent a note home to his rabbi-father, Benjamin Kahn, when they lived in the town of College Station, Pennsylvania: "Simon has written a little song, and we are getting all the class to sing it. We hope to encourage him in this activity."

Nobody knew, of course, that he would go on from there to become one of the important folksingers of his time, or that he would use his gift for poetry and music in his work as an organizer in the South. He had never even been to that part of the country until the summer before his senior year in college. It was 1965, a time of trouble in the deltas of Arkansas and Mississippi. The Student Nonviolent Coordinating Committee (SNCC) was working at the task of voter registration, which had proven at times to be a fatal undertaking. Three civil rights workers had been murdered the previous summer in Mississippi, their youthful bodies buried in a dam, and for Khan and the others who chose to return, there was a fear that never seemed to go away.

"It was with us every minute," he says, and for a while the symbolism was macabre. When he arrived in the town of Forest City, Arkansas, in the delta country just west of Memphis, the only place to stay was a funeral home, bedding down in a room next door to the corpses. The days were spent in a physical labor, building a community center where the organizers could hold mass meetings—and in furtive trips to the scattered farmhouses, where a handful of black people, old and young, decided to join the crusade for civil rights.

Kahn remembered one old woman well past a hundred, who was born a slave and had never even tried to vote in her life. Too dangerous, she said. White people didn't like it. But it was something she wanted to do before she died. The only problem was, she would have to get up from her rocking chair, the most comfortable place in her small wooden cabin, and she didn't want to do it. But Kahn and the others said, "No problem." They picked up her chair, and carried the old woman to the back of a pickup, and then to the registrar's office in the town.

There were moments like that that made it worthwhile, but the fear settled in again every night, and the only thing that drove it away was the music. All through the summer, the civil rights people would gather for meetings at the chapel up the road, and on one of those evenings the Freedom Singers came. They were a group from SNCC who sang all the standards, "We Shall Not Be Moved," "Ain't Nobody Gonna Turn Us Around," and then finally at the end of the night, as the people spilled out of the pews and joined hands, they sang the most powerful anthem of the times, "We Shall Overcome."

Si Kahn was astonished at the emotion of the moment. "The fear motivated the singing," he said, "and gave it wings"—and then in a magical transformation, the fear mutated into something very different, some rush of adrenaline that became intermeshed with a certain belief in the justice of the cause. Later, he would learn that it was almost a science, a deliberate strategy of the civil rights movement developed quite consciously on a February night in 1960. A white folk singer named Guy Carawan had met in the mountains of east

Tennessee with a group of young blacks who would soon emerge as the leadership of SNCC. Carawan began to teach them the songs—most of which had been around for years. Some of them traced to the days of abolition, while others had evolved through the labor movement of the 1930s. Many were hand-clappers, joyous anthems that were sung in the churches, while others were slow and somber affirmations that the power of the movement would not be denied.

Together they became the soundtrack of the times, and after his experience at the Arkansas church, Kahn added his own voice to the others. It was nearly ten years before he finally made a record, and even then he wasn't sure that anyone would listen. But the record companies kept wanting more. Part of it, they said, was his voice—a strong, expressive, unpolished tenor, throbbing with empathy for the people in his songs. But perhaps most of all, it was music with a message, a blend of the things he had learned in the movement.

After his summer in the delta, he worked for a while in the farming communities of southwest Georgia, where blacks were struggling to find a market for their crops. A few years later, he moved to the mountains of southern Appalachia, where he turned his attention to labor organizing and felt, if anything, even more at home. He had come of age in the Pennsylvania mountains, and just beyond the cloister of his small college town, where his father had a job as a campus rabbi, many people made their living from the mines. This was coal country, the hard anthracite extracted from the ground as fodder for the steel mills out to the west.

For the Pennsylvania miners, the living was hard, and on his trips through the coalfields Kahn became accustomed to the tarpaper shacks and burning slag heaps that were physical reminders of the unrelenting poverty. He saw the same thing in the mountains of the South, particularly when he came to eastern Kentucky to work in the Brookside strike in the seventies. Even at the time, he thought it was pivotal. The United Mineworkers Union was demanding a greater attention to safety, and Duke Power Company, the owner of the mine, was fighting the union every step of the way.

Kahn understood that it was part of a change—"the first shot across the bow," he says—in the attitudes of corporations toward labor. During the economic prosperity of the sixties, there had been a detente, when managers decided that it was easier to negotiate than to fight. Labor unions were a part of the cost of doing business. But Duke Power had no use for the unions, and that attitude that was slowly taking hold in company boardrooms all across the country. Kahn would see it a few years later in the case of the textile giant J. P. Stevens, where the workers were attempting to organize a boycott.

He felt himself drawn immediately to the struggle, as powerfully, in fact, as he had been drawn to the civil rights movement in the Arkansas delta. In many ways, it all seemed the same. He had heard the miners say so themselves—these struggling white people in the hard-scrabble towns who looked with admiration to the blacks. *If they can do it, so can we.* It was a common refrain, and Kahn understood that his calling in life was to help people organize for the fights.

"Organizers," he says, "like those I met in the civil rights movement, or the great labor struggle of the 1970s, were usually outsiders of one kind or another. They were always a minority, sometimes prophetic, sometimes not, often beleaguered, sometimes popular. They seemed to me to be the spiritual heirs of the Biblical prophets and the people who fought against slavery or for the American Revolution—some for good reasons, some for the bad. Sometimes, they—we—have been wrong about the truth. But they have been struggling against injustice for twenty thousand years, give or take. There is no reason to believe that the struggle will end in our lifetime, but our goal as organizers is to carry it on."

Through it all, of course, there has been the music. Its fundamental purpose for Kahn is political, but only in the broadest sense of that term. On his albums, there are songs of an African American farmer praying fervently for freedom and rain, and a white mill worker gazing with envy at his boss's house sitting high on a hill. There are songs of immigrants like his paternal grandfather, Gabriel Kahn, who escaped from Russia in a wagonload of hay and survived his final run for the border, as the soldiers' bullets came ripping through the snow.

All of these characters, as Kahn understands them, were moved by the fundamental promise of America, the words on the base of the Statue of Liberty, written by the poet Emma Lazarus, who was, herself, a socialist Jew. For many of the people Kahn has known in his work, that heralded vow of opportunity and fairness—*Give me your tired, your poor*—has gone unfulfilled. But if he has written most often the music of the victims, the people in his songs are much more than that. They embody, he says, the stubborn kind of courage that he found in the mining towns of Appalachia or the cotton country of the Arkansas delta.

"Despite the problems in those places," he explains, "people managed to build good lives. They hunted, fished, developed their sense of family and community, found dignity in work. Part of what I am trying to do is to paint a portrait of working-class life that has that dignity."

His efforts have evolved through more than a dozen albums, all of them done for national folk labels, including Philo, Flying Fish, and Rounder. He has performed at festivals from Newport to Vancouver, has a large following in Europe, and his songs have been recorded by other folk artist from John McCutcheon to his friend Pete Seeger. One of his most recent CDs, *Been a Long Time*, consists of twelve songs about working-class white people living in the mountains. In the title cut, a boy now grown is remembering his grandfather, a man of determination and warmth who had spent his life in the railroad yards. To a boy, it seemed like he might live forever. But he didn't, of course, and after he died, the feeling of loss never quite went away.

> *I think of him now like an engine*
> *That's pulled for so hard and so long.*
> *Rails start to slip, wheels lose their grip*
> *One day you look up and he gone.*

Kahn says his goal in every song that he writes is to honor the humanity of the people he's known. "He fuses life with song," declares Studs Terkel, the Pulitzer Prize–winning author. And Pete Seeger says, "I'm a great admirer of Si Kahn. He's a solid thinker who is able to humanize the political—an absolutely extraordinary guy. I hope he lives to be 120."

Despite such praise, music for Kahn remains a secondary occupation, or perhaps more precisely an important corner of a much bigger mission. He accepts no royalties for his albums or concerts. For the past twenty years, the money instead has gone to the budget of Grassroots Leadership, his Charlotte-based organization that works with poor and working-class communities scattered through the South.

Kahn has a mystical view of that work. He sees it, in part, as the modern extension of the civil rights movement, with roots running deep in the history of the South. Ever since the days of the abolitionist movement, which, in the early years of the nineteenth century, was stronger in the South than it was in the North, the country has been caught up in a struggle—a national tug-of-war to limit or expand the meaning of democracy. Despite its conservative reputation, says Kahn, the South has played a leading role in that struggle.

"People forget how many progressive movements came out of the South," he says. "The first sit-down strike in the 1930s occurred in Decatur, Georgia, for example, not in Flint, Michigan, as most people believe. It's a different strain in the southern character than those that are written about most often. But I believe it's there. I believe the southern movement is an unending thing. Sometimes it's weaker, sometimes it's stronger, but it's always with us. Vincent Harding (the noted African American theologian) once wrote that it's a lot like a river, sometimes on the surface, sometimes underground, but always flowing through the heart of this place."

As Kahn understands it, the movement is redemptive, often bringing out the best in everybody it touches. Sometimes it changes the shape of society. Other times it simply gives people hope, makes them feel less helpless in the face of injustice. But whatever its strength at any given movement, it seems always to keep its tie to the songs, nurtured by the ones that survive, giving rise constantly to the new compositions by writers like Kahn.

His most recent work is an album called *Threads*, in many ways the most ambitious he has done. It includes songs from every phase of his experience, from the cotton fields of the delta to the cotton mills of Massachusetts, where his immigrant ancestors first found work. His lyrics affirm a hard piece of truth: that whatever the success of the movement through the years, there is plenty of work that remains to be done.

They dream in different languages
They dance in different skins

While the bankers down in Boston
Count the money rolling in
Now the mills are empty
Like a wound across the heart
With the heirs of slaves and immigrants
Still a thousand miles apart.

Kahn understands that the day may never come when the issues that tear through American life will at last be fully and fairly resolved. His mission is simply to do what he can, sustained in part by the power of a song.

Epilogue. Not long after finishing Threads, *Kahn and his wife, the philosopher and author Elizabeth Minnich, set to work on a book called* The Fox in the Henhouse: How Privatization Threatens Democracy. *They decried the growing encroachment of for-profit corporations into the realms of prisons, health care, public land management, and even the military. Kahn has also continued writing his songs.*

PART IV

Characters

A Visit with John T. Scopes

On April 1, 1970, I reported to work as I always did, with mingled feelings of boredom and dread, taking my seat in the claustrophobic office that I shared with sixteen teletype machines. Fred Moen, czar of the Associated Press in Nashville, noted my arrival and shouted instructions above the clatter of the news: "Gaillard! John T. Scopes is speaking at Peabody. Get out there and do an interview."

I must have stood frozen for nearly a minute, trying to take in what he had said. I couldn't have been more stunned if he had told me to interview Abraham Lincoln. *John T. Scopes.* Was this some kind of April Fool's joke? As a history major fresh out of Vanderbilt University, I knew a little about the famous "monkey trial"—the trial of the century, many people said—and forty-five years later, that description still seemed to apply.

But was it possible that Scopes was still alive, that this biology teacher from Dayton, Tennessee, this apostle of science and academic freedom, was still a flesh-and-blood human being? The answer to the question turned out to be yes, for there was Scopes on the campus of the Peabody College of Education—a twinkly eyed man then seventy years old, with thinning gray hair and a dark, rumpled suit, speaking to a group of biology students.

It was his first appearance in a Tennessee classroom in forty-five years—one of four appearances he made that day, followed in order by a luncheon with the president and leaders of the college, a press conference, and a final lecture to an overflow crowd at one of the auditoriums on the campus. Until I went back and looked up the clippings, I couldn't remember much of what he said, just the dominant impression that he made, not only on me but apparently on everybody else who heard him.

He was self-deprecating about his role in the trial, seeing himself as a bit player in history. "I did little more than sit, proxylike, in freedom's chair that hot, unforgettable summer," he had written. "No great feat, despite the notoriety it has brought me."

Because of that notoriety—the melodrama of his case and the enduring controversy it produced— Scopes's humility took many of us at Peabody by surprise. Scopes insisted that the issues he had sought to raise in Dayton were not yet resolved, and because they were likely to come up again, he said it was important to understand the story. He had retained his fascination with the two dominant figures at the trial, Clarence Darrow and William Jennings Bryan, protagonists whose different understandings of the world had continued to echo down through the years.

The flamboyant Darrow was known as the greatest trial lawyer of his day, folksy and caustic, representing the leaders of organized labor and criminal defendants nobody would touch. He came to Dayton to defend John Scopes, and it was not his first high-profile case. He had defended the union leaders Eugene Debs and Big Bill Haywood and had crusaded often against the death penalty.

Among his clients were two Chicago boys, Richard Loeb and Nathan Leopold, wealthy and pampered teenaged murderers whose victim was only fourteen years old. Darrow never tried to prove them innocent—they had confessed—but he pleaded powerfully for their lives.

"I am pleading for a time," he said, "when hatred and cruelty will not control the hearts of men. When we can learn by reason and judgment and understanding and faith that all life is worth saving, and that mercy is the highest attribute of man."

That was Clarence Darrow, a man who could move a trial judge to tears and save the lives of two troubled boys when everyone else was calling for their blood.

The following year, when he asked for the chance to defend John Scopes, Darrow was sixty-eight years old. He was a craggy-faced figure with pale blue eyes and a casual, almost rumpled demeanor— camouflage for his razor-sharp mind. He was an avid reader of philosophers and poets and a believer in the rationality of science. But if he was happy to support the theories of Darwin, he was even more eager to take his shots at William Jennings Bryan, regarded by many as a "fundamentalist pope," barnstorming through the South and Midwest, stumping for laws against teaching evolution.

For Bryan, Tennessee had been the site of his greatest success. In the spring of 1925, the legislature had passed by a lopsided margin a bill that immediately made it illegal "to teach any theory that denies the story of the Divine Creation of man as taught in the Bible." The uninspiring sponsor of the bill was a politician-farmer named John Butler, who simply didn't think that a public school teacher ought to contradict the word of the Lord.

Though Bryan agreed, he was moved by a more sophisticated logic—one, in fact, that might have put him at odds with the fundamentalists who followed him a half century later. On many of the political issues of his day, he was not a reactionary at all but an ardent progressive. He supported higher income taxes for the rich and women's suffrage, and in 1915, he resigned as U.S. secretary of state, protesting his nation's drift toward war.

He was a three-time presidential candidate, unsuccessful on each of those occasions, but he was philosophical about his defeats. "The people gave and the people have taken away," he declared, "blessed be the name of the people."

Even his opponents were inclined to agree that Bryan was the greatest orator of his time, and in a curious way, his disdain for Darwin's theory of evolution—the object of his oratory in later years—may have sprung from his deep progressive inclinations. He was repelled by an explanation of life that didn't seem to leave any room for God, but just as strongly he hated the social implications of the theory, the appalling notion that the fittest should survive.

"I object to the Darwinian theory," he proclaimed, "because I fear we shall lose the consciousness of God's presence in our daily life, if we must accept the theory that all through the ages no spiritual force has touched the life of man and shaped the destiny of nations.

"But there is another objection. The Darwinian theory represents man as reaching his present perfection by operation of the law of hate—the merciless law by which the strong crowd out and kill off the weak."

Driven by his passion, and the certainty behind it, Bryan came to Tennessee in 1925 to act as the prosecutor of John Scopes. There was nothing personal about his decision. He found Scopes to be a pleasant young man, and he told him at a dinner just before the trial, "We shall get along fine."

Scopes had a similar respect for Bryan, but not for the law he had helped to inspire. Scopes, who was then twenty-five, came from a family of nonconformists; his father was a socialist union man, working in the railroad yards of Illinois, and had reared his son to swim against the tide. Scopes was happy to do it—not for Darwin or the theory of evolution but for the overarching cause of academic freedom.

Scopes had been in Dayton for nearly a year, having worked as a teacher and a football coach, and he liked the place well enough— the mountainous terrain and small-town warmth—and he was barely even curious on a May afternoon when several of the city fathers asked to see him. School was already out for the summer, and Scopes was playing tennis with some of his students.

When the game was over he made his way to Robinson's Drug Store, one of the favorite gathering spots in town. The owner, Fred Robinson, was chairman of the school board, and he was talking with some of the town's business leaders when Scopes pulled up a chair to join them. They showed him an ad in a Chattanooga newspaper in which the American Civil Liberties Union offered to pay the legal costs for anyone who would challenge the evolution law.

They asked if Scopes would be willing to do it, since he had spent a few weeks near the end of the semester subbing for the biology teacher, who was ill. Surely, they said, he had taught evolution in there at some point. Scopes wasn't sure he had actually done it, but he believed that the law should be struck down, and he agreed to test it in a Tennessee courtroom.

He could see immediately that the city fathers' motivation was different from his; their primary interest was publicity for Dayton, something they believed would be good for business. Scopes didn't mind if that was what they wanted. But as he made clear at the time, and during his later visit to Peabody, he thought there were larger issues at stake: People needed to be free to think.

"Education is something that is to mold the individual," he told his student audience at Peabody, free from the "contamination of state interference."

At the time of his visit, there were people who believed that the battle was won, that fundamentalism had died at the Dayton courthouse, its foolishness fully revealed to the world. Certainly, Scopes himself was convinced that Clarence Darrow had gotten the better of it when he summoned William Jennings Bryan to the stand and began to grill him about the pages of the Bible.

Had Jonah really lived in the belly of a whale? Had the earth stopped turning when Joshua commanded the sun to stand still? Had God really made the world in six days?

Bryan had stumbled badly in his answers, hedging and sweating in the July heat, as two hundred reporters made note of the fact. But Scopes didn't think that the contest was over. Despite the courtroom prowess of Darrow, the evolution law had remained in effect. (Scopes, in fact, had been convicted and fined one hundred dollars.) The judge in Dayton refused to find the statute unconstitutional, and for the next forty years, the Tennessee legislature refused to repeal it.

That finally changed in 1967 when a new legislature, with great fanfare, purged the monkey law from the books. "Better late than never," Scopes quipped. But he also seemed to understand clearly that the issue was likely to come up again.

"The cause defended at Dayton," he wrote, "is a continuing one that has existed throughout man's brief history and will continue as long as man is here. It is the cause of freedom for which each man must do what he can."

He said essentially the same thing at Peabody, and his warning would prove to be prophetic. Thirty-five years later, in 2005, a flurry of headlines in many parts of the country proclaimed the second coming of the Scopes trial. The setting this time was Dover, Pennsylvania, another small town with a clash of worldviews taking center stage.

The battle lines were drawn by the board of education. William Buckingham, chairman of the textbook committee for the board, had pushed through a new component on "intelligent design," a theory of the divine authorship of life, in the science classes of the Dover school district. Buckingham was a retired prison guard who walked with a cane and, as *Harper's Magazine* later noted, often wore a pin in the lapel of his coat: an American flag wrapped around a cross.

"Nearly two thousand years ago," he declared, "someone died on a cross for us. Shouldn't we have the courage to stand up for him?" Later, when pressed in court about his religious motivations, Buckingham insisted emphatically, "I'm still waiting for a judge or anyone to show me anywhere in the Constitution where there's a separation of church and state."

In 2005, after eleven Dover parents and the American Civil Liberties Union sued to overturn the Buckingham policy, U.S. district judge John Jones—described in the media as a church-going Republican—delivered a stinging judicial rebuke to the school board. As the Associated Press reported in December, "Jones decried the 'breath-taking inanity' of the Dover policy and accused several board members of lying to conceal their true motive, which he said was to promote religion."

Many science educators took heart in that. At Peabody, more than three decades after Scopes's visit, Kefyn Catley, an evolutionary biologist who teaches teachers how to deal with the subject, said the trial in Dover "really galvanized a lot of scientists. People were backing off before that."

The fundamental problem, said Catley, is that we live in a country where the population is split fifty-fifty on the theory of evolution, while the consensus among scientists is nearly overwhelming.

"Evolution," he explained, "is the overarching framework of all life science."

Not that the controversy should be surprising. As the evolutionist Eugenie Scott notes in her book *Evolution vs. Creationism*, published a year before the Dover trial, even Charles Darwin understood the painful implications of his theory. He kept it a secret for nearly twenty years, and even then, he said, "it was like confessing a murder."

In an ironic way, Darwin understood with William Jennings Bryan that there was a cruelty at the heart of natural selection, which was hard to reconcile with a benevolent God. "There seems to me too much misery in the world," Darwin wrote in a letter to one of his friends. "I own that I cannot see as plainly as others do, and as I should wish to do, evidence of design and beneficence on all sides of us."

John T. Scopes, from all indications, seemed to understand that Darwin's dilemma was not universal. There were other scientists—giants in the field—whose work took on a kind of mystical property and led them to speak quite naturally of God. Albert Einstein was certainly one of those. This towering figure of the twentieth century, whose visage was synonymous with a scientific mind, saw such an awesome symmetry in physics that in the end he could explain it only as divine.

For Scopes, as he affirmed in 1970, the issue ultimately came down to the search, the unfettered freedom to study and to think, unrestrained by the dogmas of religion or the state. Scopes never argued, at Peabody or elsewhere, that the subject of evolution was easy—that this cornerstone of scientific understanding didn't involve its share of uncertainty or angst as we struggle to understand our place in the cosmos.

Nor was it the only issue that worried him. On that April day in his seventy-first year, he spoke of his time as an oil company geologist, a profession he had entered not long after his adventure in Dayton. He decried the American tendencies to "worship at the altar of technological advance" and to run roughshod over "the environment that supports us"—tendencies, he said, that often afflicted his own line of work. But above all else, he continued to fret about "legislation that tampers with academic freedom, . . . helping to make robot factories out of schools."

There was, as I remember it now, a kind of rumpled affability that softened his warnings, the hint of a smile, the wink of an eye. He presented himself as a man overshadowed by the history he had made, though he also knew that he was, inescapably, the flesh and blood presence at the heart of it all.

It seemed fitting, somehow, that in one of his final public appearances, for he died unexpectedly the following fall, he would address himself to educators-in-waiting, reminding them again of what one student called "the fundamental right of man to ask questions."

In September 1957, several southern cities took their first halting steps toward the desegregation of their public schools. Little Rock, Arkansas, was the most famous, for it was the place where federal troops were sent in to protect nine African American students assigned to previously all-white Central High School. That same week, four students in Charlotte, North Carolina, also broke the color barrier, and one of the unnoticed implications of that story was that it attracted the attention of the great American writer James Baldwin. Baldwin, at the time, was living in Paris and had never been to the American South. That would soon change, for when he saw photographs of a white mob taunting a black student in Charlotte, he vowed to go to North Carolina and assess the situation for himself. Some of his finest writing would follow, as well as his own civil rights activism. This is the story of how that happened.

James Baldwin's First Journey South

The picture took the writer by surprise when he saw it that afternoon in Paris. There was a dignity about it that you might not have expected as the young girl made her way through the mob. She seemed so serene in the midst of her defiance. Her dress, he would learn, had been sewn by her grandmother, and it was somehow perfect for a girl of fifteen—prim and handsome with a bow at the collar, completed in time for her first day at school.

This was no ordinary school year. The date was September 1957, and Dorothy Counts—which James Baldwin would learn was the girl's name—was a racial pioneer in the American South. She had been hand-picked by the African American leaders of her city, carefully chosen for her intelligence and poise. She was one of four black students in Charlotte, North Carolina, who would cross the color barrier that fall, inflaming passions all over town. The mob she confronted on September 4 consisted mostly of her future classmates, but there were adults also on the fringes of the crowd, screaming their ugly instructions to the students: "Spit on her, people! Spit on her!"

Don Sturkey, a photographer for the *Charlotte Observer*, captured the moment in a photograph that was soon distributed all over the world. When James Baldwin saw it in a paper in Paris, his initial revulsion grew stronger by the hour, then slowly, inexorably turned into guilt. "It made me furious," he wrote, "it filled me with both hatred and pity, and it made me ashamed. Some one of us should have been there with her!"

Baldwin had lived in Europe for nearly ten years, a refugee of sorts, having fled from the agony of his Harlem boyhood. Part of it was personal. He had never known his biological father, but his stepfather proved to be unforgettable—a cruel, bombastic tyrant of a man who wrapped his terrible temper in piety. David Baldwin was a factory worker and part-time preacher who presided bitterly over the poverty around him and terrified the nine children he was raising with his violent and unpredictable moods.

On the day he died, August 2, 1943, a race riot broke out in Harlem, and on the following morning, as James Baldwin remembered, "We drove my father to the graveyard through a wilderness of smashed plate glass. . . . He had lived and died in intolerable bitterness of spirit and it frightened me, as we drove him through those unquiet, ruined streets, to see how powerful and overflowing this bitterness could be and to realize that it was now mine."

A few years earlier, as a teenaged boy, Baldwin had sought relief from his own disillusionment in the sanctuary of a Pentecostal pulpit. He became a preacher at the age of fourteen and loved the imagery and language of the church. But even in the grip of the Holy Spirit, he could never quite escape that undertow of pain that came with being a black man in America.

At the age of twenty-four, he left. A writer now, he sought a new sanctuary in the streets of Paris—the place where other men of letters had gone, from Hemingway to Fitzgerald to Baldwin's own mentor and friend, Richard Wright. He wrote his first three books in Europe—his ground-breaking novels, *Go Tell It on the Mountain* and *Giovanni's Room*, and his collection of essays, *Notes of a Native Son*. He wrestled with the agonies of sexuality and race, caught up more than ever, it seemed, with the baggage that he had brought from America.

"I was forced to admit," he wrote in *Notes of a Native Son*, "something I had always hidden from myself, which the American

Negro has had to hide from himself as the price of his public progress; that I hated and feared white people. This did not mean that
I loved black people; on the contrary, I despised them, possibly
because they had failed to produce Rembrandt. In effect, I hated
and feared the world."

But then came the afternoon in Paris, in September of 1957,
when he encountered the image of Dorothy Counts, this girl of fifteen surrounded by a mob, no trace of hatred anywhere in her face,
no hint of fear in her soft, pretty eyes. Later, she would say that yes,
it was true: she had not been afraid, for she was enveloped that day
in the love of her family, and the Sunday school certainty that God
would protect her. And she did not feel anger toward the people in
the mob. She felt sorry for them, certain that they would not have
done these things if they had been raised better, if they had come
from a family as loving as her own.

All of these things James Baldwin would learn. But his shame
was instantaneous when he saw the photograph, for here was a girl,
in her innocence and youth, confronting everything from which he
had fled. "It was on that bright afternoon," he wrote, "that I knew
that I was leaving France. I could, simply, no longer sit around
in Paris discussing the Algerian and the black American problem.
Everybody else was paying their dues, and it was time I went home
and paid mine."

He decided to travel to the American South, a place that he had
never been, and one that had always filled him with dread. He made
the trip on assignment from *Harper's Magazine* and the *Partisan
Review*, the former a mainstream monthly, and the latter a political journal in New York. He stopped in Charlotte, North Carolina,
the city where Counts had made her stand, and what he found, not
surprisingly, was a community in crisis. Charlotte was one of the first
cities in the South to attempt to desegregate its schools, and Baldwin
discovered, among other things, a mood of confusion among the
people in the town.

He learned that Dorothy was one of four children chosen to
break the color barrier that year, and in the end, the member of
the group who intrigued him the most was Gus Roberts, who had
been assigned to the city's Central High School. Baldwin would soon
hear the story of Gus's introduction to the school—how a sullen a
mob turned out to greet him, similar to the one that had confronted

Dorothy Counts. But Gus's experience was a little bit different, for he was met at the curb by the principal of the school, a wiry, crew-cut South Carolinian by the name of Ed Sanders.

Sanders, in a way, had dreaded that moment. He had no particular taste for adventure, and as Baldwin would learn, he had come of age in the segregated South. But as he sat in his office that September morning, he saw the crowd out the window below, and he knew what was coming. The stakes were greater than integrating a school. This was an assault on the southern way of life, and while Sanders had slowly come to the conclusion that the looming changes were long overdue, he had no illusion that it would be easy. He knew the mood of the crowd would be ugly, but he also knew that he couldn't let Gus face the mob by himself.

"A decision had to be made," he remembered, "as to whether you go out there and try to get the boy and bring him in, or whether you get your briefcase and go home. It was that simple. It was to me. And I didn't want to get my briefcase."

For his part, Gus was not reassured. Sanders was such an unimposing figure—scrawny almost at five-feet-seven and a hundred and thirty pounds, with ruddy features and a slow, southern drawl—but he seemed to be the only ally in sight, and together they picked their way through the crowd. Only a few steps into the journey, somebody knocked a baseball cap from Gus's head—an act of defiance, Sanders knew, that could lead to escalation. "Pick it up," the principal demanded, and for an agonizing second nobody moved. Finally, however, one of the students reached for the cap and gave it back to Gus.

The crowd, at that point, seemed to lose its nerve, and Gus was able to make it to the school. But in the coming weeks, there were mutterings and epithets in the halls, and James Baldwin, when he came to Charlotte, wanted to know what it felt like to Gus. What was he feeling when the crowd had blocked his path to the building?

"Nothing, sir," Roberts softly replied, and the writer found himself marveling again at the courage and stoicism of the young.

"He seemed to be extraordinary," Baldwin wrote, "at first mainly by his silence. He was tall for his age and, typically, seemed to be constructed mainly of sharp angles, such as elbows and knees. Dark gingerbread sort of coloring, with ordinary hair, and a face disquietingly impassive, save for his very dark, very large eyes. I got the impression, each time he that he raised them, not so much that they spoke but that they registered volumes; each time he dropped them it was as though he had retired into the library."

Throughout much of the somber interview, which occurred at the Roberts home in Charlotte, Gus sat focused on his homework, while his mother, who was with him, did most of the talking. She said the reason for changing schools was simple: the white schools in Charlotte were better than the black, and there had been too many days in the past when Gus, who had always been a straight-A student, could get his homework done in five minutes. Too many of his teachers didn't seem to care and this bright young man, now turning fifteen, had never been challenged in his all-black classes.

But things were different at Central High School, and for that reason alone, the ordeal was worth it. As Baldwin remembered the interview later, Gus remained silent while his mother talked, and when Baldwin asked again about the harassment, the boy merely shrugged.

"They just—call names," he said. "I don't let it bother me."

Even as he noted the young man's strength, Baldwin wondered about the internal damage, which he knew could not be calculated quickly. Would Gus ever wonder whether he'd done the right thing? And what about the other people around him? Could they see the human face of the drama taking shape? Had any of them given any thought to the cost?

The next day Baldwin drove down to the school, which was less than a mile from the heart of downtown, and made his way to the principal's office. Ed Sanders was waiting and greeted him cordially. He was intrigued by this curious writer from the North, a man, as it happened, about his own age, who seemed to be different from many of the others. "He was not critical of us," Sanders would recall. "He was just asking a whole lot of questions."

Despite the inevitable barriers between them—the chasm of race, the distance between Harlem, or Paris, and the South— Baldwin was impressed with Sanders as well. "I've got a job to do, and I'm going to do it," the principal had told him, and Baldwin understood that he meant it. But as he searched the face of this southern white man, he thought he detected a certain ambivalence, a confusion about the changes taking place around him.

"He explained to me, with difficulty," Baldwin wrote in *Harper's*, "that desegregation was contrary to everything he'd ever seen or believed. He'd never dreamed of a mingling of the races; had never lived that way himself and didn't suppose that he ever would. . . . The eyes came to life then, or a veil fell, and I found myself staring at a man in anguish. The eyes were full of pain and bewilderment. . . . It is not an easy thing to be forced to reexamine a way of life and to speculate, in a personal way, on the general injustice."

But if Baldwin was struck by the integrity of Sanders, that was not his dominant image of the South. He remembered his early glimpse of the land, flying into Georgia, just after his visit to North Carolina. He noticed the rust-red color of the soil and could not suppress the thought, he said, "that this earth had acquired its color from the blood that had dripped down from these trees. My mind was filled with the image of a black man, younger than I, perhaps, or my own age, hanging from a tree, while white men watched him and cut his sex from him with a knife . . .

"The southern landscape," he continued, "—the trees, the silence, the liquid heat, and the fact that one always seems to be traveling great distances—seems designed for violence, seems, almost, to demand it. What passions cannot be unleashed on a dark road in a southern night!"

But the night, Baldwin wrote, was followed inevitably by the day, and in that harsh and unrelenting light, the South would be confronted with the sins of the past—sins no greater than those of the North—and the nation as a whole would have to pay the price. In the years after that, as the civil rights movement confirmed his prophecy, Baldwin kept writing about the issue of race, not because it was all that mattered, but because it was something that he couldn't put aside. "It was," he said, "the gate that I had to unlock before I could hope to write about anything else."

In his long and distinguished career, he would produce six novels to go with his essays, the most powerful of which were written in the wake of his first visit south. He became a fixture in the civil rights movement, a speaker whose eloquence and passion would recall his own early days in a Pentecostal pulpit.

Then in 1987, he died, a victim of cancer, and at the age of sixty-three he was one of America's most venerated writers. When word of his passing reached North Carolina, a local reporter telephoned Ed Sanders to ask for a comment. Sanders, by then, had retired from a long career in education—a vocation in which his proudest achievement had been the desegregation of the schools.

Both he and his community, he thought, had come a long way since the day James Baldwin first came to town. Gus Roberts had graduated soon after, having won the respect of most of his classmates, carrying himself, in Sanders's estimation, with uncommon dignity and restraint. Sanders and Roberts had become good friends, getting together periodically to talk about their common ordeal.

"Gus," Sanders asked him on one occasion, "what did you think of me when we first met?"

As Sanders remembered the conversation later, Roberts responded with an ironic smile and mentioned the mob that had gathered at the school. "I thought," he said, "that you were the skinniest white man I ever met."

Sanders would tell the story years later as a way of demythologizing their achievement. But he knew Gus Roberts had started Charlotte on its way, and for the next twenty years, the level of integration had steadily increased. In the early 1970s, Charlotte became the national test case for busing, and adopting a plan that Sanders helped devise, its school system was, at least for a while, one of the most integrated in the country.

When Baldwin died, Sanders didn't talk about any of that. He simply paid homage to the frail young writer with the large brooding eyes, a man who seemed to be searching for the truth. He had been annoyed at the time when he first read Baldwin's article in *Harper's*—the faintly unflattering description of himself as a man "bewildered" by the changes around him. But even then, he said, he retained his fascination and affinity for a writer who seemed to be an honest man.

"At the time," Sanders said, "I didn't think we were as confused or bewildered as Baldwin indicated. But I think I would read it differently today."

That, he added, should have come as no surprise. Seeing things clearly—looking past the surface and understanding the poetry of the truth—are, after all, the first duties of a writer.

In 2003, I was asked by Vanderbilt Magazine *to write a profile of Tipper Gore, who had earned her master's degree from the university. I had met Al Gore briefly on a couple of occasions but never his wife, and I wasn't quite sure what to expect. What I discovered, as often happens in the world of journalism, was a person more formidable than I would have guessed. I was grateful to be writing for* Vanderbilt Magazine, *one of the best publications of its kind in the country, and a venue where I could discard the cynical prism of political journalism—a mindset that assumes the worst about public figures, then dares them to disprove it if they can.*

The Many Crusades of Tipper Gore

It was a July afternoon in Tipper Gore's office, one of her rare interviews these days, a moment when the memories came flooding back. There were stories of the Clintons and Nelson Mandela and the infested refugee camps of Rwanda where she witnessed the horrors of a genocidal war. But there were also the stories from closer to home, more personal and immediate, like the homeless woman outside the White House, gesturing, talking, walking in a daze, obviously in need of some kind of help.

Tipper Gore was a volunteer at the time with a homeless advocacy organization in Washington, and she often found herself searching the streets, looking for the people with no place to go. She approached the woman near the White House cautiously.

"What's your name?" she said. "How can I help you?"

The woman stared back with her large, dark eyes, looking straight into Tipper Gore's own. She was African American, thin and wispy, maybe five-feet-three, and somewhere imbedded in her quiet desperation there seemed to be a certain sweetness in her smile.

"My name is Mary Tudor," she said. "You can help me get my reality back."

They talked for a while about the places she could go—a downtown shelter where she could get a hot shower and a good hearty meal, and where they could begin to evaluate her mental health. But a cloud passed over the black woman's face.

"I can't go," she said. "My husband will worry."

"Who's your husband?"

"President Clinton."

"Oh, I see," replied Gore, a psychologist by inclination and training. "Well, I know how to get a message to the president. We can tell him you are going with me and it will be okay."

Together they went to the gate of the White House, where Gore introduced Mary to the marine on duty and told him, please, to let the president know she was fine. The marine said he would and the two women headed away to the shelter, where Mary enrolled in emergency housing and soon began treatment at a mental health center.

They visited often in the months after that, the vice president's wife and the woman of the streets. Gore would drop by the shelter to see her, sometimes talking for an hour or more, giving her encouragement as she went through her treatments. Mary (which turned out not to be her real name) came several times to the vice president's mansion, twice for lunch, and along with other homeless people from the capital, a couple of times to the Gores' Christmas parties.

As the people who have known her through the years will tell you, all of this was vintage Tipper Gore. She has long been a woman given to crusades, sometimes public, sometimes less so, sometimes quixotic in the eyes of her critics. Whatever the case, she has divided her energy, which was always considerable, between the needs of her family and the demands of the causes she has chosen to embrace.

It is a pattern in her life that continues even now. At the time of our interview in 2003, she and her husband were, among other things, putting together a national conference on the family—the twelfth in a series of meetings at Vanderbilt, which the two of them started in 1991. "We call them Family Re-Unions," she said. "We have met a lot of good people there."

She was sitting at the time in her Nashville office, just across the street from the Vanderbilt campus. She was still moving in, her professional life in cardboard boxes, as she prepared for a series of personal appearances—one in Chicago, another in Dallas, two more in California; but she was happy, she said, to take a little time to reflect on her journey. She remembered the days in the early seventies when she was still a young wife working on her master's in clinical psychology. There was a beauty about the campus of Peabody College of Education, the division of Vanderbilt where she studied, a feeling of promise as she was beginning her life with the handsome young son of a Tennessee senator.

This was before she knew where all of it would lead her, before she imagined in any realistic way what it might be like as the wife of a congressman or a U.S. senator or, later, the vice president of the United States. But she knew from the start that life with her husband would be something special. In 1964, they met at a high school party in Virginia, and the following weekend they danced to an evening's worth of rock 'n' roll records. It was like nothing she had ever felt in her life.

"He's such a sweet man," she said years later, and that was the thing that struck her from the start. It was true that he had other qualities as well. Even as a teenager, Al Gore was strong and sure of himself, as you might expect from the son of the most prominent politician in the state. His aristocratic father, Albert Gore Sr., was one of the most stubborn men in the Senate—part of the loyal opposition during the War in Vietnam, a stand that cost him politically in Tennessee. But his son often talked in the years after that about the need to follow both his conscience and his heart.

Tipper liked that about him, and even his occasional flashes of petulance seemed to fade so easily, subsiding into something more gentle and fair. Once when he was a freshman at Harvard, and Tipper was still a senior in high school, he invited her to come to Boston to see him. The problem was, Tipper's grandmother insisted on coming along, which in many ways was not a surprise. When her parents divorced when she was only two, Tipper and her mother went to live with her grandparents. For years after that, Tipper's mother, Margaret Ann Aitcheson, battled through the agony of clinical depression, and Tipper's grandmother, Verda Carlson, became a surrogate parent. She was a sturdy woman with old-fashioned values, appalled at the notion that a pretty young girl might go off to visit a boy by herself.

Al was not at all happy with the news. "I hope this isn't making you mad," he wrote, "but I don't care about spending a week with your grandmother. I want a week with you. . . . As I think more about it, I don't like it worth a damn."

But when the week finally came, the grandmother was there and there was nothing for Al to do but adjust. "He was a perfect gentleman," Tipper said years later, a fact not lost on her or her family, and whatever the various frustrations of the moment, Al Gore's stock was still on the rise.

In May 1970, they were married, and after Al did a hitch in Vietnam, they moved for a while to the Gores' family farm. It was nestled away near the town of Carthage, in the scenic hill country just east of Nashville, and Tipper thought it was perfect. She could imagine herself in such a place forever, a farmer's wife living close to the land.

In those early days of fantasy and promise, Al went to work as a reporter in Nashville, and Tipper tried her hand at journalism too. She worked for a while as a part-time photographer and soon discovered she was very good at it. She had taken a class from Jack Corn, the *Nashville Tennessean*'s chief photographer, driving the hundred-mile round trip from Carthage, absorbing his wisdom and sense of the craft. For one of the classes Corn told his students to take a photograph of somebody who loved them—a photo in which that affection was clear. Tipper took a picture of her husband shaving, his dark hair tousled, his face still lathered but a kind of smoldering softness in his eyes as he stared at the camera and the young woman behind it.

A short time later, Corn offered her a job.

She juggled her photography with work on her master's degree at Peabody, completing her studies n 1975. And then came the day in 1976 when her husband decided to run for Congress. Though it wasn't easy for her, because of her own professional aspirations, Tipper quickly made a fundamental decision. She would share in the journey as fully as she could. She would not be like those Washington wives who would make their obligatory appearances at a fundraising dinner, or perhaps at the national convention of the party. She would be there with him every step of the way.

She says it was difficult at first, that the political small talk with total strangers was hard for her to muster in those early days. But she soon discovered an aptitude for it, a natural gregariousness and an ability to look people squarely in the eye.

The people who knew her were not at all surprised.

"With Tipper Gore," says Larry Woods, a Nashville lawyer and

Democratic activist, "what you see is what you get. I've known her now for three decades, and she has impressed me as a person of wisdom and substance, who has that knack for getting things done."

As Woods had expected from the moment he met her, Tipper Gore soon emerged as a public figure on her own, and many of her passionate crusades on behalf of the causes she embraced were tied to her family. Her concern for the homeless, for example, began on a luncheon excursion with her children. They were still quite young, ranging in age from two to ten, and three of the four were attending a public school in Washington.

It was a Wednesday afternoon, an early release day to spend with their families, and they had gone to eat lunch with their father at the Senate. On the way back home, they were stopped at a light, and there on the corner was a ragged-looking woman talking frantically to nobody in particular.

"What's wrong with her, Mom?" the children kept asking. "Who's she talking to?"

"Well," said Tipper, "she's homeless and she's probably mentally ill."

The younger Gores were appalled. "You mean she's sick and she has no place to go, and we are just going to drive off and leave her?"

That night over dinner they talked about it—Tipper and Al and all four of the children, and they resolved that the time had come to get involved. Tipper had already called about the woman on the corner, alerting the people at the homeless hot line, and within a short time her husband would introduce new legislation to create housing for the people in the streets.

Her children, meanwhile, began to volunteer at a homeless shelter, making sandwiches, doing what they could, and Tipper herself began a twenty-year commitment to the issue. "I stopped turning away," she would later explain. "The children and their innocent compassion got to me. They saw the world with such total clarity."

In an effort to replicate that kind of clarity, she organized a pair of photography exhibitions, betting on the power of her favorite art form to put a human face on an abstract issue. She also volunteered at the shelters, and after her husband was elected vice president she became a regular with Health Care for the Homeless, an advocacy organization in Washington that scoured the streets and public parks of the capital, searching for people who needed better care.

It was work that took her into difficult places, which sometimes drove the Secret Service crazy. "Totally nuts," she told one reporter. But most of the agents understood the mission, and on several occasions she was glad they were there, like the time, for example, when they took away a knife from one of the desperate-looking men in an alley.

Every so often the payoff was clear, for there were homeless people who responded to the treatment and managed to turn their own lives around. But there were others who didn't, who died of AIDS or another illness in the streets, and that was a part of the reality also.

Through it all, she made no mention of her efforts to the press, for somehow that would have cheapened everything. "It was a personal commitment that I made," she explained, "that meant something to me. There didn't seem to be any need to talk about it."

That, of course, wasn't always true. Other causes on other occasions were much more visible and controversial, with Tipper Gore squarely at the center of the storm. One of those took shape in the 1980s, and once again it was triggered by her children.

In December 1984, she bought a copy of the album *Purple Rain* by the rock artist Prince. Her daughter Karenna, who was then eleven, had been asking for it because of a song she had heard on the radio. They sat down together, mother and daughter, to listen to the music and were startled by the lyrics to one of the cuts: "I knew a girl named Nikki / Guess [you] could say she's a sex fiend / I met her in a motel lobby / Masturbating with a magazine."

About the same time Karenna's two sisters, Kristin and Sarah, who were six and eight, began asking questions about videos they had seen on MTV. This time Gore was even more shocked, for she was treated to the image of a heavy metal band, Motley Crue, locking semi-naked women in cages.

She had never thought of herself as a prude. She had been raised in the rock 'n' roll generation, had been a drummer, in fact, in a high school band, and she knew that sexuality was imbedded in the music. "I understood the themes," she would later explain, "but I was like, 'Whoa.' Here I was explaining S&M to my eight-year-old."

Her husband by then was a U.S. senator, which put her in touch with other Washington wives who shared her concerns. Together they formed a nonprofit group, the Parents' Music Resource Center, and in May 1985 they set out to bring pressure on the entertainment industry. They found an ally in the National PTA and began holding public meetings and talking to the media, and after a while they began negotiations with leaders in the industry. They were seeking more responsibility and restraint, and some kind of warning labels on records, and for a while at least everything got ugly.

Frank Zappa, an aging rock 'n' roller with a national following, labeled Gore and her allies "cultural terrorists." One of the young rockers said she was afraid of the sexuality of her children, and an industry spokesman declared that her efforts "smacked of censorship."

In fact, they didn't. As others noted, from the *New York Times* to the American Civil Liberties Union, Tipper Gore and her friends were seeking voluntary labeling, not a standard imposed by the government, and that in the end was what they got. In 1987, the record industry began to rate its own product, putting warnings on albums with explicit lyrics, and Gore saw that achievement as a victory.

"It was a tool for parents," she said looking back. "It's up to us to guide our children, and as mine got older I would sometimes say, 'Ok, it's your choice. You can listen to this if you want to.' But we would talk about the values, and that's what you have to do as a parent—set the limits, and then loosen up as your children get older. The warning labels were just another tool. I thought of it really as truth in marketing."

There are those even now who say she was simply jousting at the wind. Peter Cooper, music writer for the *Nashville Tennessean*, points out that lyrics once hidden away on albums are now heard freely on the radio, and there is nothing that a label can do about that. In the largest sense, Gore and her friends were resisting the irresistible tide.

Whether it was a victory, a defeat, or something in between, for Gore herself the whole episode was soon overshadowed, obliterated by a moment of horror that quickly put everything else in perspective. It was the moment she almost lost her youngest child.

April 3, 1989—opening day of the baseball season, a day full of promise like so many others. The Baltimore Orioles, with the great Frank Robinson managing the team and Cal and Billy Ripkin anchoring the infield, were playing at home, and Al and Tipper Gore and two other couples took their children to the game.

Outside the stadium, Albert Gore III, who was not yet seven, was holding tight to his father's hand, when he suddenly jerked free and went running off in pursuit of his friends. It all happened so quickly, and the Gores could only stare in disbelief as their son ran squarely into the path of a car. He flew through the air in a horrifying arc and then lay crumpled and still on the pavement.

It took him nearly a year to recover, and during that time there were bedside vigils and moments when nobody knew whether he would live. Tipper Gore, a woman of great strength, held it together through all of those hours, but the time finally came when the crisis had passed and she felt herself slipping into clinical depression.

"I thought I had dodged that bullet," she said, recalling her mother's mental health problems. But the demons hit her with a devastating force, requiring both counseling and medication to recover.

Typically enough, she would later turn her troubles into a cause, crusading on behalf of better mental health care. She would chair a presidential conference on the subject and speak out strongly for insurance benefits comparable to those for any other illness. But for a while she struggled to make it through the day and even in the delicate period of her recovery, she depended on the love and understanding of her family.

The Gores had always been quite close. Al, she thought, was such a good father, so patient and gentle with all of the children, and now it seemed they were getting even closer. Her husband, who had run for president in 1988, coming up short in the Democratic primaries, decided not to run again in 1992 so he could spend more time with the family.

For a while at least, it appeared their time on the national stage was over—just a brief flirtation in 1988, and now it was back to the U.S. Senate, a worthy calling by anybody's measure. But then came the night of July 7, 1992.

It was eleven o'clock in the evening when Bill Clinton called, asking Al Gore to be his running mate. Clinton had confounded the political pundits by winning the nomination in the Democratic primaries, and he would surprise them again with his choice of Gore. The two men, after all, were southern moderates from contiguous states, both about the same age, and according to many political analysts, Gore didn't add a lot of breadth to the ticket.

But Clinton had a feeling, and after a little while so did the

Gores. The campaign season was inherently self-contained, the November election less than four months away, far less disruptive to their time as a family than the arduous string of Democratic primaries. Before the call, the Gores hadn't known the Clintons very well, but they quickly discovered an affinity that was rare.

"I felt Hillary was my long-lost sister," Tipper said more than once. And they would laugh sometimes when they were all four together about how Tipper was really much more like the president—more outgoing and more animated, far more at ease in the company of strangers.

All in all, they seemed to complement each other's strengths, and they shared a basic understanding of the country. They valued its diversity and hated the pitting of one group against another, and they saw the government as a tool for doing good. There was a sense in which all of them—and maybe most of all the president—had internalized the idealism of the sixties, and it gave them a feeling of possibility and hope. They would tackle the economy and the massive budget deficits, and they would talk to the Russians about nuclear disarmament and protect the environment and wrestle with the waste in the federal bureaucracy.

As they years went by, they would succeed in many of those aspirations, but eventually, of course, there were other things as well—the intricate character flaws of Bill Clinton, which in the eyes of many of the voters never fully defined him. Whatever his failings, he was also a man of resiliency and grace, and the Gores understood that as well as anybody. But in the end there were strains, as Al Gore made his own run for the presidency and sought to establish a political identity distinct from the double-edged legacy of his friend.

Today, Tipper Gore is much more guarded in talking about the Clintons, more reluctant to go into personal detail. When a reporter recently asked about Hillary, her answer was enigmatic and abrupt: "I have my life, she has hers. But we do talk."

And yet, for Tipper, whatever the weight of the personal history, the memories of those eight years in Washington were as rich and compelling as any she had known. Some of them, of course, were deeply disturbing, including her visit to the killing fields of Rwanda. Her poignant photographs tell the story of the trip—pictures of children and occasionally their parents, staring at the camera with emptiness or pain.

But she will also tell you that on the same troubled continent at about the same time, there was a moment of inspiration so powerful and pure that it stands far above all the rest. In 1994, she was part of the official American delegation attending the inauguration of Nelson Mandela.

She had never met anyone quite like him. She knew his story, how he had spent twenty-seven years in a cell on Robben Island, and later she would see it—the claustrophobic rectangle that he had somehow known was only temporary. At one of the inauguration ceremonies, she and the other Americans in Pretoria watched in astonishment as Mandela called his former jailer to the podium, put an arm around his shoulder, and talked to the country about the power of forgiveness.

"Al and I were just blown away," she remembered, and the image was never very far from her mind. It was a source of perspective, a lesson against bitterness and regret, as the Gores encountered their own disappointments—the controversial loss of the 2000 election, and the decision in December 2002 to abandon their presidential dreams altogether.

The latter decision was made in New York City, and somehow the richness of memory made it easier—the simultaneous feelings of accomplishment and gratitude for all of the opportunities they had had.

So they came together in New York—Tipper and Al and all four of the children—for a week of rehearsals for *Saturday Night Live*, where Al, improbably, would appear as guest host. The show itself went remarkably well (later it was nominated for an Emmy), and those who were watching had no way to know that the host was working toward a difficult decision.

He had long been worried that the American media had little interest in a Bush-Gore rematch. He thought it was possible to beat George Bush, and because of the economy and the looming war in Iraq, he also thought it was critically important. But would it be possible, if the press corps were bored, to get his own message out?

More and more he was afraid the answer to that question was no, and he told all this to the members of his family. Later, he would say the same thing to Leslie Stahl, stunning a national *60 Minutes* audience. Tipper Gore thought it was typical of her husband, putting the interests of the country ahead of his own, and she bristled at even the vaguest suggestion that some more cynical strategy was at work—an angling, perhaps, for a Democratic draft.

She said she knew him as well as anybody, and understood the subtlety of his political ambition. "You win some, you lose some," he had said in his speeches, and if that sounded glib to many of his listeners, particularly the reporters out there taking notes, maybe it was because they were looking through a lens that simply didn't fit. They insisted on seeing every national politician as a man or woman of naked ambition—some of them caught in a grand sense of destiny, others obsessed with the concept of power.

But Tipper was certain that the man she was married to was not like that. There were ideas and issues in which he believed, and he was deeply confident of his own understandings. But when he made the decision not to run a second time, there was never any feeling of a destiny denied, or a burning ambition that could never be replaced. What he said was exactly what he meant. He was trying to do what was right for the country.

Tipper was certain of that in her heart, believed it as much as she believed anything. "My husband," she said, "is an honorable man."

By late afternoon, as our interview was ending, she glanced across the room toward a picture of Al Gore hanging on the wall—a color photograph she had taken herself.

"Cute picture, isn't it?" she said with a smile, and her face was suddenly the face of a girl. For anyone who had seen it, it was easy to flash back to her wedding photograph, as her blue eyes sparkled and she brushed back a strand of blond hair. She said they had come a long way in the past thirty years, and whatever the twists and turns still ahead, she was caught in the same old spirit of adventure.

Already, since the end of the White House years, they had written two books on the American family, and she knew that other opportunities were out there, and perhaps some teaching possibilities as well.

"Al is a natural teacher," she said, knowing from conversations with his students that most of them seemed to share that opinion.

Rodney Crumpton, for example, was a former Tennessee truck driver who decided in his forties to go back to college. He took a course under Gore, a seminar on the family, and he found the whole experience surprising. For one thing, there at the front of the room every time was the former vice president of the United States—a man who had missed being president by a handful of votes, and who, in the aftermath of that defeat, could have taught at any school in the country. But he had chosen Middle Tennessee State University, a blue-collar institution tucked away in the hills, and Gore seemed to revel in that opportunity. He was not at all like what some people expected, not stiff or awkward, as he sometimes appeared on the campaign trail, but a teacher who seemed to "bubble over" with his knowledge.

Crumpton got to know Gore outside of class, and soon met Tipper Gore also. He thought of her then, as he does today, as a woman who knew how to light up a room.

"I'm so proud of the Gores," he said. "They could lead the elite lifestyle, but they choose not to. You can be real with them—anybody of any race or any background. Professor Gore was so accessible to his students, and Tipper is like your cousin, your mother, your long-lost friend. There's no pretense about them at all."

Mrs. Gore smiles at such testimonials. She is proud of Al and his ability to reach out and is ready to push ahead with her own work as well. "I'll continue to make speeches on health care and the status of women and families," she explains. "I'll continue to be an advocate on these issues."

As you listen to her talk, it is easy to believe that life after Washington is exactly as she says. It may be a little less visible now, a little less public in between her appearances. But she still has the passions she has always had—her family and her causes, made richer by her memories—and what more, really, could anybody need?

The answer, she says, is nothing at all.

Until I was asked to write this profile, I had not heard of Robert Howard Allen, a Vanderbilt Ph.D. who had never gone to a school of any kind until he went off to college at the age of thirty-two. Ordinarily, I am not drawn to stories that seem to be mere curiosities. But when my perceptive editor, GayNelle Doll, lent me a copy of Robert Allen's book, Simple Annals, *I could see immediately that this was a writer of extraordinary substance. As I was to learn more clearly in the course of my research, here was a man who had internalized the story of his family and turned it into the essence of his art.*

The Education of Robert Howard Allen

There's a small framed portrait in Robert Allen's office, a bearded ancestor from the nineteenth century peering out across the clutter of the desk and the bookshelves crammed full of classical texts. It's hard to say which is more important to him—the musty hardbacks of Tolstoy and Dickens, or the dark-eyed visage of Hosea Preslar, Allen's maternal great-great-great grandfather, who preached against slavery in west Tennessee and spent the Civil War hiding in a cave.

The truth of it is, all of these symbols of his heritage and learning are so mixed together in Robert Allen's mind that he probably couldn't separate them if he tried. Allen is a poet, now living and teaching in east Tennessee, and his improbable story is unlike any other. He grew up poor in the hard-scrabble country northeast of Memphis, where the hills give way to the Mississippi delta, and until he entered college at the age of thirty-two, he had never set foot in a school.

He was raised in a house full of aging relatives—his grandfather, an uncle, and his great aunt Ida, a round-faced woman, gray-haired and blind, who was born in 1885 and was the self-appointed keeper of the family history. Hour after hour, he would listen to her stories, which she told with matter-of-fact precision, even though none of them had been written down. In the cumulative certainty of Aunt Ida's memory, there were heroes and scoundrels and people in between, and the old woman seemed happy to talk about them all.

"Aunt Ida fig-leafed nothing," Allen says, and after a while he began to write it all down—the stories of pioneers and Tennessee soldiers who fought for the Union and adulteries committed in the haylofts of barns. He carried that legacy of family identity on his belated pursuit of a formal education, first to Bethel College in west Tennessee, where he received his undergraduate degree, and then to Vanderbilt University, where he earned his master's and his Ph.D.

He began writing poetry in the course of that journey, much of it about the members of his family, and he left some dazzled professors in his wake. "I thought he was a genius," said a teacher at Bethel; and at Vanderbilt, his adviser, Donald Davie, summarized Robert Allen this way: "He has the most single-minded appetite for learning of anyone I've ever taught. A good mind, yes, an extremely retentive memory, a very good sense of humor, all that; but the greatest thing is his unquenchable thirst for knowledge. The man simply can't get enough learning."

As Allen understands it, the thirst took hold in that rambling farmhouse in west Tennessee, last painted, he said, in 1909 and rented by his family for twenty dollars a month. It offered only the bare rudiments of shelter, and as the winter wind whistled in across the delta, it was easy for a boy growing up in such a place to find himself drawn to the flicker of the wood stove, and the reassuring warmth of Aunt Ida's stories. There wasn't much formal education in the house. Aunt Ida had none, and his grandfather, James Ethridge Jones, was a farmer and carpenter who had never been to school and saw little reason why anyone should.

But there was a darker reason, talked about in whispers, for the old folks' decision to keep the boy at home. Robert's parents had been involved in a nasty divorce, his mother running off with a traveling shoe salesman, and the boy's new guardians were afraid that the father would come back one day and steal him from the schoolyard. There was some wrangling for a while with the local school board, producing an agreement that Robert would simply be taught at home. A teacher did come to his house on occasion, but the arrangement didn't last, and after six months or so, Allen says, "I just sort of fell through the cracks."

By the age of twelve, he had taught himself to read, mostly through the medium of comic books, and then his horizons began to grow a little broader. His original introduction to the outside world came from a warm and familiar source, the family Bible that he began to read to Aunt Ida in the evenings. They started with Genesis and worked their way through, proceeding at the rate of five chapters a night, and they were startled sometimes by the stark humanity of the biblical characters—the kings such as David, insatiable in their sexual appetites but caught up also in that heroic odyssey of the Hebrew people.

To Robert Howard Allen, it sounded a little like the story of his family, all those people that Aunt Ida talked about who had made the journey across the Tennessee mountains, looking for a place they could build a better life. More and more in his teenage years, he felt himself drawn to nearly any kind of story. Most nights, in the sanctuary of the farmhouse, he would ply his aunt for everything she remembered, and at least a couple of times a month, he made the four-mile trek to the Carroll County Library. The librarian there was a middle-aged woman by the name of Pearl Harder, who saw great promise in such an eager young mind, and for Robert Allen, she became his fellow pilgrim in the world of greater learning.

"In many ways," he says, "she was a typical librarian, but not the kind to shush an eager child."

Among other things, she introduced the boy to the collected works of William Shakespeare, a well-worn volume that became more so in Allen's eager hands. He read everything—*Hamlet, Romeo and Juliet*, but his favorites, he discovered, were less conventional. He loved *King Lear* and *The Tempest*, and when he read Mark Twain, it was not *The Adventures of Huckleberry Finn* that captured his fancy but rather the hilarity of *Innocents Abroad*. And then came the day when a prominent doctor in Carroll County died, leaving the library his twelve-volume set of Will Durant's *Story of Civilization*. Allen decided to read the whole thing.

"It took me two and a half years," he says, "but I read all of it and retained a lot of it. Even today, off the top of my head, I could probably write a small book on the history of the world."

And so it was for young Robert Allen, living without any friends his own age. His books and his family and a county librarian made up the expanding boundaries of his world. By sometime late in his teenage years, he had turned his hand to writing stories of his own— journal entries first, written in a flowing, old-fashioned script that his grandfather taught him. But the world of poetry called to him early, and by his mid-twenties he was sending submissions to prestigious journals, unaware of the odds that were weighted against him.

When his work was accepted, he took it in stride. "That just seemed like what ought to happen," he said. "The purpose of the journals was to publish people's poems." And whatever his relative level of inexperience, he had studied the work of Longfellow and Yeats, Shakespeare and Poe, and he thought he understood what they were doing. Not that he saw himself as Shakespeare. But the intertwining power of eloquent language and a captivating story was now the primary passion of his life.

Pearl Harder, among others, was impressed. "I identified with Robert," she said. "He was his own person, unassuming, but very bright, and with a keen sense of humor. I knew he was exceptional."

In addition to his mind, she told a journalist in 1988, she was struck by the dignity of Allen and his relatives, who sometimes came to the library with him. "Poor, but not ashamed," she said. But she couldn't help worrying that the young man's brilliance would inevitably be cramped, circumscribed by the peculiar isolation of his family. She thought it was time for him to go to college.

She talked to Robert about it off and on, and sometime late in the 1970s, he said he began to think about it too. He was pushing thirty by then, working as a handyman and upholsterer, and when a recession hit hard in Carroll County, drying up his work, he decided he needed to do something different. Bethel College was just a few miles away, a little Presbyterian school that had opened in the 1840s. After taking his high school equivalency test and passing easily, Allen decided he might as well apply.

He came to Bethel in 1981, and both he and his teachers say it was a jolt. "He was pretty lonely," his philosophy professor William Ramsey remembered, "and lacking in social graces." And his English professor Bill King added, "He's just not like anyone else—and no one is remotely like him."

Allen himself more or less agreed, and in his memories of his early days at Bethel, one occasion in particular stands out in his mind. He was talking with a fellow student, a young man who was studying to go into the ministry and who seemed to be brighter than some of their peers. Having read the Bible from cover to cover and having studied other works, including John Milton's *Paradise Lost*, Allen was eager for a conversation of substance.

"What do you think of Milton's theology?" he asked.

For a moment, the ministry student stared at him blankly, then finally answered with an uncertain shrug, "Milton who?"

For Allen, it was not a moment that made him feel less awkward, for it revealed the chasm between himself and his peers. But it did make him feel as if he might be prepared. Like any college freshman he had wondered about it, and perhaps at first even more than many others. School, after all, was completely new to him. But he threw himself into the process of learning, just as he had as a teenaged boy, and without any trace of self-consciousness or pride, he began to show what he could do in class. Having tested out of freshman English, he took a literature course under Professor Bill King, and one day when the conversation turned to poetry, he stood and recited Thomas Gray's "Elegy Written in a Country Churchyard"—every word of it, without missing a line.

> Let not Ambition mock their useful toil,
> Their homely joys, and destiny obscure
> Nor grandeur hear with disdainful smile
> The short and simple annals of the poor . . .

In 1984, at the age of thirty-five, after only three years, he graduated summa cum laude at the top of his class. He shared the graduation stage with the commencement speaker Al Gore, then a U.S. senator, and Gore was amazed when the cameras from *60 Minutes* arrived—not to record anything from the senator but to do a piece on Robert Howard Allen. The award-winning southern journalist John Egerton also profiled Allen about that time and summarized his story this way: "It's not often that middle-aged poor people finish college at all, let alone as classical scholars leading the academic procession."

But as the years would reveal, Robert Allen was just getting started.

He left Bethel College for Vanderbilt to work on his master's degree in creative writing. By then, he had already started on a project, more ambitious than anything else he had done. He wanted to write down the story of his family—that journey that began in North Carolina, back around the time of the American

Revolution. It was a brutal time, as Allen understood it. In the South especially it was neighbor against neighbor, people forced to choose between competing imperatives—loyalty to the king, a long-held value among British subjects, and the great, intoxicating notions of liberty.

Allen's ancestors were peaceable people, caught in the gathering fury of that choice. They fought when they had to, for after a while, there was no way to avoid it, but eventually they decided to move to the West. It was Allen's ambition to document that journey in verse, expanding on the power of Aunt Ida's stories. He relied in part on the example of the Bible. He had been reading the Old Testament one night, he said, first the Psalms and then the Book of Samuel—the psalms containing the poetry of King David, and Samuel a narrative account of his life. He decided he wanted to try to do both, to write the narrative of his own family's odyssey with the lyricism of a poet.

At Vanderbilt, as he worked to find his own writer's voice, he came under the tutelage of Donald Davie, one of the great elder statesmen in the English department. As Davie's colleague Vereen Bell later put it, "Davie was English, a very distinguished poet of his generation, and a really important literary critic. He came to Vanderbilt after being at Stanford, and he was classically educated, which was something that he and Robert Allen shared."

As Allen was working on his master's thesis, he gave Davie some of his poems to read. They came back to him with a note in the margin: "This won't do!"

"And he was right," says Allen today, smiling his wry and enigmatic smile. "What he was trying to get me to see was that I was imitating writers I admired. His point was, I had to be original. What do I know that no one else knows?"

That question marinated for a while, as Allen earned his master's degree and then his Ph.D., with a dissertation on William Butler Yeats. In 1990, with those milestones behind him, he started working more deliberately on the book that he decided to call *Simple Annals*, taking the title from the poetry of Thomas Gray. At this point, he says, he knew he was ready.

The family stories beckoned more powerfully than ever, and at the age of forty-one, he was more his own person as a writer and a man. But most of all, his poems were beginning to take on a shape, individually and as a group. He began his collection with "Elias Butler," an epic reminiscence on an early ancestor who went to war reluctantly against the British king. A few poems later, there was the story of Rebecca Singleton Thomas, a Civil War–vintage relative who, by the sheer, improbable power of her defiance, cowed the Rebel soldiers who were threatening her farm. But in addition to these heroic accounts, there were also the memories of degradation and tragedy—for example, the story of Nate, a black man lynched in west Tennessee for the simple crime of loving a white woman.

In that poem, Allen let his imagination run free—"as is every poet's right," he said—and he wrote about the star-crossed lovers with all the gentleness he thought they deserved.

Tell the story: a love story
Tender touched the lovers, proper as spring;
But death was the ending of it.
For loving,
Oh, for weeping in secret and longing
When the fat red sun
Lumbered to rest,
For the caring and the dreaming,
Standing with his hoe
In the weedy corn

For that
Death.

Because he whispered to her
The common secrets of an honest heart,
Death, because his finger
Traced words he could not write upon her cheek, death,
Death for caring, hoping, death—for the dance of love
The dance in the noose

For this reason:
That she was white, he black.

When *Simple Annals* came out in 1997, published by the literary press Four Walls Eight Windows in New York City, there were those who compared it to *Spoon River Anthology*. But the reviews in the end were few and far between, and the sales, says Allen with a winsome smile, "might charitably be characterized as modest." And so it was that in the chilly and unpredictable world of publishing, Allen's great literary labor of love appeared and then quietly slipped away, leaving barely a trace. But Allen seemed to know, as good writers do, that this was not a reflection on him. The stories were there, and there was art in the telling, and so he simply went on about his life.

He turned his attention, in part, to writing plays, including one soon to be staged at Murray State University, telling the story of a family maverick, who built a cabin for his mistress within a stone's throw of the one for his wife. He has also written a work of scholarship, *The Classical Roots of Modern Homophobia*, also published in 2006, which traces the prejudice against homosexuals from the time of the Roman Empire.

In that particular book, he was returning to a subject he had taken on before, when a mainstream publisher, having seen the segment on *60 Minutes*, asked him to write his autobiography. He wrote it as he thought Aunt Ida would have wanted, "fig-leafing nothing," including the difficult matter of his own sexuality. But as one of his Vanderbilt advisers later noted, this was not what the publisher had in mind, and in the end, the manuscript was rejected.

Allen, as always, took it in stride and simply pushed ahead as a writer. It seemed there was always a poem or a play, and often something larger, taking its inevitable shape in his mind—and he also found new rewards as a teacher, seeking to impart his own love of learning to the diversity of students who passed through his classes.

He left Vanderbilt to return to Bethel College, a professor this time, and from there he moved to Murray State University, and then to the University of Tennessee-Martin. In 2001, he moved across the state to Hiwassee College, a Methodist school built in the 1840s in the rolling foothills of the Great Smoky Mountains.

On Tuesdays and Thursdays, you will find him in his classes, freshman composition and British literature, orchestrating the far-flung discussions, which range from the shooting spree at Columbine High School to the iambic pentameter of Alexander Pope. At fifty-six, with his tuft of a beard and his wire-rimmed glasses, he looks the part of a lifelong scholar—his seriousness tempered by a dry sense of humor that his students seem to love.

"He's a lot of fun," says Josh Debity, one of his Brit-lit students. And Ashley Wise, a sophomore English major agrees. "I love Dr. Allen's classes," she says. "Normally, there are some pretty heated discussions, some really good arguments about all sorts of things."

Allen seems to feel the same affection for his students, especially those who are eager and bright. "I've had my share of good ones," he says, and one night in his office just before Thanksgiving, he settled back in his chair and reflected on the various ingredients of his life. His Civil War ancestor, Hosea Preslar, stared down from the wall, a flinty-eyed man in a Wal-Mart frame, an apostle of abolition in the South.

"This is his book," said Allen, pulling out a hard-back volume from the classics. "It's a book about slavery, but it's also partly an autobiography." He stopped for a moment and thumbed through the pages, then returned the book to its place on the shelf. He knew, of course, that it was much like his own—not famous or commercially successful in its time—but the writer's reward is not a short-term thing.

He had learned long ago, in the rambling old farmhouse back in Carroll County, that there is meaning simply in handing down the story. It was a curious way to grow up, he admitted, lonesome at times, but he was surrounded by members of a family who loved him, and more than that, who knew who they were. They had kept alive a history of pathos and grace, and they had given their blessing when he began to expand it—when he made those treks to the Carroll County library and filled his mind with the knowledge it contained.

"It was a good beginning for a poet," he explained. "I couldn't have asked for anything more."

As our conversation wound down on that November night he shuffled through a handful of papers on his desk, then locked up his office and shut out the light. He nodded goodnight to a student in the hall and again reaffirmed the quiet and lasting satisfactions of his work. Barring anything unexpected, he said, he planned to stay at Hiwassee for a while—writing his poems, teaching his students—doing what he thinks would make the old people proud.

One of the most eloquent commentators on the life and culture of the American South was a fellow Alabamian, Dr. C. Eric Lincoln. After a long career of brilliant scholarship, he published a novel in 1988, a thirty-year labor of love called The Avenue, Clayton City. *This profile of Lincoln, which appeared in an earlier book,* The Heart of Dixie, *tells the story of a writer and his work.*

Pride and Prejudice

Blind Bates began to caress the strings of his battered old guitar. . . . This time he was playing for love. Love for a woman he had never seen, but whose love he had known not only through the meals she had fixed for him, or the shirts she had patched, but through the sharing of her time, her wisdom and her compassion. Tears flowed from beneath the dark glasses covering his sightless eyes as he riffed the steel strings with the glass bottleneck on his little finger and launched into a song he had written in his mind for Mama Lucy. It was a sad, lonesome song.

Train done gone
Train done gone

The funeral scene stays with you for a while. The prose itself is haunting in its rhythms—elegant in its cadence and its vivid word pictures—as C. Eric Lincoln describes the little church, hot and crowded and overflowing with grief. A leading black citizen has died, a matriarch of tenderness and strength, and her funeral was, as Lincoln writes, "an occasion licensed by the whole community to break down—to scream and to shout, to moan and to weep, to engage in the delirium of temporary relief from sadness, from fear, from hatred and frustration. All in the name and the presence of God."

Lincoln was a scholar by trade, a professor of religion at Duke University, author of nineteen works of nonfiction, but never a novel until 1988. Then, with the publication of *The Avenue, Clayton City*, he established his place in the front ranks of black writers. The book was an alternate selection of the Literary Guild, with a large first printing of about twenty-five thousand. Paperback and movie rights were already sold at the time of publication, and critics called it a "masterpiece."

Lincoln said he worked on the novel for more than thirty years, writing a chapter here and there and then putting it aside, and for much longer than that he carried the stories and the characters in his head—the prototypes of life in the black rural South.

He knew the story firsthand. He was born in Alabama in 1924, coming of age in the little town of Athens, in the cotton country near the Tennessee line. He found bits and pieces of heroism there, traces of nobility during a time of segregation. But mostly what he saw—the enduring image that took shape in his novel—was the crazy futility of life in those times, the lost and squandered dignity among his neighbors black and white.

Lincoln was reared by his grandparents. His mother went away when he was four; she married a preacher and moved off to Pittsburgh, leaving her son in the care of Less and Mattie Lincoln. Mattie worked for white families as a cook and a maid and, in many ways, ruled her own family with a kind of ferocious generosity—quick to punish a misbehaving child but ready to go to war if they were ever abused.

"She taught us," Eric Lincoln remembered, "You got to respect everybody respectable," for that was the only way you could expect the same treatment.

Less Lincoln, meanwhile, was a farmer. He did odd jobs for white people, but his passion, his calling, was tilling his own fields: three acres of cotton behind his wood-frame house. He was a gentle man, his grandson remembered, dignified, with iron gray hair that was tight and springy to young Eric's touch, and the two of them were great friends. They would sit by the fire on many a Sunday evening, roasting sweet potatoes on the hearth while Mattie was off at church.

For Lincoln, such memories were mingled with those of deprivation—the six-room house so cold some nights that ice formed on the floor—and also of cruelty, an ever-present possibility in a time of white supremacy.

"My experiences with white people were varied," he said. "I played with white kids and loved some of them. It was not unusual for poor whites and blacks to eat together, to hunt and fish together, whore together. Yet there was supposed to have been a hatred. I didn't see much of that, but then, I wasn't looking. I do remember one time that I was cheated and kicked in the head, for the reason that I unwittingly challenged a white man.

"I was thirteen or fourteen. My grandfather was on his deathbed. There was no food in the house, no fire in the house, no money in the house. My grandmother and I went out to the fields where the cotton had already been picked, not only our fields but those nearby, and we pulled the only bolls that were left."

That night, he said, they picked the cotton from the bolls and put it in a bag, and the next morning, Eric put it in a wheelbarrow and took it to the gin. It was seven o'clock in the morning when he arrived, and the owner, Mr. Beasley, was sitting on the porch.

"Whatcha got there, boy?" he said.

"Cotton, sir."

"Well, dump it out."

So they put it on the scales, and the weight came to forty pounds, and young Eric made a quick calculation: At 9 cents a pound, that would mean $3.60 for food, firewood, and other family necessities. He was startled, therefore, when the white man casually flipped him a quarter.

"Mr. Beasley," he said, after a long hesitation, "I think you made a mistake."

Beasley's face turned red, and he got up abruptly and bolted the door. At first, the boy was merely puzzled. But then he found himself gasping, his lungs suddenly empty from a blow to the midsection, as the white man began to kick him and stomp at his head.

"He was in a frenzy," Lincoln remembered, "and I'll never forget his words: 'Nigger, as long as you live, don't you never try to count behind no white man again!'"

There were times, for Lincoln, when that story came hard— when he told it with such emotion that he had to stop for a moment and wipe the tears from his large, expressive eyes. But there were other stories, too, he said—other experiences with white people of a very different kind. One man, for example, a high school principal named J. T. Wright, praised and encouraged Lincoln's gift as a writer, and lent him fifty dollars so he could go off to college. "I was four-teen," Lincoln remembered. "I had just graduated from high school in May of 1939, and I had an uncle in Rockford, Illinois, who worked at what he called an 'auto laundry'—a car wash, we would call it today. I was going to go there and take a job, and the principal, Mr. Wright, loaned me some money and said, 'C. Eric, while you're up that way, stop on by the University of Chicago.'"

Lincoln did and eventually emerged with a divinity degree. But there were some stops in between his enrollment and graduation—a couple of years in the navy, several more at a black college in Memphis, and a strange and singular job opportunity one summer that caused him to travel extensively across the South. He became secretary and road manager to a Negro League baseball team, the Birmingham Black Barons. It was an outstanding collection of talent (among its players was an Alabama teenager by the name of Willie Mays), and as Lincoln handled the team's financial affairs, renting stadiums, negotiating with the management of the teams they were playing, he got to know the South in a way that stayed with him.

Every town, it seemed, was remarkably the same. Despite some colorful differences in detail, each had a similar cast of characters: a wise man, a fool, a chief bootlegger, a white patriarch. They were prototypes, and they provided, for Lincoln, the images and building blocks of a novel about the South.

Not right away, however, for his major energies were soon chan-neled into scholarship. He taught for the next thirty years at Clark College in Atlanta and Fisk University in Nashville, at Columbia University and Union Theological Seminary in New York, before finally coming to Duke in 1976. His best-known books during that time were *The Black Muslims in America* and *The Negro Pilgrimage in America*, which together sold more than a million copies.

The Muslim book especially was a seminal work, the first seri-ous study of Islam in America, and it introduced Malcolm X to the country. Eric and Malcolm soon became fast friends, and when the Black Muslim leader decided to write his autobiography, his first choice for a collaborator was Lincoln. Lincoln, however, turned down the assignment, citing the demands of his work and steered Malcolm instead to a long-time friend, Alex Haley.

A few years later, while teaching at Brown University, Lincoln invited Malcolm to the university to speak. Malcolm's affectionate answer was disturbing: "I would do anything you ask," he said, "but I may soon be dead."

Only a couple of days later, in one of the great tragedies of the 1960s, Malcolm X was murdered in New York City.

All the while, as the racial melodramas unfolded in America, Lincoln continued his scholarship on the subject—and also continued to work on his novel. Finally, in 1988, he sent a copy of the manuscript to Alex Haley, whose response was encouraging: "C. Eric," Haley wrote back, "you can write your ass off! Ain't nothing wrong with this manuscript except that you wrote it instead of me."

When the book appeared a few months later, Lincoln was braced for mixed reviews. The prose and the passion made it easy to read, but the structure of it was unorthodox. Each of the ten chapters was a self-contained story, and though some characters appeared more than once, the chapters were connected more by theme than plot. They read almost like a collection of short stories that together produced a powerful portrait of a place.

In addition to that departure from the standard form, Lincoln also knew the novel might offend. It was as unflinching in its portrayal of blacks as it was of whites, for the people of the Avenue in Lincoln's Clayton City are not always admirable, or even sympathetic. There were some heroes—Mama Lucy, based loosely on Lincoln's grandmother, and Roger McClain, a white educator who resembled the real-life principal at Lincoln's high school. But there were also petty criminals and assorted other hustlers whose choices were self-centered and sometimes disastrous—who added to the debasement white supremacy had produced.

Most of the characters, meanwhile, were somewhere in between, well-intentioned perhaps, but fundamentally bewildered, trying to survive the vagaries of the South as it was. And then there were one or two who fought back, taking their desperate and fateful stands against the order of the day.

One of the latter was Dr. Walter Pinkney Tait, an enigmatic physician who had a profitable practice, a position of prominence among Clayton City's blacks, and who had even grown accustomed to a certain respect among whites. Still, he hated segregation and the slow death of the spirit it inevitably produced, and he decided one day that he had had enough.

His decision took the form of a simple act of defiance, the

refusal to obey the desperate order of a white man—a prominent citizen who was addicted to drugs and who wanted the black doctor to give him a shot. Tait refused, not because what was being asked would violate his principles, but because he was simply tired of the way things were, including his own life.

"If the canvas is rotten to begin with," he said, "no matter what you paint on it, the colors will run and the texture will blister." He knew his decision, at the least, would cost him his practice and maybe get him killed. But he also knew that the time had come.

> All his life he had tried to walk the thin, wavering line between what it took to live in the white man's world and what it took to hold on to some semblance of self-respect, but he had never been so blunt with any white man before.
>
> Often, when his dignity was cornered, he had resorted to professional jargon to say what he would never say in plain speech, but never before had he had the temerity to look a white man—not just some poor cracker, but The Man himself—squarely in the eye and tell him precisely what he wanted him to know. It was a good feeling—a liberating feeling—and <u>he felt no fear except for the fear of not being afraid</u>. . . .
>
> He sat motionless in his swivel chair and watched the evening shadows blot the dying sunlight from the room.

Epilogue. Before he died in 2000, there was a graceful symmetry in the life of Dr. Lincoln. In addition to his far-flung symbols of acclaim—the Lillian Smith Award for his novel, a lectureship in his honor at Clark Atlanta University—he was invited home just before his death to deliver the commencement address at Athens College. The little liberal arts school in Lincoln's hometown had been all-white when he was a boy—a piece of turf where he had been forbidden to go. But when he returned in the 1990s, treated like the dignitary he became, Lincoln said he was deeply moved. In his life and work, he had come a long way from the cotton fields of Athens, and in the welcome he felt near the end of his days he found reason to believe—or at least to hope—that the country was slowly making changes as well.

Of all the characters I've met in writing about the South, none has been more important than my own grandfather, Palmer Gaillard, whom I profile here along with his friend Robert Croshon. In their ways, each was a symbol of the old South—particularly my grandfather—but his story and Robert's contain their own revelations of hope.

The Last Confession

He exists for me in bits and pieces of memory: the high cheekbones and slightly hooked nose, the wispy white hair and the frailties that slowly whittled away at his vigor. He was ninety years old by the time I was born, but our relationship lasted for thirteen years, and for only two or three of those did he seem really old. Certainly, he didn't when he was a mere ninety-five and tilled a half-acre garden with a hand-held plow. His friend Robert Croshon, an ageless black man of indestructible good humor, was usually there for encouragement and to tug and chop away at the meanest clumps of wild onions.

My own contributions were a little more random. I chased away the Indians in the bamboo hedges and practiced high-jumping across the rows of collard greens. But it was, nevertheless, a splendid partnership that grew with the years, as my grandfather offered more and wider glimpses into his treasury of recollection. In the beginning, there were the stories. He talked occasionally about The War, by which he meant the War Between the States, which did not end until he was nine. His memories of it, like my memories of his stories, were those of a child. But they were enlarged by time to an epic dimension somewhere in the realm between myth and allegory: Yankee soldiers marching toward the family plantation, servants rushing to hide the silver in the woods.

The specifics, after a while, began to seem unremarkable, for he offered them simply as something he had known. What really mattered to him, as I later came to understand, was a symbolism that rang with clarity and meaning. The Northern soldiers, however menacing, were ultimately ineffective in their assault on the spirit.

The grace and elegance of the Southern way of life were essentially too powerful, protected in the end by that body of knowledge and understanding that each generation passes to the next.

Nearly everyone, it seemed, looked to my grandfather for that sort of wisdom. They hung on his words and paid him more homage than anyone should endure. And if he grew accustomed to the accolades and attention, accepting them calmly as the rewards for his antiquity, he nevertheless considered it unseemly to boast.

He was a lawyer by trade, and even at the age of 102, he went regularly to his office, offering advice to his partners and writing articles carefully rooted in traditional scholarship. His last one appeared in 1959 in the journal of the Alabama Bar Association. It was a vigorous defense of southern segregation, and though it was filled with certainty and passion, it also revealed the limits of his vision.

"I am not seer enough to forecast what can be done by force of autocratic nationalism in the course of time, but from my 102 years of life, I predict the deep South will never accept integration by force. The spirit of Thaddeus Stephens may force upon us a second Reconstruction era with its humiliation and tragedy, but the white race of the South cannot accept forced integration in their private, social and family life."

As I read that passage many years later, my mind flashed back to a day when I was five. It must have been some time in the fall, for the leaf piles were burning, and the sweet scent drifted through the neighborhood. Robert Croshon was there with his wheelbarrow, and I was, as always, ready for a ride. It was something of a ritual for us by now. Every Saturday on his way to work, Robert would stop to pick up his "helper." That was me, the youngest grandchild, who soaked up the spirit of those innocent days, as my grandfather and Robert worked together in the garden.

They seemed to enjoy each other's company, talking about all manner of things, from my grandfather's Presbyterian theology to the background of Robert's own family. On his mother's side, Robert was the descendant of runaway slaves, people who had fled their Georgia plantation expecting to follow the Drinking Gourd north. But on the night of their escape, the Big Dipper had been obscured by a sudden thunderstorm, and by the time they recovered their bearings, they found that they had been headed south. They spent a night in a cave with another runaway, then decided to keep pushing to the town of Mobile, where they knew there was a community of free Negroes.

There, they stayed and sometime near the turn of the twentieth century, Robert's family came to work for mine. The association had continued for more than fifty years, and in the closing years of my grandfather's life, there were clearly strong feelings of affinity and warmth. "Robert," the old man had told him more than once, "you've been blessed with good ability. Don't let anybody think they are better."

Even years later, Robert had no doubt that my grandfather meant it, but on the day I'm remembering, all of us came face to face—suddenly and without any warning—with the myopia and contradictions of the times. After a morning spent in the garden, it was time for lunch, and we headed for the Big House, as my grandfather's dwelling was known in those days. The extended family was beginning to gather, and it was an impressive spread on the dining room table—fried chicken, turnip greens, a platter of biscuits. But as we took our places around the great cluttered feast, Robert found a chair by himself in the kitchen.

To a five-year-old it made no sense. "Robert!" I called. "Come on in here."

I knew immediately that I had made a mistake, for my aunt quickly shot me a look that could kill. "Shame on you!" she said with a hiss. "Shame on you for hurting Robert's feelings."

It was my first encounter with the great southern sin, and I remembered the moment as the years went by and the civil rights movement descended on the South. I was a teenager when the movement hit its stride, and for me at least, those festering doubts that began when I was five—the secret suspicions that the world around me didn't make a lot of sense—finally erupted into full-blown rebellion. What I didn't know until many years later was that my grandfather was struggling with the same set of issues, the same misgivings about the southern way of life.

His struggle played out most clearly in the church, for my grandfather was a man of deep faith. Every night in the Big House, precisely at nine, he would take his place in the rocking chair by the hearth and thumb through the well-worn pages of his Bible, selecting the verses to be read aloud. The psalms were his favorites, those bits of poetry that were written by kings, but there were others also that were scattered through the Book—the words of the prophets and the Sermon on the Mount.

He served as an elder in the Presbyterian church, an office he had held for sixty-five years, and his minister, John Crowell, was a learned young man of stunning eloquence, with the kindest heart the old man had ever known. He was one of a handful of Alabama ministers who preached a few sermons on the issue of race, calling essentially for an end to segregation. For many years, my grandfather disagreed. He had grown accustomed to the codes of segregation, which seemed to resemble what God had intended, and many of his fellow church members concurred. And yet, they were drawn to this brilliant young preacher, with his spell-binding words and a faith that was clearly a match for their own.

Perhaps the most basic issue they faced was what to do on Sunday if a black person came to worship at the church. Would he be made welcome, or as some in the congregation suggested, turned away in deference to the southern way of life? To the minister, of course, the answer was clear, for he regarded segregation in any form as wrong—a patent affront to the dignity of black Americans. His stance, however, drew fire from many of the people in the church until the day my grandfather rose to speak. Palmer Gaillard was an amazing figure at the age of ninety-nine, nearly six-feet-one, if a little bit stooped, with clothes that were beginning to sag on his frame. But his voice was strong as he cleared his throat and proclaimed that the minister this time was right. Even in the days of their ancestors, he said, slaves had been allowed to worship in the balconies. Surely today, they would not retreat from the wisdom and generosity of their fathers. But more than that, they should also remember that "our Lord looks not on the color of skin, but on the quality of a man's heart and his character and soul."

It was a powerful performance, as it usually was when the old man spoke—as if his words, somehow, should be inscribed on a tablet. And yet it left the young minister perplexed. In John Crowell's mind, the leap was so small from such professions of faith to a support for the end of segregation in the South. But Palmer Gaillard resisted that connection. Kindness was one thing, a welcoming spirit at a Sunday church service, but racial equality was something else again, and for the rest of his life he wrote letters and articles supporting segregated schools and public transportation and limits on the right of black people to vote. He and Crowell continued to debate it until the day in 1959 when the minister got word that the old man was dying.

It was a day he had dreaded for more than a decade—the end of a life so spirited and grand—and he drove out quickly to the house on the hill just west of Mobile. The old man was now 103, and he looked so fragile as he lay in the bed, his breathing shallow and his skin ghost-white. He couldn't have weighed more than a hundred pounds, and his voice when he spoke was barely a whisper. The preacher took a seat on the side of the bed and my grandfather slowly reached out his hand.

"Pastor," he whispered, letting the word hang there as he gathered his breath. "I must tell you now, I see that you were right."

There were just the two of them in the half-darkened room, where the shadows fell softly on the old man's bed. He didn't say anything after that, just shut his eyes as the preacher held his hand. The next morning he was gone.

As the 1950s drew to a close, John Crowell thought often about that confession, and it somehow gave him a reason to hope. Palmer Gaillard was such a symbol of the South. He had lived through more than half of its history if you began counting time with the founding of the country, and he had seen everything since the great Civil War—the temporary upheavals of Reconstruction, and the eventual restoration of his family and his race. He was proud of the legacy he had sought to pass on—that code of honor and generosity and kindness, but in the clarity of those final moments of his life, he may have understood that it was not enough.

John Crowell thought so, and the question, he believed, for the American South—confronted with the darker implications of its past—was whether those still living could understand it as well. Many years later, I told that story to Robert Croshon. He was an old man himself by then, having worked for my family for more than sixty years. I had kept up with him as the years went by, visiting whenever I came back to Mobile, and marveling at his gentle dignity and strength. He could have been bitter, as I knew very well, but he had simply rejected that option—perhaps for his own sake as much as those around him. It was clear as we talked that he understood the limits of my grandfather's vision, as well as the cruelty at the heart of segregation. But when I told him the story of the deathbed confession—a story I had recently learned from John Crowell—Robert simply smiled.

"Your grandfather," he said, "was a good, kind man."

I decided to push him on that point, for despite my childhood reverence for my grandfather, I had also seen his inconsistency—his ability to work side by side with Robert, treating him apparently as a friend, then sentence him to dinner alone in the kitchen. And while he supported in principle allowing black people to worship at his church, he also supported the laws of segregation, understanding quite well the effect of those laws in a white man's world.

Robert nodded as I spoke and offered what I knew was a wistful smile. "That was a different day," he said. "Things are better now."

And so they are. The thing that Robert Croshon understood, and affirmed several times in the course of our talks, was that civility and kindness were a powerful force in the South, tied to the religious heart of the place. When the civil rights movement finally came along, demanding simple justice as the price of racial peace, there were too many people like Palmer Gaillard—resistant at first, but eventually and inevitably worn down by the truth.

Oddly enough, it was Robert and not the family he worked for who saw the whole thing coming from the start.

Acknowledgments

The majority of the stories assembled here have appeared in other forms in other places. Most of the introductory piece, "The Heart of Dixie," appeared in the fine anthology of Alabama writers *The Remembered Gate*, edited by Jay Lamar and Jeannie Thompson and published by the University of Alabama Press. Parts of it were also adapted from my own book *Lessons from the Big House*, and one of the anecdotes appeared in slightly different form in an essay I wrote for *Close to Home*, an anthology of North Carolina writers edited by Lee Harrison Child and published by John F. Blair, Publisher.

In Part I, "A Change Is Gonna Come," I first wrote about the Greensboro Four for *Creative Loafing* and later expanded that article into a book, *The Greensboro Four*, published by Main Street Rag Publishing Company. Another version of the profile appeared in the anthology *The North Carolina Century*, edited by Marion A. Ellis and Howard Covington. The version of the story that appears here includes elements of all three previous publications, though it most closely resembles the original piece in *Creative Loafing*. The second story, recounting the round of sit-ins that followed the breakthrough in Greensboro, was written for *Creative Loafing* and was based in part on an impressive exhibit at the Levine Museum of the New South. The profile of Perry Wallace appeared in *Vanderbilt Magazine*, as did the stories on Lewis Baldwin and Robert Kennedy's visit to Vanderbilt. "The Sheriff Without a Gun" is adapted from my book, *Cradle of Freedom*, published by the University of Alabama Press.

In Part II, "Amazing Grace," the story about Will Campbell incorporates elements from stories I wrote for the *Progressive*, *Sojourners*, the *Oxford American*, and the *Charlotte Observer* and in a previous book, *The Heart of Dixie*, published by Down Home Press. The Billy Graham profile is adapted from many different stories I have written on Graham through the years, appearing in such diverse publications as the *Washington Post,* the *Charlotte Observer,* the *Progressive,* the *(NC) Independent,* the *Chicago Tribune,* and others. The story on the religious debate in the New South city of Charlotte appeared originally in *Creative Loafing* and was later expanded into a monograph, *Charlotte's Holy Wars,* published by Main Street Rag Publishing. The Karen Graham profile is expanded from one written originally for *Creative Loafing.* The story on Millard and Linda Fuller and the birth of Habitat for Humanity is adapted from my book *If I Were a Carpenter: Twenty Years of Habitat for Humanity,* published by John F. Blair, Publisher. A similar version of the piece also appeared in the anthology *No Hiding Place: Uncovering the Legacy of Charlotte-Area Writers,* which I co-edited with Amy Rogers and Robert Inman. The story about Jimmy Carter appears here for the first time, though I cover some of the same ground at greater length in a new book on Carter, *Prophet from Plains,* published by the University of Georgia Press.

In Part III, "Soundtracks," the story about Johnny Cash is adapted from my book *Watermelon Wine: The Spirit of Country Music,* published originally by St. Martin's Press and updated twenty-five years later by NewSouth Books. A similar version of the profile appeared in *Creative Loafing* at the time of Cash's death. The chapter on southern rock also appeared in slightly different form in *Watermelon Wine,* having been adapted from an original story in *Country Music* magazine. "Old Fashioned Notions of Love and Music" was published originally in the *Oxford American* and reprinted in *Creative Loafing.* The version here has been modified slightly. The stories on Emmylou Harris and Marshall Chapman appeared originally in *Creative Loafing,* as did the profile of the folk singer Si Kahn.

Part IV, profiling intriguing characters I've written about over the years, begins with the story of John T. Scopes, different versions of which were written for *Vanderbilt Magazine* and the *Peabody Reflector.* By far the best account of the Scopes trial appears in the book *Summer for the Gods* by Edward J. Larson. I also read and quoted from Scopes's autobiography *Center of the Storm,* and from Matthew Chapman's article "God or Gorilla," in the February 2006 *Harper's Magazine.* I read the essay "Who Is Clarence Darrow?" by Douglas O. Linder at the University of Missouri, and the *Nashville Tennessean* reports on Scopes's visit to Peabody, written by Elaine Shannon. The story of James Baldwin's first visit to the South appears here for the first time, though it is based in part on coverage of the Charlotte school desegregation story for the *Charlotte Observer*, which I later expanded into a book, *The Dream Long Deferred*. I wrote an obituary of James Baldwin for the *Observer*, and one of the people I quoted was Ed Sanders, the other main character in the story as it appears here. Carol Polsgrove, in her fine book *Divided Minds*, recounts Baldwin's decision to travel to North Carolina, and I relied also on Baldwin's own account, which appeared in *Harper's Magazine* in October 1958.

The profiles of Tipper Gore and Robert Howard Allen appeared originally in *Vanderbilt Magazine*. The profile of C. Eric Lincoln was written originally for the *Charlotte Observer* and was reprinted in a slightly different form in my book *The Heart of Dixie*. I also wrote an obituary on Dr. Lincoln that appeared in the Alabama publication *First Draft*, and the epilogue for the story as it appears here is adapted from that obituary. I wrote the story of my return to Mobile, and my reunion with my old friend Robert Croshon, for an anthology called *Cornbread and Sushi*, edited by a group of students and faculty at Wofford College and published by Holocene Publishing. The article was reprinted in the *Mobile Register*.

I am grateful to all these publications and their editors for the chance to do this work. I'm especially grateful to Michael Schoenfeld, vice chancellor at Vanderbilt University, for his belief in this project; Ken Schexnayder and GayNelle Doll, editors at *Vanderbilt Magazine*, for making their pages available to my work; and Michael Ames, director of Vanderbilt University Press, for his patient suggestions that have made this a better book.

Special thanks also to my wife, Nancy Gaillard, who supported me in all these projects, and to the six fine writers and friends to whom this book is dedicated.